The Court Magician in Medieval German Romance

MIKROKOSMOS
BEITRÄGE ZUR LITERATURWISSENSCHAFT UND BEDEUTUNGSFORSCHUNG

Herausgegeben von Wolfgang Harms

BAND 44

Stephan Maksymiuk

The Court Magician in
Medieval German Romance

PETER LANG
Frankfurt am Main · Berlin · Bern · New York · Paris · Wien

Stephan Maksymiuk

The Court Magician in Medieval German Romance

PETER LANG
Europäischer Verlag der Wissenschaften

Die Deutsche Bibliothek - CIP-Einheitsaufnahme
Maksymiuk, Stephan:

The court magician in medieval German romance / Stephan
Maksymiuk. - Frankfurt am Main ; Berlin ; Bern ; New York ;
Paris ; Wien : Lang, 1996
  (Mikrokosmos ; Bd. 44)
  Zugl.: Seattle, Univ., Diss., 1992
  ISBN 3-631-30099-9

NE: GT

ISSN 0170-9143
ISBN 3-631-30099-9
US-ISBN 0-8204-3176-1
© Peter Lang GmbH
Europäischer Verlag der Wissenschaften
Frankfurt am Main 1996
All rights reserved.

All parts of this publication are protected by copyright. Any
utilisation outside the strict limits of the copyright law, without
the permission of the publisher, is forbidden and liable to
prosecution. This applies in particular to reproductions,
translations, microfilming, and storage and processing in
electronic retrieval systems.

Printed in Germany 1 2 3 4 6 7

TABLE OF CONTENTS

INTRODUCTION 1
   1. Summary of Existing Scholarship 2
   2. Approach 4
   3. Procedure 5
      a) Seeking Out Mentalities 5
      b) Determining and Ordering Mentalities 6
   4. Selection of Sources 7
   5. Definitions of Magic and Court Magicians 8
      a) Magic 8
      b) Court Magicians 10
   6. Plan for this Book 11

Chapter I:
THE PREDECESSORS OF THE COURT MAGICIAN: MAGICAL
ADMINISTRATORS IN ROMAN, CELTIC AND GERMANIC SOCIETY 13
   1. Magic and Politics in Antiquity 14
   2. Magic and Politics in Celtic Society 21
   3. Magic and Politics in Germanic Society 27
   4. Conclusion 37

Chapter II:
MEDIEVAL CHRISTIAN RESPONSES TO MAGICAL KNOWLEDGE 39
   1. High and Low Culture in the Middle Ages 39
   2. Orthodox Church Policy Towards Magic 41
   3. Popular Culture and Christianity 46
   4. Popular Beliefs Connecting Wisdom and Magic 50
      a) Hagiography 50
      b) Gerbert of Aurillac 52
   5. Historical Clerics and Magic 54
      a) Magic in the Schools 55
      b) The Theoretical Legitimation of Magic 62
   6. Conclusion 64

Chapter III:
THE ADAPTATION AND TRANSFORMATION OF MAGICAL
CONCEPTS IN MEDIEVAL COURT SOCIETY 65

1. High and Low Culture at the Medieval Courts 65
2. Charismatic Rule 66
3. The Dissemination of Power at Court 72
4. Magicians in Court Writings 74
5. Magicians at Historical Courts 78
6. Conclusion 86

Chapter IV:
LANZELET 87

1. Introduction 87
2. The Function of the Malduc Episode 87
3. Malduc and Historical Magicians 93
4. Conclusion 98

Chapter V:
PARZIVAL 99

1. Introduction 99
2. The Function of the Cundrie and Clinschor Episodes 99
   a) Cundrie 99
   b) Clinschor 104
4. Clinschor, Cundrie and Historical Magicians 109
5. Conclusion 117

Chapter VI:
WIGALOIS 119

1. Introduction 119
2. The Function of the Roaz Episode 119
3. Roaz and Historical Magicians 124
4. Conclusion 129

Chapter VII:
DIU CRÔNE 131

   1. Introduction 131
   2. The Function of the Gansguoter Episodes 131
       a) The Adventures at the Bridle Castle and Castle Salie 133
       b) The Recovery of Arthur's Treasures 134
   3. Gansguoter and Historical Magicians 138
   4. Conclusion 146

Chapter VIII:
WILHELM VON ÖSTERREICH 149

   1. Introduction 149
   2. The Function of the Merlin/Parklise Episode 149
   3. Magicians in Wilhelm von Österreich and Historical
      Magicians 153
   4. Conclusion 162

CONCLUSION 165

BIBLIOGRAPHY 169

   I. Primary Sources 169
   II. Secondary Literature 173

ACKNOWLEDGEMENTS

This book is a revised version of my dissertation, which I submitted to the University of Washington (Seattle) in the Spring of 1992. I would like to express my sincere appreciation to my advisor, Professor C. Stephen Jaeger, for his invaluable assistance. In addition, special thanks to the German Academic Exchange Service for having granted me a scholarship which allowed me to conduct research at the Westfälische-Wilhelms-Universität in Münster, F.R.G. from October 1990 to July 1991. While there, I received valuable advice from Dr. Hans-Jörg Spitz, who offered a colloquium on "Mentalitätsgeschichte" in the Winter Semester of 1990-91. Parts of this book appeared in an article entitled "Knowledge, Politics, and Magic: The Magician Gansguoter in Heinrich von dem Türlin's *Crône*" in Volume 67.4 (Fall 1994) of *The German Quarterly*, pp. 470-83. I would like to thank the editors of this journal for granting me permission to incorporate the article in my book. Thanks as well to Professor Wolfgang Harms for accepting my book in his *Mikrokosmos* series. I am also grateful to both Professor Harms and Dr. Otto Neudeck for their valuable editorial comments. And last but not least, I am deeply indebted and grateful to my mother, Lore Maksymiuk, whose constant love and support made this book possible.

INTRODUCTION

Magic is attracting attention today. Students of folklore and of the history of religion cannot afford to neglect it. Anthropologists have found that it colors much of the life of primitive man, and sociologists have begun to deal with it as an important social manifestation.

Lynn Thorndike, author of the monumental *History of Magic and Experimental Science*, made this observation in 1915.[1] Today, over three quarters of a century later, magic is again attracting the attention of medievalists.[2]

These scholars have begun to question the long-held assumption that medieval European society was "essentially Christian" in nature. They believe that only a small clerical minority were actually Christian, and that the vast majority of people subscribed to a "folkloric" belief system, dominated by prevailing magical-superstitious patterns of thought. Keith Thomas, for example, states: "The line between magic and religion is one which it is impossible to draw in many primitive societies; it is equally difficult to recognize in medieval England." (50) John Van Engen's comments in his 1986 article "The Christian Middle Ages as an Historiographical Problem" show the impact of the new attitude towards medieval Christianity:

> This newest historiographical shift has proved so powerful that even authors kindly disposed to Catholic Christianity have summarized the state of late medieval religious life as 'in broad stretches a religious consciousness that can hardly be called Christian' (Van Engen, 519-520).

These popular religious beliefs also influenced the "high" culture of the nobility. Marc Bloch, one of the first historians of learned and popular beliefs, demonstrated the reciprocal influence of "high" and "low" cultures in his

---

1 "Some Medieval Conceptions of Magic," p. 107.
2 For example, see Richard Kieckhefer, *Magic in the Middle Ages*; Christa Habiger-Tuczay, *Magie und Magier im Mittelalter*; (review of both books by author in *Arbitrium* 1/94, pp. 27-30); Gabor Klaniczay, *The Uses of Supernatural Power*; Keith Thomas, *Religion and the Decline of Magic*; John Van Engen, "The Christian Middle Ages as an Historiographical Problem".

study of sacred monarchy in France and England. Bloch examined the belief that French and English kings could heal scrofula, a notion whose origins he traced to pagan beliefs in sacred royalty, and Christian ideas of saintliness and divine unction.

In this study I also wish to examine how the sensibilities of "high" and "low" culture interact when they associate supernatural skills with political ones and attribute these skills to another member of the court. I intend to study the medieval mentality that equated knowledge with magic, and to look at this concept personified in the figure of the court magician in medieval German literature.

Magicians are portrayed repeatedly in medieval romance as educated and knowledgeable men with great administrative and advisory skills. In English and French Arthurian Literature, Merlin appears as a wise and powerful royal advisor, continually using his magic and learning to counsel and help Uther Pendragon and his son Arthur. Conversely, in Gottfried von Straßburg's *Tristan,* the title hero's political success at King Marke's court aroused the jealousy of other courtiers who denounced him as a sorcerer. Magicians were active at real courts as well. John of Salisbury condemned the great influence of magicians at Henry II's court in his *Policraticus* and chided his friend Thomas Becket for turning to soothsayers. Accusations of sorcery were used to discredit successful courtiers, clergymen and other influential advisors. Pope Sylvester II's great erudition and political skill led to rumours that he had signed a pact with the devil. It is this connection between knowledge, magic and power in both fact and fiction that I want to examine. I intend to investigate the mentality in medieval Europe which considered learning to be magical and examine how this notion was reflected in literary portraits of court magicians.

1. Summary of Existing Scholarship

Several scholars have studied magicians in medieval German literature. In 1933 both Adelaide Marie Weiss and E.A. Schiprowski wrote dissertations on Merlin in German literature. Their works both included medieval treatments of Merlin, but concentrated primarily on his appearance in modern works. Merlin, however, did not find the resonance in German literature that he did in English and French literature. He only appears in one extant work before 1478, Johann von Würzburg's *Wilhelm von Österreich*, written in 1314. This work will be discussed in the last chapter of this study. There are also several studies of the Clinschor figure in medieval German literature, for example Theresa Holländer's dissertation from 1927 entitled *Klingsor: Eine stoffgeschichtliche Untersuchung*, and Norbert Wolf's 1967 essay "Die Gestalt Klingsors in der deutschen Literatur des Mittelalters". Holländer's and Wolf's works are both source studies, and use approaches quite different from my own. Ernst S. Dick has also written an essay dealing in part with the magicians Clinschor and Gansguoter;[1] yet he only looks at the structural implications of the relationship between these magicians and Gawan. Several essays have also been written on Cundrie, but they have concentrated on her function within the romance or have been source studies.[2]

The magician in English literature has received more attention than his German counterpart, and there have been several books on the topic published in recent years. Interest has focused on Merlin; an example is Norma Lorre Goodrich's work of popular scholarship, *Merlin* (1987). Her study is, however, an attempt to determine Merlin's historical origins, rather than an examination of the medieval mentality which brought together sorcerer and court advisor in this figure. There are also several works on English magicians from later periods, such as *White Magic and English Renaissance Drama* by David Woodman (1973), *Five Ceremonial Magicians of Tudor-Stuart Drama* by Robert Goltra Jr. (1984), and *Heavenly Necromancers: The Magician in English Renaissance Drama* by Barbara Howard Traister (1984). These works all deal with Renaissance magicians and focus on the rise of Neo-Platonic thought in that period. While comparing the qualities of fictional magicians with the historical reality of the period, these approaches do not look at the

---

[1] Ernst Dick, "The Hero and the Magician. On the Proliferation of Dark Figures from *Li Contes del Graal* and *Parzival* to *Diu Crône*."
[2] Franz Rolf Schröder, "Cundrîe"; Phyllis Ackerman, "Who is Kundrie - What is She?"; Andree Kahn Blumstein, "The Structure and Function of the Cundrie Episodes in Wolfram's *Parzival*"; Fritz Peter Knapp, "Die hässliche Gralsbotin und die Victorinische Ästhetik."

mentality also present in Renaissance society which associated magicians with learning and power.

2. Approach

In examining the medieval notion equating learning and magic, I will make use of a methodology known as the history of mentalities. This methodology has attracted the attention of a growing number of scholars. Realizing the limitations of a strictly economic, political, philosophical or religious point of view, they are turning their attention to the structures of thought which determine social behaviour both in real life and in literary production and reception. Peoples' value systems, their particular view of the world and their culturally determined reactions are now the focus of an increasing number of historical studies. These studies strive to transcend purely political or economic interpretations through an interdisciplinary socio-economic analysis of how "material civilization and culture interpenetrate one another."[1]

Such an approach brings the historian of mentalities closer to the anthropologist and the ethnologist, and indeed this methodology is sometimes referred to as "historical anthropology" or "ethno-history".[2] The ethnologist's approach is useful because it brings attention to the common people and their beliefs, which have been neglected in traditional histories written from the point of view of the ruling classes. The history of mentalities, however, is not identical with an ethnological approach. Nor is it just a history of ideas. A history of mentalities does not restrict its focus to either popular or learned culture. It examines the spheres of both ruler and subject in order to determine the ideas and beliefs pervading the collective consciousness of a society and the beliefs that shaped everyday life in that society.

---

1 Jacques Le Goff, *Time, Work & Culture in the Middle Ages*, p. xiii.
2 Aaron J. Gurevich, "Medieval Culture and Mentality According to the New French Historiography", p. 174.

Literary scholars have also adopted the history of mentalities methodology.[1] Ursula Peters sees it as a great help in understanding medieval literature:

> Eine *histoire des mentalités* würde mit ihrem Insistieren auf den gruppentypischen emotionalen Einstellungen, auf den Selbstinterpretationen und Verhaltensmustern genau diese für das Verständnis literarischer Produktion und Rezeption entscheidende psychische Zwischenschicht zwischen der gesellschaftlichen und literarischen Wirklichkeit in den Blick rücken. (183)

A history of mentalities approach thus enables the literary scholar to discover the mental structures which influenced and shaped literary production.

3. Procedure

In attempting to seek out a particular mentality the historian of mentalities must differentiate between the different layers of mentality present in a particular example.[2] These mentalities, although not necessarily ordered in a logically coherent manner, are nevertheless ordered according to certain criteria. Once these mentalities are identified, the historian can then turn his attention to the various systems of organization that shaped the thoughts in his sources.

a) Seeking out mentalities

How and where does one find evidence of a mentality? Mentalities are ideas pervading the collective conscious of a particular society. They crystallize into the institutions and social practices that determine the rituals of interaction, the patterns of everyday life and the forms of expression of a society. They are shared by groups as diverse as kings and serfs, popes and monks alike. Mentalities are reflected in almost all aspects of human thought:

---

1 Ursula Peters, "Literaturgeschichte als Mentalitätengeschichte? Überlegungen zur Problematik einer neueren Forschungsrichtung."
2 Jacques Le Goff, "Mentalities: a history of ambiguities," p. 175.

> jene Bilder und Vorstellungen, die die Menschen einer bestimmten Epoche von sich und der Welt haben, ihre geheimsten Befürchtungen und Hoffnungen, ihre emotionalen Einstellungen zu den grundlegenden Lebenssituationen wie Geburt, Krankheit, Sexualität und Tod (Ursula Peters, 180).

As Jacques Le Goff states, "What men say, whatever the tone in which they say it - conviction, emotion, bombast, - is more often than not simply an assemblage of ready-made ideas, commonplaces and intellectual bric-à-brac ...".[1]

These sensibilities often reveal themselves in the automatic gestures and spontaneous words "which seem to lack any origins and to be the fruits of improvisation and reflex" (Le Goff, "Mentalities: a history of ambiguities", 170). They have, however, long traditions and are well established in systems of thought. Mentalities may be most clearly evident in irrational and abnormal behaviour and attitudes, as for example belief in supernatural phenomena. In magical explanations the "interpenetration between the tangible and supernatural, the common nature of the corporeal and the psychic" (Le Goff, "Mentalities: a history of ambiguities", 173) become apparent. The conditions necessary for a supernatural ordering of the world become visible.

b) Determining and ordering mentalities

The historian of mentalities must also realize that the presence of an example in a text does not necessarily reveal a sensibility currently at work in that culture. It may simply be a topos left over as a vestige of a once active mentality or thought structure. It is therefore necessary to try to determine whether any given example indicates an active mentality, or an archaic survival, remaining only as a hollow convention. An active mentality tends to have reverberations in a number of different types of sources, whereas a vestigial topos usually appears only in a very specific and isolated text tradition. Although mentalities are resistant to transformation, they do indeed change

---

[1] Le Goff, "Mentalities: a history of ambiguities", p. 169.

and disappear. The historian must determine the continuity or discontinuity of a mentality and to what degree it is still operating in a society.

4. Selection of sources

Since the history of mentalities approach distinguishes itself through its analysis rather than its choice of sources, a great number of sources can be useful. There are texts, however, which lend themselves better than others to this approach. The traditional and formulaic aspects of sources, such as topoi in introductions and descriptions, require particular attention. Topoi are of great help in revealing the framework of mentalities.[1] In my study it will be important to see if there are certain topoi used in describing learned men, magicians and court advisors. Are there similarities in these descriptions? Where do they overlap?

Sources which reveal marginal aspects of a society's attitudes and behaviour are of particular interest to the researcher. Religious and supernatural writings such as church histories, hagiographies and Christian legends serve as a point of intersection for natural and supernatural orderings of the world. These texts show the reciprocal influence of official church doctrine and popular religion in establishing which supernatural powers are accepted by people and institutions.

Literature is also useful because of its representation and interpretation of reality. The portrait of the magician in literature reflects contemporary conceptions of him that were active in the minds of both author and audience. In choosing literary sources, however, it is important to determine whether or not these sources are indeed representative of the mentality of a culture. The medieval German literature I am examining was directed at a courtly audience, a relatively small segment of society. The sensibilities of that audience were not necessarily identical to those of medieval German society in general. Therefore it is important to substantiate my findings in other written

---

1 Le Goff, "Mentalities: a history of ambiguities", p. 175.

sources, where the presence of popular and ecclesiastical culture makes itself felt.

Mentalities tend to develop within certain social groups and institutions. On the other hand, there are groups or institutions that act as intermediaries in their diffusion. I will look at the areas where knowledge is transmitted and at those where it is applied. The centers for magical and political education will be considered, as well as the worldly and ecclesiastical centers where this knowledge was applied.

Through this selection of sources I hope to achieve a broad perspective of medieval attitudes towards knowledge and magic; broader than could be gained by an analysis restricted to magicians in German or even European literature.

5. Definitions of Magic and Court Magicians

a) Magic

In order to examine the beliefs associated with magic in the Middle Ages it is first necessary to establish a working definition of magic.[1] In antiquity the word *magos* was first applied to the practices of the *magi*, the Zoroastrian priests who accompanied Xerxes into Greece.[2] The Greeks' understanding of the magi's actual practices was unclear, but these practices included astrology, healing and the search for occult knowledge in general. Because of the magi's foreign origin, the term carried all of the negative connotations associated with the hated Persian invaders. After the fifth century B.C. the *magos* was no longer associated with the Persians and the word became the general term for any practioner "of arts that elicited the aid of gods or *daimones* for his own benefit or for that of his clients, usually for criminal purposes" (Edward Peters, 1). Although the foreign connotations had disappeared, the negative ones remained.

---

[1] My definition of magic is greatly indebted to the insightful studies of Edward Peters, *The Magician, the Witch and the Law*, especially Chapter I, "The Transformations of the Magus," Richard Kieckhefer, *Magic in the Middle Ages*, especially Chapter I, and Lynn Thorndike, "Some Medieval Conceptions of Magic."
[2] Edward Peters, p. 1.

Early Christians propagating their religion played on the negative connotations of magic to denounce all forms of its practice.[1] Of the early Christian theologians, St. Augustine was the most influential in his condemnations of magic, denouncing all forms as the work of the devil and his demonic minions.[2] Augustine's concept of magic was so influential among later theologians that until the end of the twelfth century,

> if you asked a theologian what magic was you were likely to hear that demons began it and were always involved in it. You would also be likely to get a catalogue of different forms of magic, and most of the varieties would be species of divination (Kieckhefer, 10-11).[3]

In the 13th century, however, a more positive view of magic began to gain acceptance among many intellectuals. Theologians like Thomas Aquinas[4] and Albertus Magnus[5] allowed for the possibility of natural magic, which did not involve demons but relied on occult powers occurring in nature. These powers had many different origins.[6] Plants or stones, for example, could have symbolic powers from their shape, color or relationship to other items. Draconium, a plant whose leaves resemble dragons could be used to counteract snakebite or parasitical worms.[7]

> Other items gained their power from animistic principles. The mandrake root with its "human" shape was considered so powerful a magic plant that people feared uprooting it. Magicians requiring the root for their operations used ropes tied to animals to pull it out of the ground so that any retaliatory magic the plant might release would be directed at the animal and not the magician.[8]

---

1 Edward Peters, p. 4.
2 Augustine, *On Christian Doctrine*, especially Book 2, and *City of God*, Books 9-10.
3 Also Thorndike, "Some Medieval Conceptions of Magic," pp. 108-12.
4 Thorndike, "Some Medieval Conceptions of Magic," p. 115.
5 Thorndike, "Some Medieval Conceptions of Magic," pp. 116-21.
6 My examination of natural magic is based on Kieckhefer's discussion (pp. 12-14).
7 Kieckhefer, p. 13.
8 Kieckhefer, pp. 13-14; also illustration p. 14.

Still other powers came from stellar or planetary influence on terrestrial objects. These heavenly bodies emitted rays which gave objects on earth their occult powers.

Since medieval theologians disagreed on which kinds of magic were natural and which were demonic, I will take magic to include occult powers deriving from both natural and demonic forces.[1]

b) *Court Magicians*

Magical feats pervade medieval literature and any attempts to describe and analyse all examples of magic in courtly romance quickly become an endless task. Therefore I will concentrate on the magic practiced by magicians at court. For the purposes of this study the court magician will be either a member of the court who is a magician or a magician working for a member of the court. By magician, I mean someone who extensively studies and practices magic, a "professional", so to say. This definition excludes characters (such as knights) who occasionally resort to magical devices or spells without actually working the magic themselves. I will not include Morolf, the crafty royal advisor from the epic *Salman und Morolf*. As Maria Dobozy has pointed out, Morolf's seemingly supernatural knowledge is in fact not supernatural at all:

> the poem attempts to explain most events rationally and treats the construction of Morolf's leather boat, the use of numerous disguises, herbs and potions not as magic, but as technological skill, cunning, and understanding of natural phenomena. (39)

Morolf's "rational" knowledge thus serves as a contrast to the magic of Fore and Salme: "Thus, Morolf proves that knowledge is essential and beneficial to man, for without it, the dark forces of magic used exclusively by the heathen would prevail." (Dobozy, 39). My definition of court magician also ex-

---

[1] In my definition of magic I am following the one developed by Richard Kieckhefer:
   Magic will be used for those phenomena which intellectuals would have recognized as either demonic or natural magic. That which makes an action magical is the type of power it invokes: if it relies on divine action or the manifest powers of nature it is notmagical, while if it uses demonic aid or occult powers in nature it is magical (14).

cludes magician-monarchs such as Gottfried von Straßburg's Queen Isolde or Konrad von Würzburg's Meliur. Here another mentality, that of magical kingship, is predominant.

6. Plan for this Book

Before turning to the Middle Ages, it is important to first examine the equation of knowledge and magic in the cultures which shaped and influenced Medieval Germany: Classical, Celtic and Germanic cultures. I will begin by looking at the connections between magic and knowledge in these societies and the influence magicians had in government and politics.

Another important influence on medieval culture was the Bible and its presentation of magic and magicians. Closely related to this is Orthodox Christianity's view of magic and the extent to which these teachings were internalised by medieval clergy and laity.

Next, I turn to medieval court culture and the role magic played there. I will investigate the influence of the church and clergy as well as of popular beliefs regarding magic. The education of courtiers and their access to magical knowledge will also be considered.

In light of the various views of magic circulating at court, it is important to explore how the court adapted, transformed and legitimized magical power for its own ends. I will look at the distribution of power at the court and how magic and charisma were used as means of establishing power by both rulers and their advisors.

After having examined the historical courts' notions and adaptation of magic, I will turn to the presentation of court magicians in Medieval German literature. The works I discuss cover a period of roughly 120 years, beginning with Ulrich von Zatzikhoven's *Lanzelet* (1194), continuing with Wolfram von Eschenbach's *Parzival* (1200-1205), Wirnt von Gravenberg's *Wigalois* (1215), Heinrich von dem Türlin's *Diu Crône* (1225), and concluding with Johann von Würzburg's *Wilhelm von Österreich* (1314). In my analysis of the magicians in these works, I will begin with their description and the role they played within the romance. Then I will compare them to their historical counterparts in order to determine to what degree they correspond to actual magicians and how medieval notions of magic were incorporated into these figures. Although the literary magicians in this study are fictional creations of medieval writers, it will become apparent that there are nevertheless strong parallels between them and actual magicians: both historical and fictional magicians are educated clerics; their magic is closely associated with learning and science, and the lines between magic and technology are indistinct; their knowledge grants them access to the court and allows them to move in the highest circles of society. At the court magicians are valued (and feared), and their assistance is often invaluable to rulers.

I hope to determine to what extent and, if possible, *why* knowledge was considered magical. Taking medieval German literature as a point of departure, I will examine the sphere of influence of the concept of knowledge as magic and thereby hope to gain insight into the nature of power, its exercise and self-representation in the Middle Ages.

Chapter I

THE PREDECESSORS OF THE COURT MAGICIAN: MAGICAL ADMINISTRATORS IN ROMAN, CELTIC AND GERMANIC SOCIETY

The origins of the magical court advisor can be traced back to the mythologies of Indo-European cultures. According to George Dumézil's comparative myth studies, the concept of a magical administrator existed in most European societies. Dumézil proposed that these societies were characterized by a hierarchical tri-partite social division which manifested itself both in their mythology and social organization.[1] Because each of these three parts plays a role in the maintenance of a social and mythological organization, Dumézil called them functions. The first and most important function was concerned with the magical/religious and juridical administration of the universe. The second was concerned with physical strength and war and the third with fertility, prosperity and health. In social organization the respective offices are those of priest-king, warrior, and farmer/herder. Dumézil has found this classification to varying degrees among all Indo-European societies. In Indian society (the one which Dumézil most often uses as an example) the first function is embodied mythologically in the gods *Varuna* and *Mitra* and socially in the *Brahman* caste; the second function in the god *Kshatriya* and the warrior caste; the third in various fertility deities including the *Ashvins* and the *Vaishya* or farmer caste.

It is the first function, that of administrator of the universe, which I will examine in Roman, Celtic and Germanic society, the three major cultures influencing Medieval Germany. This function is of particular interest because it embodies the two major skills found in the court magician; rational/juridical skills on the one hand and magical/religious ones on the other. I want to determine to what degree the function of magical administrator influenced the mythological organization of these three societies and to what degree this function manifested itself in their social organization. Fi-

---

1 A good English overview of Dumézil's work (with extensive bibliography) is C. Scott Littleton's *The New Comparative Mythology: An Anthropological Assessment of the Theories of Georges Dumézil*.

nally I will examine how magic was used to achieve political goals in each of these cultures.

1. Magic and Politics in Antiquity

According to George Dumézil, there are indications that a tri-partite structure existed in early Roman culture.[1] Mythologically, this structure was reflected in the Pre-Capitoline triad Jupiter, Mars and Quirinus. Jupiter was the god responsible for the cosmic order and therefore represented the magical/religious aspect of rule. The obscure god Dius Fidius was responsible for the maintainance of moral order and thus represented the judicial administrator. Together, Jupiter and Dius Fidius made up the Roman equivalents of *Mitra* and *Varuna* and embodied the first function. Mars was the god of war and the warrior caste. Quirinus was god of those people responsible for the day-to-day well-being of society.[2]

Although Jupiter represents the magico-religious aspects of rule, his characteristics reflect both political and supernatural skills. Dumézil notes that he is *"Rex,* colleague and celestial aspect of the earthly *rex* - it is to this title as well that he owes his position and prestige" (179). Jupiter is also the god of transactions, and occupies the role "as witness, as guarantor, as avenger of oaths and pacts, in private as well as in public life, in commerce between citizens or with foreigners" (179). As ruler of the Roman panthenon and the god associated with transactions, Jupiter clearly has an important administrative role.

Yet, Jupiter's magical side is a vital aspect as well. He is the god of the sky, and "causes to appear there the *auspicia,* the signs which as sovereign god he gives to the heads of Rome through the flight of birds and which the au-

---

[1] Dumézil, *Jupiter, Mars, Quirinus; Essai sur la conception indo-européenne de la société et sur les origines de Rome* (1941), overview in Littleton, pp. 67-79. See also Dumézil, *Archaic Roman Religion*.
[2] Dumézil admits that there are, of course, differences between the Roman and Indic systems (Littleton, p. 59). The Indic system reflects a rigidly defined class system, the Roman system only three modes of activities. Ancient Indian society was a royal society and Rome a state of citizens. Finally the Indic *brahman* (and Celtic druid) "could exercise his duties over the whole range of the pantheon, while the Roman *flamen* was confined to the service of a single God" (Littleton, p. 59).

gurs ... observe in a portion of the sky" (Dumézil, 179). And he is also associated with the Vinalia festivals, at which he receives the first ceremonial offerings of wine. In interpreting this ritual, Dumézil emphasizes the intoxicating effects of the drink: "Drunkenness is not only a plebeian debauchery; through it, in an illusion stronger than reality, man goes beyond himself" (185). Dumézil sees Jupiter's association with alcohol to be similar to those made with Indra and Odin.

> The thief and principal user of the *soma* is not a divine protector of the plants; it is Indra, the warrior god, who performs his exploits while drunk. The thief and possessor of the best mead is not one of the Vanir, the gods of the fertility of beasts and fields, but Ódinn, the sovereign magician, the king of the gods; and the drunkenness which it creates in him is that which produces science and poetry. Finally the acknowledged right of Jupiter over this intoxicating drink, the *epulum* which is served to him on the Capitol, and the *daps* with which the peasant regales him - consisting essentially of wine - all derive from the same conception: they are homage rendered to the celestial sovereign, not bargains with an agrarian god. (185-86)

In this brief sketch of Jupiter's characteristics, both sides of the magical administrator come to light: the juridical, embodied in his association with transactions and kingship, and the irrational, supernatural aspect, reflected in augury and intoxication.

According to Dumézil, the tri-partite division of Roman society was also reflected in the three groups of *flamen* or priests. These groups consisted of: the *flamen dialis*, associated with Jupiter and the king; the *flamen martialis*, associated with Mars and soldiers; and finally the *flamen quirinalis*, associated with Quirinus (later with the *tranquillus* of Mars) and the agricultural *quirites*. These *flamines* were the most sacred and important of the priests. In monarchical and early republican Rome, the ruler's fortune depended on the prosperity of the *flamines*.[1]

The great significance of the *flamen Dialis* becomes apparent in the special powers accorded to him. The *flamen Dialis* was above the law and not

---

1 Littleton, p. 55.

bound by any oaths. He could suspend the execution of punishments and free prisoners,[1] and, he was also the "incarnation of the sacred" (Dumézil, 153). This meant that no day was a secular one for him, and that he always had to keep with him some item which expressed his sacred function. He also was to avoid contact with anything which could defile him, "especially with what is dead or suggests death: corpses, funeral pyres, and uncooked meat" (Dumézil, 153). The *flamen Dialis*, like the god he served, also embodied a combination of juridical and sacred aspects.

As Roman society developed, however, the triad of Jupiter, Mars and Quirinus gave way to the so-called Capitoline triad of Jupiter Capitolinus, Juno and Minerva.[2] Of the original triad, only Jupiter remained, but in "a much altered and, in later times, Hellenized form" (Littleton, 69). Although Jupiter was still the main god, his magical aspect was less emphasized. Mars continued to enjoy a devoted following, but the gods Dius Fidius and Quirinus faded from popularity. They were seen as archaic already by the beginning of historical times. As the relative importance of the Jupiter-Mars-Quirinus triad diminished, so too did that of its priests. Yet elements of the tri-partite structure continued to exist in Roman culture:

> ... the functions, administrative and sacerdotal, military, and agricultural, remained distinct; and it is as the summation of these functions, which is tantamount to saying the summation of Roman society, that these three deities were canonical. (Littleton, 69-70)[3]

The equation of magic and administrative skills was not restricted to the Roman gods and priests. There was also a tradition of political sorcery running throughout Roman antiquity, which continued up into the fourth century A.D. It would be beyond the dimensions of this study to trace the

---

1 Dumézil, p. 153.
2 Dumézil, pp. 283-310.
3 Dumézil also has shown that many of the historical legends of monarchal Rome were in fact historicized Indo-European Myth: *Archaic Roman Religion*, pp. 60-79, also Littleton, pp. 70-72.

Magical Administrators in Roman, Celtic and Germanic Society   17

history of magic in Antiquity,[1] but it is enlightening to briefly examine its applications in political circles.

Rulers often turned to sorcery to achieve their aims.[2] According to Pliny, Nero had studied magic with the best teachers. Pliny also notes that Caesar, before departing on a journey, would repeat three times a prayer for safe travel (XXVIII. 4. 21). Philostratus *(Vita Apollonii,* viii. 3) mentions that the emperor Domitian (81-96 A.D.) consulted the magician Apollonius of Tyre.

The Roman historian Ammianus Marcellinus notes that the emperor Julian the Apostate (361-363 A.D.) was proficient in the magic arts and used them to learn of the imminent death of Constantius II (XXI. i. 6ff). Julian had learned these arts from Maximus, whom he had chosen as his teacher, after he had heard that Maximus, "using incense and incantations in front of a statue of the goddess Hecate, had in the presence of his followers brought it about that the face of the goddess came to life" (Barb, 115).

Magic, however, was not only used by rulers; it could also be directed against them. Julius Caesar Germanicus, the adopted son of the emperor Tiberius, was apparently the victim of such an attack. He died in 19 A.D., presumably by poisoning. Tacitus (Annals, 2.69) reports that shortly before his death, a number of strange objects were found under the floor and between the walls of his house. They included exhumed body parts, blood-smeared ashes, and lead tablets with the name Germanicus engraved on them. It seems likely that one of his enemies had resorted to black magic to dispose of Germanicus.

The fear of treasonous sorcery reached a high point in fourth and fifth century Rome: there were a number of sorcery accusations and trials during the reigns of Constantius II, Valentian I and Valens. Draconic penalties were instituted for anyone remotely connected with any sort of magic. The severity of these laws shows to what degree the emperors feared sorcery. Ammianus Marcellinus recorded some of these laws:

---
[1] A useful guide to magic in antiquity is Georg Luck´s *Magie und andere Geheimlehren in der Antike.*
[2] Kieckhefer, p. 24.

> Nam siqui remedia quartanae vel doloris alterius collo gestartet, sive per monumentum transisse vesper, malivolorum argueretur indiciis, ut veneficus, sepulchrorumque horrores, et errantium ibidem animarum ludibria colligens vana, pronuntiatus reus capitis interibat. (XIX. xii. 14)
>
> ... if anyone wore on his neck an amulet against the quartan ague or any other complaint, or was accused by the testimony of the evil-disposed of passing by a grave in the evening, on the ground that he was a dealer in poisons, or a gatherer of the horrors of tombs and the vain illusions of the ghosts that walk there, he was condemned to capital punishment and so perished. (XIX. xii. 14)[1]

As a result of these laws, some scholars have found this period to "closely resemble the worst witch-hunting centuries at the end of the Middle Ages" (Barb, 105). What is interesting about these trials is that the accused were not simple and ignorant people from the peasant classes, but people around the emperor: "the scene is usually the inner ring of the court: it is played out among officials, ex-officials, local notables. All of these men would have had personal contact with the emperor as a man, and not only as a remote figure of authority" (Brown, "Sorcery, Demons and the Rise of Christianity: From Late Antiquity into the Middle Ages", 125).

The most infamous of these trials occurred in 371 A.D. in Antiochia. Hundreds of people from aristocratic and plebeian classes were tortured and executed for their involvement in a plot to replace the emperor Valens with a young man named Theodorus. According to Ammianus (XXIX. i. 28-33), two soothsayers had by means of magical ceremonies attempted to discover who would succeed Valens.[2] When Valens learned of the plot he rounded up the magicians and sentenced them to death.

---

[1] Translated by John C. Rolfe (*Res gestae*, dual language edition).
[2] They had learned the first four letters of his name [Θ,E,O,Δ] when the ceremony was interrupted by one of the diviners who cried out the name Theodorus. When the emperor sentenced them to death, they prophesied that the emperor himself would die by "evil fate while Ares rages on the plain of Mimas". Interestingly enough, the soothsayers were correct in predicting a successor to Valens (a man named Theodosius) and the emperor's fate, even though Valens did not die near the mountain Mimas. He fell on the plain of Adrianople, near the tomb of a man named Mimas (Barb, 112-114).

Magical Administrators in Roman, Celtic and Germanic Society

Peter Brown has developed an interesting theory about the increase of magical trials in fourth-century Rome. He sees the increase of political sorcery accusations not simply as "pretexts for suppressing political conspiracies" ("Sorcery, Demons and the Rise of Christianity: From Late Antiquity into the Middle Ages", 125), but as the result of the competitive and constantly changing life at court combined with the current political instability and discord between the ruling classes. These accusations continued from the fourth until the end of the sixth century A.D., when stability was once again reestablished. Brown sees the cause of conflict as the clash between two systems of power, one which he calls "articulate" power and the other which he calls "inarticulate". He defines articulate power as "power defined and agreed upon by everyone (and especially by its holders!): authority vested in precise persons; admiration and success gained by recognized channels" ("Sorcery, Demons and the Rise of Christianity: From Late Antiquity into the Middle Ages", 124). Inarticulate power consists of "the disturbing intangibles of social life: the imponderable advantages of certain groups: personal skills that succeed in a way that is unacceptable or difficult to understand" (Brown, "Sorcery, Demons and the Rise of Christianity: From Late Antiquity into the Middle Ages", 124).

According to Brown, the representatives of "articulate" power, such as the emperor's official administrators, whose position and influence were clearly defined by their office, levelled charges of sorcery against those holders of less clearly defined positions of personal power. The latter group's "inarticulate" power was "based largely on skills, such as rhetoric, which, in turn, associated the man of skill with the ill-defined, inherited prestige of the traditional aristocracies" (Brown, "Sorcery, Demons and the Rise of Christianity: From Late Antiquity into the Middle Ages", 125). Brown sees the Roman concept of misfortune as responsible for accusations of sorcery. Roman society often associated a man's identity with his skill. "When an incongruity suddenly appears in his performance, he defends his image of himself by treating it as an intrusive element, placed there, from the outside, by some hostile agent" ("Sorcery, Demons and the Rise of Christianity: From Late Antiquity into the Middle Ages", 134). Thus a man suffering a lapse in skill could attribute this lapse to the machinations of a jealous colleague who had resorted to sorcery in order to bestow misfortune onto the victim.

Brown sees the rise of Christianity as responsible for a new sense of identity which resulted in a decline in sorcery accusations:

> In the fourth and fifth centuries, therefore, the sense of a fixed identity in a stable and well-oriented world, that would encourage the blaming of sorcerers and would single out incongruities in public behaviour as *the* misfortune *par excellence,* was being eroded in both the social milieu and the religious ideas associated with the leaders of Christian opinion. ("Sorcery, Demons and the Rise of Christianity: From Late Antiquity into the Middle Ages", 135)

Early Christian church fathers like Augustine saw misfortune as inextricably linked with the Christian concept of human frailty. Christians saw misfortune as the result of mankind's sinful nature and God's anger at mankind's fall. As a result, one's identity was no longer seen as fixed and stable, but frail and unreliable. As the Christian penitential system became more developed, "the idea of ill-defined guilt hardened into a sense of exposure to misfortune through the neglect of prescribed actions" (Brown, "Sorcery, Demons and the Rise of Christianity: From Late Antiquity into the Middle Ages", 135). The early Christian church viewed the struggle between good and evil as one between God and His supernatural agents: angels and saints on the one hand, and Satan and his demons on the other. This new view changed the relation of the sorcerer to misfortune. "The confrontation of Saint and Devil stole the scene from the sorcerer" (Brown, "Sorcery, Demons and the Rise of Christianity: From Late Antiquity into the Middle Ages", 135). As Christian doctrine developed in the sixth and seventh centuries, the image of divine social structure came to mirror the earthly one: "Angels were the courtiers and bureaucrats of a remote Heavenly Emperor, and the saints, the *patroni,* the 'protectors', whose efficacious interventions at court channelled the benefits of a just autocrat to individuals and localities" (Brown, "Sorcery, Demons and the Rise of Christianity: From Late Antiquity into the Middle Ages", 142). This concept of immanent justice removed the secular court's responsibility to punish the sorcerer as it allowed the sorcerer to be punished "by the direct intervention of these divine governors [angels and saints]: the sorcerer received short shrift, as a traitor from a well-regimented celestial society" (Brown, "Sorcery, Demons and the Rise of Christianity: From Late Antiquity into the Middle Ages", 142). Although the changing concept of immanent justice in late Antiquity caused the Roman magician to step into the background, his Celtic and Germanic counterparts remained active.

2. Magic and Politics in Celtic Society

A triad of Gods corresponding to Dumézil's three functions also existed in Celtic society. The Roman poet Lucan in his *Pharsalia* (I.445-46) names three Celtic gods; *Teutates, Esus* and *Taranis*, to whom human sacrifices were made. Mythologists have attempted to find the three functions in these three gods, but their efforts have been hampered by meager records and Roman historians whose records were anything but painstakingly accurate.

Jaan Puhvel retains Lucan's triadic division of *Esus, Taranis,* and *Teutates* but also equates the god Lug with Esus. "Esus-Lugus, Taranis and Teutatates ... may thus roughly match the Scandinavian set of Odin, Thor and Freyr ... They, like *Jupiter-Mars-Quirinus*, were a stylized Western Indo-European embodiment of the erstwhile tripartite pantheon..."(172). Jan De Vries sees the Celtic gods *Nodens/Teutates* as occupying the first function, *Taranis* the second, and the Gods called *Minerva* and *Apollo* by Caesar (*The Gallic War*, VI. 17) the third.[1]

Yet De Vries' and Puhvel's disagreements about the god of the first function are not as irreconcilable as might at first seem. Their views can be brought into harmony if we look at the god *Lug*, whom Puhvel[2] and De Vries[3] also equate with the first function. Called Mercury by Caesar, (*The Gallic War*, VI. 17) he is generally considered to be the most widely worshipped god among the Celts.[4]

Lug was the god associated with acquired skill. Caesar describes him as "omnium inventorem artium" (VI. 17) (inventor of all arts) and the Irish referred to him as "*(sam) ildánach*, 'possessing, or skilled in, many arts (toge-

---

[1] De Vries, *Kelten und Germanen*, pp. 93-94.
[2] Puhvel, p. 172.
[3] De Vries, *Kelten und Germanen*, p. 92.
[4] Mac Cana, p. 27, Rankin, p. 267.

ther)' " (Mac Cana, 28). *Lug* is indeed multi-talented, being an expert wright, smith, champion, harper, hero, poet-historian, sorcerer, leech, cupbearer, and metal craftsman[1]. Here, too, we can discern the fusion of knowledge and magic similar to that in the Indian god *Varuna* and Roman Jupiter.

De Vries sees a further relationship between *Lug* and *Nodens*, the god of the heavens, who was called Jupiter or Mars by the Roman chroniclers[2]. According to De Vries, the pair of *Nodens/Teutates (Lug)* reflects first function of the Indo-European mythological structure.

> Es kann kein Zweifel bestehen: die keltische Götterwelt zeigt eine ähnliche Struktur wie die der übrigen indogermanischen Völker. Die höchste Gewalt hat überall, wo sie noch klar zu erkennen ist, zwei Aspekte: der Gott der Verträge und im allgemeinen des gesetzlichen Verhaltens neben einem anderen, der auf gewaltsame Weise mit magischen Kräften die Welt-Ordnung behauptet: den Götterpaaren Mitra-Varuna bei den Indern oder Tyr-Odin bei den Germanen entspricht Nodens-Teutates bei den Kelten. *(Kelten und Germanen*, 93)

Puhvel also agrees that Nodens (Irish: *Nuadu*) completes the divine pair which occupies the first function.

> At the same time, "Mars" and "Mercury" alternated in Lucan's scholiasts as interpretations of *Teutates* and *Esus*, and in inscriptions both take similar epithets (e.g., *Vellaunus*, of unknown meaning). Thus "Mars" may hide yet another divine figure, structurally akin to *Esus-Lugus* and perhaps partially syncretized with him ... The Gaulish name of such a "Mars" is not known, but he appears in Ireland as *Nuadu* beside *Lug*. (172-73)

Dumézil's triadic division was not restricted to Celtic mythology; it also manifested itself in their social structure. Caesar categorized Gaulish society according to the groups *druides, equites* and *plebs,* which corresponded to the early Irish classes of "druids, warrior nobles *(flatha)* and freemen *(bó-airigh)"* (Mac Cana, 60). The druids are of interest to us.

---

[1] Mac Cana, p. 28.
[2] De Vries, *Kelten und Germanen*, p. 92.

Magical Administrators in Roman, Celtic and Germanic Society 23

The druids were part of the intellectual class in Celtic society.[1] When comparing the roles of the druids and warriors, Caesar says: "Illi rebus divinis intersunt, sacrificia publica ac privata procurant, religiones interpretantur"(*The Gallic War* VI. 13) [The Druids officiate at the worship of the gods, regulate public and private sacrifices and give rulings on all religious questions][2]. In addition to their responsibilities as religious leaders, they also exercised a great amount of judicial power:

> Nam fere de omnibus controversiis publicis privatisque constituunt et, si qod est admissum facinus, si caedes facta, si de hereditate, de finibus controversia est, idem decernunt, praemia poenasque constituunt; (VI. 13)

> They act as judges in practically all disputes, whether between tribes or between individuals; when any crime is committed, or a murder takes place, or a dispute arises about an inheritance or a boundary, it is they who adjudicate the matter and appoint the compensation to be paid and received by the parties concerned. (VI. 13)

The druids were highly learned; they spent up to twenty years studying druidic lore (VI. 14). Because of their great erudition, they were responsible for the education of their people:

> Multa praeterea de sideribus atque eorum motu, de mundi ac terrarum magnitudine, de rerum natura, de deorum immortalium vi ac potestate disputant et iuventuti tradunt. (VI. 14)

> They also hold long discussions about the heavenly bodies and their movements, the size of the universe and of the

---

[1] Also included among the intellectuals were the *bardoi* or bards, mentioned by Diodorus (V. 31. 2), Strabo (4. 197), and Lucan (*Pharsalia*, 1. 45 ff). The *bardoi* were concerned primarily with singing the praises of Celtic heroes. Another group was the *ouateis* (Latin *vates*) mentioned by Strabo (4. 197) and Diodorus (V. 31. 2). Ammianus referred to them as *euhagis* (XV. ix. 8). Their duties were as follows:
> The *vates* are generally represented as experts in divination, but it is not possible to make any rigid distinction between their functions and those of the druids, and some would argue that they do not constitute a separate class but rather a subordinate division of the druidic order. (Mac Cana, p. 14)

Since the *vates* are not clearly distinguishable from the druids, they will be included in the discussion of the druids.

[2] All translations by S.A. Handford, *The Conquest of Gaul*.

> earth, the physical constitution of the world, and the power and properties of the gods; and they instruct the young men in all of these subjects. (VI. 14)

The lore of the druids was secret and only transmitted orally:

> Neque fas esse existimant ea litteris mandare ... id mihi duabus de causis instituisse videntur, quod neque in vulgum disciplinam efferri velint neque eos qui discunt litteris confisos minus memoriae studere. (VI. 14)

> The Druids believe that their religion forbids them to commit their teachings to writing ... but I imagine that this rule was originally established for other reasons - because they did not want their doctrine to become public property, and in order to prevent their pupils from relying on the written word and neglecting to train their memories. (VI. 14)

From these accounts, it becomes quite clear that the druids fulfilled the offices of religious leader, intellectual, educator and political advisor, exactly the combination of functions which is of interest to us. Is there, however, a link between the druids and the medieval court magician?

In order to answer that question, it is necessary to look at the fate of the druids. The emperor Claudius abolished the order in 54 A.D., though this action was not immediately successful. In 71 A.D. Tacitus reports that druids prophesied the destruction of Rome *(The Histories.* 4. 54. 2). The druids did, however, disappear from the continent relatively soon after.

> The decline and death of druidism proper is related to the fact that it was an upper-class religion with little depth of affection in the minds of ordinary people, Celtic or subjects to the Celts. Its esoteric teachings, which were the substantial core of druidic prestige, had little popular appeal, for the simple reason that they were, in the first place, too complex; and secondly, were in no respect designed for popularisation. (Rankin, 292)

The insular druids, not subject to Roman subjugation, enjoyed greater success in survival. St. Patrick, upon arriving in Ireland in the fifth century, found the druids to be "a force which was by no means trivial" (Rankin, 293). There are several legends about magical contests between St. Patrick and druids in which St. Patrick demonstrated the superiority of his god.[1] In one encounter, St. Patrick raised a druid into the air and then let him fall to his death on the rocks. In another episode, "a druid put into a hut of green wood was burned alive, while Patrick remained unharmed when fire was set to his hut of dry wood." (Kieckhefer, 54).

How long druidism continued to exist as an organized religion is uncertain. After the arrival of Christianity on the British Isles, the druids were prosecuted by the church. The *Canones Hibernenses* or Irish Canons, dating from ca. 675 A.D., prescribe a penance of seven years on bread and water for *magi* or wizards. The word *magus* or *magi* was "frequently used in Hiberno-Latin documents as the equivalent of 'drui' a druid" (McNeill, Gamer, 119, fn. 12). As seen in this canon, the church still prescribed penance for them at the end of the seventh century. As well, the office of magical advisor carried out by the druids was taken over by another figure, the *filidh*, who displayed a greater ability to co-exist with the Catholic church:

> ...already by the seventh century A.D. the *filidh* had become virtually the sole inheritors of such druidic functions and privileges as survived the stresses of the first few centuries of Christianity ... the *filidh* succeeded in establishing a remarkable *modus vivendi* with the ecclesiastical authorities which allowed the two bodies separate but complementary spheres of authority and permitted the *filidh* to continue many of their ancient functions and prerogatives, including some which had formerly belonged to the druids. Thus the *filidh*, whose title is often translated as 'poets', were in fact very much more: they were seers, teachers, advisers of rulers, witnesses of contracts ... (Mac Cana, 14-15)

Druids did continue to exist in literature, and there are several works which attest to their political influence. Although some of these tales were already written down in the eighth century A.D., most of them are preserved in manuscripts dating from the twelfth century or even later. These late recordings show that these accounts of druids were remembered and still popular in the High Middle Ages. In *The Destruction of Da Derga`s Hostel*, dating

---

1 Kieckhefer, p. 54.

back to the 8th Century A.D.,[1] a druid is instrumental in bringing about the downfall of Conare, king of Ireland. Conare's foster brothers have besieged him and his men inside Da Derga's hostel, but the hostel cannot be taken. Druids cause Conare to be overcome by thirst, and he sends Macc Cécht, his chief champion to fetch him a drink. Macc Cécht is away for three days, and when he returns, his king has just been killed.

Druids also figure prominently in the stories of Cú Chulaind, one of the great heroes of Irish literature. The druid Cathub raises and educates Cú Chulaind, and his prophecies spur the young hero to perform great deeds.[2] In the tale *The Intoxication of the Ulaid*, Cathub and his fellow druid Senchae act as political negotiators. Ireland has been divided into thirds, ruled by Conchubur, Cú Chulaind and Findtan. In order that the province may once again be united, Cathub and Senchae arrange it that Cú Chulaind and Findtan relinquish control of their thirds to Conchubur.[3]

The druids' negotiating finesse is also seen in other tales. In *Bricriu's Feast*, Cú Chulaind competes for the title of champion with two other warriors, Loégure Búadach and Conall Cernach. The rivalry between their peoples repeatedly threatens to break out into an all-out battle, and it is only the mediating intervention of Senchae which prevents this from happening. In *The Exile of the Sons of Uisliu*, Senchae and Cathub again prevent warriors from fighting after the fetus of Fedilmid's wife screams from inside the womb. Cathub then predicts that the child will be a girl, and that she will bring about the death and exile of many great heroes.

Although druids had ceased to exist as an official caste by the early Middle Ages, the *flildh* and literary portraits of druids allowed the concept of magical advisors to live on in medieval Celtic culture.

---

1 Jeffrey Gantz, *Early Irish Myths and Sagas*, p. 20.
2 Gantz, pp. 140-142.
3 Gantz, pp. 191-193.

3. Magic and Politics in Germanic Society

Germanic culture also shows elements of the Indo-European tri-partite social and mythological division. Although most of the written sources come from thirteenth century Scandinavia, the few existing continental documents show southern Germanic peoples to have worshipped the same group of gods. The interpretation of gold medallions by Karl Hauck and other mythologists has indicated a tripartite division in Germanic religion, corresponding to the functions of Magical Ruler, Warrior and Fertility God. The respective deities were Odin/Tyr, Thor and Freyr.

Odin, the god representing the first function, is relevant to this study. Odin was a many-sided deity; he was father of the gods as well as the god of poetry, the dead, war, magic, runes and ecstasy. Odin was also the god associated with knowledge.

Odin's knowledge stems from several supernatural sources. One of these was the preserved head of Mímir. The story of Mímir's head is mentioned in Snorri's *Ynglinga saga* (4 & 7).[1] Mímir was the wise advisor of the god Hœnir. Hœnir and Mimir had been given by their fellow gods as hostages to the rival race of gods known as the Vanir. Impressed by Hœnir's supposed knowledge, the Vanir made him their king. When the Vanir finally discovered that Hœnir was in fact helpless without Mímir, they decapitated Mímir. Odin rescued the head and, through his skillful use of magic, preserved it as his personal advisor.

Odin had two ravens, Huginn and Munin, who sat on his shoulders. Every morning, these birds would fly round the world and gather news for him (*Gylfaginning* 37).

Odin also possessed magical knowledge. According to *Völuspa* 18 and Snorri's *Prose Edda* (*Gylfaginning* 14), Odin drank the magic waters from the well of Mímir. *Hávamál* 138-141 recounts the story of how Odin hung wounded on a tree for nine nights in order to learn the secret of the runes.

---

1 Also *Völuspa* 48 and *Sigrdrifumál* 14.

The knowledge of this magical alphabet gave Odin mastery of both poetry and magic.[1]

As in Roman and Celtic cultures, divination played a very influential role in Germanic society. Roman sources mention numerous Germanic prophetesses. Tacitus reports in his *Germania* (8) that the Germans considered women to have holy and prophetic qualities. Strabo (7. 45) mentioned that Cymbrian women travelled with their soldiers and examined the blood and entrails of executed war prisoners, presumably to divine the outcome of future battles.[2] The Romans' belief in these predictions was sometimes exploited by the Germans for their own ends: "Die Achtung, die den germanischen Seherinnen von den Römern gezollt wurde, haben die Germanen bisweilen für politische Verhandlungen zu nutzen gewußt" (Volkmann, 9). In 69 A.D. Vitellius consulted an unnamed Germanic prophetess as to whether or not he should challenge the rival emperor Otho (Volkmann, 9). In 91 A.D. Masyas, the king of the *Semnones*, visited the Roman emperor Domitian on an unspecified political mission accompanied by his sibyll Ganna. According to Cassius Dio (Hist. Rom. 67. 5), both king Masyas and Ganna were highly honored by the emperor.

The best known of all the Germanic prophetesses, however, was most likely Veleda, member of the *Bructeri*. Her name is probably related to Celtic *filidh*, an indication of a possible common origin of prophets in both cultures.[3] Veleda was considered almost a deity among her people and also enjoyed considerable respect among the Romans. She was often called upon to determine the outcome of military operations. She prophesied success for Julius Civilis and the *Batavi* when they rose against the Romans in 69 A.D. The citizens of Cologne, under siege by the rebel Germans, sent for Veleda to decide their fate.

---

1 Odin's magical skills are documented in one of the few continental sources for Germanic paganism: in the second Merseburger Zauberspruch (10th century), Odin heals an injured horse's leg by means of incantation. Images depicting the head of Odin over a horse with an injured leg appear on about half of the approximately 700 Germanic medallions dating from the 5th-6th centuries, which indicate that the spell is considerably older than the written version which we possess.
2 This Germanic ritual is similar to the druids' examination of the blood of war prisoners.
3 Simek, p. 438

In addition to their prophetesses, the Germans also had a priestly caste. Information about the continental Germanic priest, however, is scant. Caesar, in his *The Gallic War*, even insinuates that the Germanic people, unlike the Celts, did not have priests (VI. 21). Admittedly, the Gemanic priest-caste was not nearly as highly developed as that of the druids, but the absence of druidic priests does not mean that the Germans had no specific office for religious matters. One should not forget that Caesar's report on the Celts and Germans exhibits a pro-Celtic bias.

Other Romans, however, do comment on the Germanic priests. Tacitus writes in his *Germania* that the priests interpret at the public drawing of the lots (c. 10). Tacitus also mentions a priest among the Cult of Nerthus (c. 40). The exact religious duties of the priests is difficult to ascertain, and their duties were not restricted to solely religious functions. De Vries notes, "sie scheinen sogar im ganzen denselben weltlichen Charakter gehabt zu haben, den wir später noch in Skandinavien vorfinden" *(Altgermanische Religionsgeschichte*, § 276). According to Tacitus, their powers included invoking silence before the Thing had passed judgement and administering the severest punishments *(Germania,* c. 7).

In addition, the Pan-Germanic presence of the word êwarto, (OHG) and æweweard (OE) points to the priests' role as "Wärter des Gesetzes" (De Vries, *Altgermanische Religionsgeschichte*, § 277). De Vries warns against confusing this with êsago (OHG), eosago (OS), asega (OFRI), meaning "lawspeaker":

> Eher darf man sagen, daß die Sorge für die êwa, womit nicht nur das ewige Gesetz, sondern auch die sittlichen und religiösen Ordnungen im allgemeinen gemeint sind, ein Hauptmerkmal der priesterlichen Funktion war. Gesetzsprecher oder Urteilfinder war er nicht, aber er ahndete die als Frevel betrachteten Verletzungen der heiligen Ordnung *(Altgermanische Religionsgeschichte,* § 277).

In Scandinavia the priest was referred to as the *godi* (plural form *godar).* The earliest known use of this title is inscribed on the Runestone of Nordhuglen in Norway which dates from the 5th century. Several runestones from the Viking age also mention *godar.* The *godi's* duties, like those of his continental counterpart, were not limited strictly to religious activities. On Iceland the position of *godi* "war erblich und ist nach der Organisation des Freistaates und der Einrichtung des Allthings besonders zu einer politischen Macht geworden" (De Vries, *Altgermanische Religionsgeschichte*, § 278). According to the interpretation of Erich Moltke (83-96), the Glavendrup Runestone inscriptions (10th c.) were inscribed in honor of a certain Alli who was concurrently an important member of the royal court and a priest who may have been in charge of the Temple of North Fünen. The Tune-Runestone, inscribed in honor of WoduridaR, describes this man as the secular leader of his district and perhaps also a priest of Odin, "wenn man dessen Namen, der 'der wütende Reiter' bedeutet und somit ein Odinsheiti sein konnte, als kultischen Decknamen betrachten dürfte" (De Vries, *Altgermanische Religionsgeschichte*, § 278).

Medieval Germanic society may have had another religious representative. Although the evidence for this figure is meagre, his existence is hinted at by the enigmatic word *thulr*, which appears several times in various Old Norse writings. The *Hávamál* (111) mentions the seat of the *thulr* which is located at *Urdr*, the well of fate.[1] It was at this spring that the Gods held council. The speaker of life wisdom calls himself the old *thulr* (*Hávamál*, 134), and so does the giant Vafthrudnir who engages in a contest of mythological knowledge with Odin *(Vafthrudnismal,* 9). Odin is called the *fimbulthulr* 'mighty *thulr*' *(Hávamál,* 80 & 142), which reflects his position as god of poetry and magic.

The term *thulr* was used in reference to actual people as well. A Danish runestone at Snoldelev dating from the 9th century connects a certain *thulr* named Gunnwaldr Hróaldsson with the hill Salhaugum. In interpreting this inscription, De Vries refers to the cultic significance of hills in Germanic religion and mentions that several places in Denmark are called Tulshøj or Tulehøj. He comes to the conclusion, "daß wir hier eine Würde anzunehmen haben, in der weltliche und religiöse Elemente miteinander verknüpft waren" *(Altgermanische Religionsgeschichte,* § 279).

The word *thulr* also appears in later sources with religious connotations. In the 12th century Rognvaldr jarl kali, as a pilgrim on his way to Jerusalem,

---

[1] According to Snorri (*Gylfaginning* 14, 15), Urdr lies at the roots of Yggdrasill, the tree of life.

Magical Administrators in Roman, Celtic and Germanic Society 31

says of himself: "'kross hangir thul thessom fyr brjósti ... en pálmr medal herda' (Das Kreuz trägt dieser thulr [ich] auf der Brust und die Palme auf dem Rücken" (Vogt [with own translation], 255). Two centuries later, Orm, a frightened cleric is ridiculed for praying at a church door during a fight. The words the warrior Snjólfr uses to describe him are *"thylja vess"* (Vogt, 255). Just what the activities of the *thulr* were is not known, but the word is related to *thylja*, 'to murmur' and to *thulur*, which is "stabende Wissensdichtung, ursprünglich wohl magisch-religiösen Inhalts, die schon durch ihre gebundene Form auf den Zweck der Weitergabe ausgerichtet [ist]" (Simek, 410). On the basis of this relationship Vogt has taken the *thulr* to be the keeper of tradition, primarily religious but perhaps also legal, who recites these rules; a "Kultredner". De Vries sees the *thulr* as keepers of the sacred tradition of the tribe *(Altgermanische Religionsgeschichte,* § 279).

The *thulr* was also associated with magic. Vogt notes:

> Als Zauberer bezeichnet Hauks Islendinga drápa v. 18 den Thorleif jarlsskáld durch dies Wort; der kleine Rest des Zauberliedes, durch den er nach seinem Thatt Finsternis und Tanz der Waffen erregt haben soll (Thoku-vísur), ist durch und durch und in höchster Potenz Zauber-Inhalt und Form; Thorliefr stammt aus zauberkundiger Familie: sein Vater - sein Lehrer, sein Bruder Olafr - volubrjótr (Hexenbrecher), seine Schwester Ynbvildr - die intellektuelle Überwinderin des Unholdes Klaufi (254).

In the Rímurdichtung the magician Vóli is called "thulr enn galdra vísi" (the *thulr* with magic knowledge); in the *Fáfnismál* (34), the magical dwarf Reginn, who gains magical knowledge from the heart of Fáfnir, is called pejoratively "hárr thulr", the "hoary *thulr".*

There is also an English equivalent, *thyle,* and in *Beowulf,* the character Unferth is the *thyle* at the court of King Hrothgar. As with the Germanic *thulr,* the precise duties of Unferth are unclear. He plays an ambivalent role in *Beowulf.* Joseph Baird observes that Unferth, although a schemer, apparently occupies a prominent position at the court of Hrothgar and enjoys the confidence of both Hrothulf and Hrothgar (4); he is called *eafodes cræftig* (l. 1466) and *widcudne man* (l. 1489) and owns one of the best swords in the kingdom. At the same time, however, Baird notes that "the poet is at times clearly hostile to him (ll. 501-5; 1164b-8a; 1468b-71a), and, most important, condemns him through Beowulf to the fires of hell" (4). Because of this ambivalent image of Unferth, Old English scholars have variously considered the *thyle* to have occupied a role as anything between "(1) an honoured and trusted king's counsellor possessing his own seat of distinction, and (2) a motley fool assigned an ignoble position at the feet of the king (with varying gradations of meaning between these two extremes" (Baird, 5). Old English glosses are not much help, as they define *thyle* rather vaguely as an *orator* and in a compound word as a *scurra* (Ogilvy, 370). Joseph Baird suggests that the difficulty in defining the term is due to the fact that

> the designation of a heathen office handed down to a new Christian age is likely to be subjected to a rapid speeding up of the normal process of semantic shift, particularly if the word itself was still redolent (as *thyle*, I believe, was) of dark unacceptable heathen associations; that such an old word in such a new context is especially subject to the process of pejoration; that the word in pre-Christian times was likely to have been fairly stable. (5)

Baird turns to the Germanic position of *thulr* as an aid in understanding the attitude toward Unferth. He, too, finds an explanation for the attitude towards Unferth in the priest-role of the *thulr*. Baird sees in the position of *thulr* not only a Germanic priest, but specifically a priest of an Odin-cult:

> Unferth seems to have been, somewhere back in the dark matrix whence the poem arose, a servitor of the one-eyed god, a divine favourite, a Woden's man, a *thyle*; and vestiges of this Wodenism are still discernible in the poem as we have received it. (9)

Baird refers to the warrior Starkadr from *Gautrekssaga* and the treacherous dwarf Réginn from the *Fáfnismál* to illuminate the character and function of Unferth. He sees in both Starkadr and Réginn the Odinic characteristics of the *Friedenstörer*, or promoter of strife, especially between kinsmen (8). In Baird's opinion, Unferth shares these qualities:

> He might better be compared, however, with Starkadr or Reginn, for, more than simply an evil counsellor, he is like these, a *Friedenstörer*, a peace-disturber, an evil speaker, a Mar-peace, not only in his clash with Beowulf, but also in

his darkly hinted role in the eventual Hrothgar-Hrothulf confrontation, in which, it is worthy of note, he was apparently to play the part of setting kinsman against kinsman (9).

Norse literature is another source of information about Scandinavian magicians. Scandinavia was the last region of western Europe to be christianized (Iceland in 1000 A.D.), and so the influence of pagan culture was felt much longer there than on the continent. Although the majority of sagas were written in the thirteenth century, they still contain a good deal of information, not necessarily about actual pagan customs, but about how medieval Scandinavians perceived them to be. The magic practiced by the witches and sorcerers in the sagas does not happen in the fairy world or the mythical realm of King Arthur but in Iceland, and to historical people whose names are recorded in the *Landnámabók* and *Islendingabók*. Of course the actual existence of these people does not mean that the sagas are to be read strictly as historical accounts. The historical accuracy of the sagas has been discounted for fifty years. Scholars like Sigurdr Nordal have shown that sagas once considered to be factual accounts were in fact pure fiction.[1] Yet as Richard Kieckhefer has pointed out, magic "takes place within the familiar context of Icelandic life ... Nor is the situation that gives rise to magic anything out of the ordinary" (50). Magic was, after all, considered a part of everyday experience in Medieval Iceland.

> At first glance it may seem paradoxical to assign the host of witches, berserkers, magicians, shape-shifters, attendant spirits, ghosts, and demons to the realm of the real and actual, but nevertheless they belong to the common experiences of all primitive people and are not mere trappings or supernatural "machinery" for literary or entertaining effect. (Bayerschmidt, 44)

These pagan beliefs were considered evil by the church and therefore condemned, but the church did not deny their existence. Adam of Bremen in his *History of the Arch-Bishops of Hamburg-Bremen* (1070 A.D.) describes a heathen temple made completely out of gold at Uppsala, Sweden. According to

---

[1] For example *Hrafnkels saga Freysgoda*, in the article "Hrafnkatla" in *Studia Islandica* 7 (1940).

Adam, the pagans worship the gods Thor, Wodan and Frikko (Freyr) here. Although it is unlikely that this temple was indeed constructed of gold, Rudolf Simek notes, "die Existenz eines Tempels in Uppsala steht jedoch außer Zweifel" (425). In an Icelandic penitential from the twelfth century we find written:

> ... if anyone going about by night seeks illicit knowledge or practices a magical trick or anything pertaining to magic, or if anyone does what the heathen do, the bishop shall indicate the penalty, provided it is confessed to the priest before being confessed to the bishop. (McNeill & Gamer, 356)

These church documents show us that, in spite of the church's efforts, the old gods were being worshipped well into the eleventh century, and magic was still practiced in the twelfth. Thus it is not surprising that magicians and supernatural events appear in a great many medieval sagas.[1]

Because the medieval Scandinavian church was not sympathetic to the Germanic religion, magicians and witches in literature were generally presented as negative characters.[2] Yet magic was not used exclusively by antagonists in the sagas. Several examples where magic is also used by positive characters show that, at least in the literature of the Scandinavians, magic was viewed much more pragmatically than the position of the church might indicate. When benevolent characters resorted to magic, they often used it to maintain or restore political order in Icelandic society.

One example of a magician who acts to avenge injustice and restore civil order occurs in *Hœnsa-Thóris saga*. In this tale, Herstein Blund-Ketilsson tries to avenge the death of his father Blund-Ketil. He turns to his foster-father Thorbjorn Stegandi. Thorbjorn is "rumoured to be more of a warlock than appeared on the surface" (V). Thorbjorn uses a mixture of magic and diplomacy to resolve the dispute. When Tungu-Odd, the murderer's father, tries to cheat Herstein out of his property, Thorbjorn foils him by using magic to

---

1 An essay which gives a good overview, although only of malevolent magic, is "Hostile Magic in the Icelandic Sagas," by H.R. Ellis Davidson, in *The Witch Figure*, pp. 20-41.
2 There are many examples in the sagas. Two better known examples are the magician Kotkel and his family who cast a spell to murder Hrut's son Kari in *Laxdœla saga* (XXXVII) and Thorbjørn's foster-mother, who uses magic runes to injure Grettir in *Grettis saga* (LXXVIII).

save Herstein's possessions (V). Then he negotiates an alliance between Herstein and Thorkel Trefil to avenge Blund-Ketil.

Kings and local chieftains often looked to magicians in order to help them achieve their ends. In *Eiriks saga rauda*, Thorkel, leader of a settlement in Greenland, seeks out the seeress Thorbjorg during a famine. As the community's leader, Thorkel is responsible for organizing the seance. "Because Thorkel was the leading house-holder there it was thought to be his responsibility to find out when these hard times which now troubled them would cease ..." (III). The community expects its leader to care for its well-being, and this includes seeking magical assistance, if necessary.

This pragmatic view of magic in medieval Scandinavia is seen in the author's description of the seance. Thorkel, who organizes the seance, is described by the author as an "excellent man" (III). Although Gudrid, a practicing Christian, at first hesitates to sing the chant that will summon the spirits, she agrees after Thorbjorg reassures her that she "could prove helpful to folk in this affair, and still be no worse a woman than before" (III). In spite of her Christian beliefs, she sings so well that many spirits appear. None of them are malevolent and they do not harm anyone during the seance. Nor were the prophecies simply demonic illusion; according to the author of the saga, "little indeed of what she said failed to come about" (III). In this incident, the author appears to regard this magic as an alternative religion, not on the same ethical level as Christianity, but certainly helpful in times of need.

Other examples in the sagas show how even Christian rulers turned to magic. The stories surrounding Olaf Tryggvason serve as an example. In her essay on the conflict between paganism and Christianity in the sagas of Olaf Tryggvason,[1] Jacqueline Simpson points out that "the traditions about Olaf current in Odd's time tended to attribute various forms of sorcery to men who opposed him" (172). Yet she also refers to an incident where Olaf himself consults a magician. "Early in his struggle for the kingship, Olaf, preparing for a crucial battle, is advised by his men to consult a Lapp who

---

[1] Jacqueline Simpson: "Olaf Tryggvason versus the Powers of Darkness," in: *The Witch Figure*, pp. 165-187.

could foretell its outcome and reveal the enemies' plans" (172). Although Olaf is unwilling, he agrees and goes to the Lapp. On the way he is almost sucked into a bog, apparently a warning to avoid magical assistance. But Olaf continues and receives the necessary information from the Lapp. As a sign of his gratitude, Olaf allows the magician to keep his faith.

In *Hrólfs saga kraka* a magician saves two princes from the malevolent magic of an evil king. In this saga, King Frodi treacherously murders his brother King Halfdan and then searches for Hroar and Helgi, Halfdan's sons. Their only chance for survival lies with Vifil, an old friend of Halfdan's, "deeply versed in ancient wisdom if danger threatened him" (I).[1] Vifil hides the boys on an island. King Frodi fetches wise women, soothsayers and finally wizards to locate his nephews. Yet Vifil's magic is even stronger. He conjures up thick mist and fog so that the wizards cannot see what is on the island. The king then sends messengers to search the island, but Vifil hides the boys so successfully that they cannot be found, even when the king himself finally comes to the island. Saved from death, the boys return to kill Frodi and regain their kingdom. In this episode, both Frodi and Halfdan rely on magical advisors and it is only the malevolent use of magic which is life-threatening.

A highly effective method of magical retaliation one could use against an unjust ruler was a verse called a *níd*, or lampoon. In *Flateyjarbók*,[2] Jarl Hakon burns the skald Thorleif's ship. In revenge, Thorleif recites a *tongunid* in the Jarl's presence. His verses cause the Jarl's groin to itch intelsely. The hall is then plunged into darkness and all weapons clash together, killing several of the Jarl's men. The Jarl faints and when he regains consciousness, his beard and all of the hair on one side of his head have permanently fallen off.

Another master of the *níd* was the skald and politician Egil Skallagrimmson. Egil was one of the most shrewd and ruthless of all Icelandic chieftains, a descendant of supernatural ancestors and a master of poetry, warfare, and magic. Like Starkadr and Unferth, he was one of Odin's chosen warriors; a man to be feared. Yet Egil was not simply a negative character. His opposi-

---
[1] "Ancient wisdom" is often a euphemism in the sagas for magical knowledge.
[2] Noted in Davidson, "Hostile Magic in the Icelandic Sagas", p. 33.

tion to King Harald Fairhair's unification of Norway made him a hero to many of his independent-minded countrymen. On one occasion Egil sets up a *níðstöng*, or pole with runic inscriptions, which he directs at Harald's son King Eirik Bloodaxe and his wife Queen Gunnhild. Eirik and Gunnhild had deprived Egil of an inheritance in Norway. During the ceremony Egil calls upon the spirits of Norway to torment the king and his wife: "and I direct this insult against the guardian spirits of this land, so that every one of them shall go astray, neither to figure nor find their dwelling places until they have driven king Eirik and Queen Gunnhild from this country" (LVII). He then places a horse's head on the *níðstöng* and carves his speech onto the pole with runes.[1]

Egil also uses his knowledge of magic to counteract royal intrigues. On one occasion (XLIV) Queen Gunnhild has a poisoned drink brought to Egil. Egil carves runes into the drinking horn and rubs them with his blood. The horn splits and the poisoned ale flows onto the floor. Here the runes are used not for any harmful purpose, but to save Egil from the queen's intrigues.

4. Conclusion

The concept of magical administrator was present in Celtic, Germanic and Roman mythology. It manifested itself in the persona of Jupiter, *Lugus* and Odin, the gods of Dumézil's first function. Magical administrators could also be found in the social organization of all three cultures, in the priestly castes of *flamen*, druid and *thulr*. Although the Christian church condemned and suppressed pagan religions and their adherents, magicians continued to practice magic well into the Middle Ages. Their magic often served political purposes: rulers turned to it to consolidate their power, just as their enemies used it to bring about their downfall.

---

[1] This type of magic also finds an echo in Book V of Saxo's *Gesta Danorum*. Here a group of wizards sacrifices a horse and sets its head up on a pole to thwart Erik the Eloquent, an advisor of King Frodi's. Upon seeing the head, Erik recognizes the possible supernatural danger and bids his companions to be silent. "No one must blurt out any words in case unguarded speech gave a loophole for sorcery" (*Gesta Danorum*, V. 134). In order to counteract the curse, Erik commands the magic to turn on its casters. True enough, the spell recoils on the magicians: the head and pole fall on the man holding them, crushing him to death.

Chapter II

MEDIEVAL CHRISTIAN RESPONSES TO MAGICAL KNOWLEDGE

1. High and Low Culture in the Middle Ages

Another important influence on medieval perceptions of magic was Christianity. Yet the influence of Christianity on medieval culture is not as straightforward as was long thought. Until recently the Middle Ages were seen as an "Age of Faith" where the "absolute and complete dominance of Catholic ideology was unshaken" (Gurevich, *Medieval Popular Culture*, xiv). No difference was made between the religious views of the clergy and laity with the notable exception of heresy. The general medieval *Weltanschauung* was equated with that of the orthodox church and the "high" or Latin culture of its educated theologians. It is important to realize that Christianity was not a single monolithic force, but a doctrine interpreted in different ways and to diverse ends by various social groups within medieval society. The large majority of the medieval populace did not have access to the high Latin culture of Christian theologians. This majority constituted the laity or "low" culture which "was barely if at all influenced by schools of classical or patristic tradition but which had preserved vital links with the mythopoetic and folkloric-magic consciousness" (Gurevich, *Medieval Popular Culture*, xv).

The origins of high and low culture can be found in the early Middle Ages. Jacques Le Goff sees the development and separation of these two cultures from the fifth to eighth centuries "as the gap widened between the uncultured masses and the social elite" *(Time, Work and Culture in the Middle Ages,* 155). Le Goff finds that, as the two cultures grew apart, the educated clergy tried to establish its domination over the low culture. This conflict resulted in

> a blockage of the 'lower' by the 'higher' culture, a relatively hermetic stratification on two cultural levels, more than a hierarchization incorporating means of transmission between the levels for the purpose of facilitating unilateral or bilateral influence. *(Time, Work and Culture in the Middle Ages,* 158)

Although Le Goff admits that clerical and folkloric culture shared some common ground, such as the belief in the supernatural, he sees the clerical acceptance of such similarities as "a practical and tactical necessity for evangelical purposes" (*Time, Work and Culture in the Middle Ages*, 157). For Le Goff "the essential point, however, is that folkloric culture was *refused* by ecclesiastical culture" (*Time, Work and Culture in the Middle Ages*, 157).

The relationship between high and low cultures is more complex than the labels may at first indicate. These labels have led some historians to equate these concepts with the respective social groups. Georges Duby, for example, finds that the absence of sources originating from the lower strata of medieval society makes it impossible to study anything but the upper classes.[1] Aaron Gurevich has countered this opinion arguing that "cultural models which have been created within this [aristocratic/clerical] milieu or for this milieu have spread and been vulgarized in other strata of society, but Duby seems to deny that these strata have cultural autonomy" ("Medieval Culture and Mentality According to the new French Historiography", 185).

It is an oversimplification to consider low culture as the culture of the lower social classes. As Gurevich points out, "it should be remembered that in the Middle Ages the uneducated were by no means identical with the lower orders of society, as the great majority of lords were also illiterate" (*Medieval Popular Culture*, xv). Le Goff, too, notes that

> the formation of a clerical aristocratic culture did not, however, coincide with the social stratification. Beginning in the Carolingian era, the "folkloric" reaction would involve all lay strata. It would burst upon Western culture beginning in the eleventh century, alongside the great heretical movements. (*Time, Work and Culture in the Middle Ages*, 158)

Duby is certainly correct in saying that the lower levels of medieval society have left few, if any records of their culture, yet Le Goff[2] and Gurevich have

---

1 Aaron Gurevich has observed that Duby's studies focus solely on the court and clerical culture. Aaron J. Gurevich, "Medieval Culture and Mentality According to the New French Historiography".
2 Le Goff, "Mentalities: a history of ambiguities" (pp. 166-180).

shown that there are several sources (exempla, hagiographies, visionary literature, etc.) which lend themselves well to such folk culture analyses. Although these works were written by the literate clergy, they reveal "the imprint of a popular and folkloric tradition and a specific world view, which differs essentially from official doctrine" (Gurevich, "Medieval Culture and Mentality According to the new French Historiography", 185). The presence of low culture mentalities within the records of high culture is indicative of their intertwined relationship:

> ... in the early and high Middle Ages learned and popular cultures represented different traditions within the context of one culture. It may be surmised that the dialogue-conflict of both traditions, which were constantly interacting and opposing one another, formed the basis of the cultural and religious development of the West in that period; they can only be properly understood in correlation to one another. (Gurevich, "Medieval Culture and Mentality According to the new French Historiography", 185)

It is therefore more useful if we regard medieval popular culture as "that world-perception which emerges from the complex and contradictory interaction of the reservoir of traditional folklore and Christianity" (Gurevich, *Medieval Popular Culture*, xv).

Both high and low culture influenced medieval perceptions of magic. I will first look at the orthodox church's attitude towards magic. Then, I will turn to popular notions regarding religion, magic and knowledge. Finally, I will examine the historical situation of learning and magic at the clerical schools.

2. Orthodox Church Policy Towards Magic

The medieval church was clearly hostile to magic. Its antagonism was supported by explicit condemnations of magic in the Bible. There are several instances in the Old Testament where magical practices are listed and condemned. In Leviticus 19:26 God says: "neither shall ye use enchantment nor observe times". In 19:31 He goes on to say: "Regard not them that have familiar spirits, neither seek after wizards, to be defiled by them". In Deuteronomy 18:10-11 further magical practices are listed and condemned:

> There shall not be found among you *anyone* that maketh his son or his daughter to pass through the fire, *or* that useth divination, *or* an observer of times, or an enchanter, or a witch, or a charmer, or a consulter with familiar spirits, or a wizard, or a necromancer.

Perhaps the most infamous passage condemning magic is Exodus 22:18: "Thou shalt not suffer a witch to live."

The Bible also gives examples of Christian superiority over pagan magic. In Exodus 7:8-12, for example, the Pharaoh's magicians demonstrate their skills by turning their staffs into snakes. God gives Aaron the power to turn his staff into a snake as well. His snake devours those of the magicians. God's miracles are shown to be more powerful than those of pagan sorcerers.

It is not within the scope of this study to trace the church's attitude to magic throughout the Middle Ages;[1] however, mentioning a few of the most influential condemnations of magic can give us some indication of church polemic against magic.

In *On Christian Doctrine*, written between 396 and 427 A.D.,[2] Augustine states that

> Omnes igitur artes hujusmodi vel nugatoriae vel noxiae superstutionis, ex quadam pestifera societate hominum et daemonum, quasi paeta quaedam infidelis et dolosae amicitiae constituta, penitus sunt repundianda et fugienda christiano (2.23)
>
> all acts pertaining to a trifling or noxious superstition constituted on the basis of a pestiferous association of men and

---

[1] For more detailed accounts of the medieval church's attitude to magic see Dieter Harmening, *Superstitio*. Harmening's thesis is that medieval penitentials include topoi copied from earlier authors like Caesarius of Arles and thus do not reflect contemporary social reality. His interpretation is successfully countered by Gurevich in *Medieval Popular Culture*, p. 36. Another valuable source of information about medieval policies on magic is Edward Peters, *The Magician, the Witch and the Law*.

[2] *Patrologia Latina*, vol. 34, col. 53.

demons as if through a pact of faithless and deceitful friendship should be completely repudiated and studiously avoided by the Christian.[1]

In describing supernatural phenomena, Augustine carefully distinguished between miracles and magic. For Augustine, miracles were a legimate part of Christian religion: "haec et alia multa hujuscemodi ... fiebant ad commendandum unius Dei veri cultum, et multorum falsorumque prohibendum. Fiebant autem simplici fide atque fiducia pietatis"(City of God, Book X. c. 9[2]) [These miracles and many ohers of the same kind ... were intended to support the worship of the one true God, and to prevent the cult of many false deities. They were achieved by simple faith and devout confidence[3]]. Magic, on the other hand, was achieved by "incantationibus et carminibus nefariae curiositati arte compositis" (City of God, Book X. c. 9) [spells and charms composed according to the rules of criminal superstition (Book X. c. 9)].

Augustine is one of the first church fathers to reject the inclusion of magic among the legimate branches of knowledge:

> qui quasi conantur ista discernere, et illicitis artibus deditos alios damnabiles, quos et maleficos vulgus appellat (hos enim ad goetiam pertinere dicunt); alios autem laudabiles videri volunt, quibus theurgiam deputant; cum sint utrique ritibus fallacibus daemonum obstricti sub nominibus angelorum. (City of God, Book X. c. 9)

> For people attempt to make some sort of distinction between practitioners of evil arts, who are to be condemned, classifying them as "sorcerers" (the popular name for which is necromancy) and others whom they are prepared to regard as praiseworthy, attributing to them the practice of theurgy. In fact, both types are engaged in the fraudulent rites of demons, wrongly called angels. (Book X. c. 9)

Another important influence on the medieval condemnation of magic was Bishop Isidore of Seville (ca. 560-636). In his *Etymologiae*, an encyclopedia of

---

1 Translated by D.W. Robertson, *On Christian Doctrine*.
2 *Patrologia Latina*, vol. 41, col. 286.
3 All passages translated by Henry Bettenson, *City of God*, here Book X. c.9.

the knowledge of his time, he included a section entitled *De Magis*. Here Isidore extensively lists the different kinds of magic, emphasizing the different kinds of divination (by water, fire, air, earth, the flight and calls of birds, the entrails of animals, and astrology). He also describes medicinal magic, which for him can involve incantations or magical objects fastened to the patient. Isidore, in the vein of Augustine, denounces all such practices as the commerce between evil humans and fallen angels. This denunciation was taken up by other writers until well into the thirteenth century.[1]

Clerics looking for condemntions of magic only needed to turn to their Bible commentaries. The standard Bible commentary for the Middle Ages, the *glossa ordinaria* (completed early in the 12th century), reflects the church fathers' hostile attitude towards magic. The gloss on Leviticus 19:31 (quoted above) for example states "Veneficis, qui daemonum scilicet nomina invocant, et aliquando corpus curant, vel animam interficiant" (*Patrologia Latina* 113:1 col. 354). In discussing Saul's consultation with the Witch of Endor, the gloss to I Samuel 28:9 says:

> Magi utuntur sanguine humano, et contactu mortuorum in maleficiis et divinationibus arioli solis verbis, id est incantationibus divinant. Pythius dicitur Apollo harum artium cultor, a quo Pythonissae, id est divini: Hol Saul quasi zelo legis delevit, quia, ut aiunt, a daemonibus coacti David regem esse futurum praeconabantur. (*Patrologia Latina* 113: 1 552-3)

The tendency among the glossators, when they do elaborate on magicians in the Bible, is to denounce the workings of magic as the illusions of demons.[2] Edward Peters, in his examination of twelfth-century theological discussions of magic, finds that the small interest in Biblical magicians was due to the fact that "the observations of the fathers and the glossators were probably satisfactory as far as the needs of theologians went" (70).

As punishment for practicing magic the twelfth-century commentators call for excommunication. Exodus 22:18 (quoted above), later to become the most

---

[1] For a more detailed discussion of Isidore's description of magic, see: Valerie Flint, *The Rise of Magic in Early Medieval Europe*, pp. 51-57.
[2] For a more detailed discussion of the *glossa ordinaria* see Edward Peters, pp. 68-70.

infamous passage concerning witches, was interpreted as sentencing magicians to excommunication. The *glossa ordinaria* states:

> Maleficos non parteris vivere. Qui praestigiis magicae artis et diabolicis figmentis agunt, haereticos intellige, qui a consortio fidelium qui vere vivunt, excommunicandi sunt, donec maleficium erroris in eis moriatur. (*Patrologia Latina* 113:1, col. 261)

In this gloss the magician is not condemned to a physical death, but instead to a spiritual one. He is to be excommunicated and driven away from the community of the faithful. This interpretation is very similar to God's judgement in Leviticus 20:6, "And the soul that turneth after such as have familiar spirits, and after wizards, to go a whoring after them, I will even set my face against that soul and will cut him off from among his people".

A similar fate is accorded magicians in the *Canon Episcopi*, a chapter concerning magic from a collection of canonical laws dating back to Regino of Prüm in the early tenth century. The canon[1] states:

> Ut episcopi episcoporumque ministri omnibus viribus elaborare studeant ut perniciosam et a diabolo inventam sortilegam et maleficam artem penitus ex parochiis suis eradant, et si aliquem virum aut feminam huiuscemodi sceleris sectatorem invenerint, turpiter dehonestatum de parochiis suis eiciant.

> Bishops and their officials must labor with all their strength to uproot thoroughly from their parishes the pernicious art of sorcery and malefice invented by the devil, and if they find a man or woman follower of this wickedness to eject them foully disgraced from their parishes.[2]

In the thirteenth century, Thomas Aquinas also concerned himself with the question of magic. In the tradition of Augustine, he denied that it could function without the help of demons, because they cannot defy the laws of

---

1 Quoted by Jeffrey Russell in *Witchcraft in the Middle Ages*, p.292.
2 Translated by Jeffrey Russell, *Witchcraft in the Middle Ages*, p. 76.

nature, but can only deceive the practitioners of magic.[1] Moreover, magicians are criminals, since they commit adultery, murder and theft.[2] Aquinas also condemned most divination as the work of demons, although he did allow that some kinds had a natural basis, and saw much of astrology as science, rather than magic.[3] Aquinas' works, however, can not be viewed as a defence of magic, and it is his systematic condemnation of it which allowed subsequent clerics to use his opinions in their fight against magic. As Edward Peters notes,

> Although his views on magic are scattered throughout the vast body of his work, Aquinas' views are remarkably consistent and logically rigorous. Probably no writer before him systematized the condemnation of magic on so many different levels ... Aquinas provided formidable influence both toward the traditional condemnation of magic and toward the linking of magic with service to or subjection to the devil. (97)

From these condemnations, the orthodox church position becomes clear. Magic was always demonic illusion and had no place among the legitimate branches of knowledge, just as magicians were criminals, who had no legitimate place in society.

3. Popular Culture and Christianity

In spite of the church's condemnations and threats of excommunication, the laity (and many clerics) turned to magic as an alternative source of supernatural power. One of the reasons magic enjoyed continued popularity was the lack of clear distinction between magic and religion. This indistinction made a qualitative difference between magic and religion difficult to determine. It was in part already present in the Bible itself. There are several occurrences in both the Old and the New Testament where miracles are difficult to distinguish from magic. In II Kings, 13:20-21 a dead man is placed into a grave where the bones of Elisha rest, "and when the man was let

---

1 Habiger-Tuczay, p. 72; Thorndyke, "Some Medieval Conceptions of Magic", pp. 113-115.
2 Habiger-Tuczay, p. 72.
3 Thorndike, "Some Medieval Conceptions of Magic", p. 115.

down, and touched the bones of Elisha, he revived, and stood up on his feet". In the Acts of the Apostles, Peter's shadow (5:12) and handkerchiefs have the power to cure the sick (19:12). Theologians could explain these acts as God working through his followers, but to an ordinary layperson the divine origin of these powers might be too far removed to be attributed to God. The laity might interpret these wonders as originating from the magical powers of Elisha and Peter. It was not unusual for medieval Europeans to attribute magical powers to people. It is important to remember that for the inhabitants of medieval Europe, the borders between the natural and supernatural spheres of existence were not located where they are today. In our rational and secular world we have separated the supernatural realm from our conception of "reality" and dismissed it as the fantasy world of children and the bugaboos of primitive or superstitious peoples. In the Middle Ages, the supernatural pervaded the natural realm and supernatural events were part of everyday experience. As Aaron Gurevich stated, people in medieval Europe

> bauten ihre Beziehungen zur Natur nicht nach dem Typ der "Objekt-Subjekt-Beziehung" auf, sondern gingen von der Überzeugung aus, daß Natur und Mensch organisch und magisch gleichermaßen beteiligt sind, daß sie eine intime Einheit bilden und sich wechselseitig durchdringen. *(Das Weltbild des mittelalterlichen Menschen, 379)*

They saw the universe as an organic whole in which they were just a part, and as in any organism, the actions of one part influenced the others. "Die 'Elemente' können den Menschen helfen, und diese ihrerseits sind fähig, durch bestimmte Verfahren in der für sie notwendigen Richtung auf die 'Elemente' einzuwirken" (Gurevich, *Das Weltbild des mittelalterlichen Menschen*, 378). Because nature's effect on humans was so direct and crucial, magical spells could be used to influence nature in order to bring success and health to its practitioners.

The magical view of the world also explains the laity's willingness to turn to magic. As Bob Scribner observes:

> ... the demonic was not regarded by the laity with the same abhorrence as it was by the clergy or theologian. Rather, it was an alternative means of access to efficacious sacred

power. Thus, one turned to the professional magician or sorcerer, folk who knew how to deal with spirits or demons and their power. (25)[1]

The laity's belief in and tolerance of magic influenced the way in which they understood Christianity. In the early conversions, the Christian religion was seen as a new form of magic which was more powerful than the native sorcery. The Venerable Bede tells the story of the missionary Augustinus, sent by the pope to convert King Ethelbert of Kent. The priests were considered to be magicians, and the king prevented them from entering any of his rooms, so that they could not harm him.[2] Keith Thomas observes:

> It was also inevitable that around the Church, the clergy and their holy apparatus there clustered a horde of popular superstitions, which endowed religious objects with a magical power to which theologians themselves had never laid claim. (Keith Thomas, 32)

In his book *Religion and the Decline of Magic,* Thomas has collected the medieval superstitions surrounding the mass, the sacraments, consecrated objects and the clergy.[3] As Thomas has observed, magical powers could be attributed to almost any ritual or object connected with the church. Relics could be used to control weed growth on fields and the Host was thought effective in curing sick humans and animals. Prayers could be recited backwards to inflict harm on one's enemies. Anyone attending church "would not lack meat or drink for the rest of the day, nor be in any danger of sudden death or blindness" (Keith Thomas, 35).

Magical powers were also attributed to the clergy, who, by virtue of their training, celibacy and ritual consecration, were special intermediaries between humans and God. The clergy also regularly performed a ritual which could be interpreted as a powerful act of magic. During the Mass the priest was able to transform bread and wine into the body and blood of Christ. Just how the common people interpreted this ritual cannot be completely determined. Keith Thomas is most probably correct in his assessment: "What

---

[1] Bob Scribner, "Cosmic Order and Daily Life: Sacred and Secular in Pre-Industrial German Society," pp. 17-32.
[2] Gurevich, *Das Weltbild des mittelalterlichen Menschen,* 367.
[3] See pp. 25-50 in *Religion and the Decline of Magic.*

stood out was the magical notion that the mere pronunciation of words in a ritual manner could effect a change in the character of material objects" (33). The Bible was seen by many as a magic book that contained not only supernatural information, but could also be used as a magical tool.

> The Bible could be an instrument of divination, which opened at random would reveal one's fate. The gospels could be read aloud to women in childbed to guarantee them a safe delivery. A Bible could be laid on a restless child's head so as to send it to sleep. (Keith Thomas, 45)

Thomas concludes that "the medieval Church thus acted as a repository of supernatural powers which could be dispensed to the faithful to help them in their daily problems" (Keith Thomas, 32).

Yet the confusion between magic and religion was not only the result of the *Weltanschauung* of lay culture, it was also encouraged by the church in an effort to hasten the conversion process. The church's recognition of the supernatural view of the world influenced its emphasis on Christian supernatural power as an effective argument for conversion. Significant aspects of pagan worship were assimilated into the Christian religion. Pagan holy days were renamed and associated with Christian events. Sacred wells associated with pagan beliefs were now given patron saints. An example of the supernatural emphasis in proselytizing is seen in Hincmar of Reims' ninth century biography of St. Remigius. In the text Hincmar marked out passages which should be read by the clergy versed in theology and others which should be read out to the simple people. The passages for the laity were mainly moral exempla or descriptions of miracles.[1] Thus the line between superstition and official religion was not clearly defined; neither in the minds of the people, nor always in the policies and doctrines of the church. Thomas comments, "in general, the ceremonies of which it [the Church] disapproved were 'superstitious'; those which it accepted were not" (49). Bob Scribner concurs, stating "the church's commitment to a sacramental view of religion made any hard and fast distinction between 'religion' and 'magic' almost impos-

---

1 *Monumenta Germaniae Historica. Scriptores rerum Merovingicarum* III, pp. 239-349.

sible" (26). The church was often prepared to incorporate magical beliefs in order to strengthen its hold on its members.[1]

4. Popular Beliefs Connecting Wisdom and Magic

a) Hagiography

The church employed certain genres of literature to address the laity. The subject matter of these works was aimed at the particular concerns and beliefs of the lay audience. Such works can be used to determine the laity's beliefs regarding magic and knowledge, albeit from the clerical point of view. As Hincmar's aforementioned *vita* illustrates, hagiographies were especially useful in reinforcing the Christian beliefs of the common people. In the deeds of the saints, as in the acts of the apostles, the common people could see the omnipotence of God manifesting itself in the actions of a mortal human being. Hagiographies did not just emphasize the ethical worth of the saint, but the supernatural feats made possible by devout faith. For an audience which considered occult supernatural forces to pervade the world, the church's monopoly over an even greater magic was the quickest and most effective proof of the validity of Christianity. The church's use of magic/miracle was especially effective in dealing with those who might not appreciate the finer subtleties of complicated church doctrines. Gurevich notes: "aus den Viten geht ganz klar hervor, daß das Volk in der Gestalt des Heiligen einen in Kirchengewänder gekleideten und vom Heiligenschein gekrönten Magier sah" (Gurevich, *Das Weltbild des mittelalterlichen Menschen*, 367).

Medieval hagiographies show how saints were not only credited with divine powers but also supernatural knowledge. There are numerous examples in which saints use divine knowledge[2] to demonstrate the powers of Christianity.

---

1 Valerie Flint finds that the Church actively adapted and saved certain magical practices, which it incorporated into its own teachings and practices. For more information, see her important study: *The Rise of Magic in Early Medieval Europe*.
2 For a detailed study of the various kinds of magic practiced by saints see C. Grant Loomis, *White Magic: An Introduction to the Folklore of Christian Legend*, especially the chapter

Saints often engaged pagan sorcerers in magical contests reminiscent of the one between Peter and Simon Magus.[1] In one contest between saint and magician, St. Cainnicus saw through the illusions of a magician deluding a crowd of spectators. Whereas the spectators believed the magician to be walking through a tree, St. Cainnicus realized that he was in fact walking around it. Although the object of these stories was to show the superiority of Christianity, such contests lent themselves to the equation and confusion of Christianity and magic.

In addition to showing Christian wisdom to be superior to illicit magical knowledge, hagiographies also show how God could accelerate clerical learning. Several saints receive their erudition in a wondrous fashion: "Indractus, as a boy, was able to read perfectly all in a moment. Mercurius and John learned to read and to write Coptic and Arabic without a teacher" (Loomis, 72). In other hagiographies, saints miraculously acquired knowledge of foreign languages, usually in order to proselytize in foreign lands. Dominicus learned German in four days; Bertrandus and Cambertus were able to pray in German, although they had not been able to speak the language before. Vitalis preached in French to an English audience which had no difficulty in understanding him. Birinius learned French in three days and Patient could speak it immediately. In these examples, erudition comes from supernatural origin. The saints do not learn through effort and practice, but instantly by miracle. For an audience in an oral culture which still believed in the magical efficacy of letters and words, such miracles were powerful magic.

Saints often used their divine knowledge to give advice to rulers. Neot was able to predict victory for King Alfred at a time when his luck seemed to have deserted him. Dunstan was able to predict Ethelred's defeat because the king as a baby "polluted the sacred font during the course of the [baptismal] rites" (Loomis, 71). A king approached St. Abban asking him to say what fraction of a particular rock was buried beneath the ground. Abban was able to give the correct answer. Albeus requested an island from a king

---

"Divine Foresight and Knowledge", pp. 71-77. All of the following examples are taken from this chapter.
1 Acts 8:9-24.

for the purpose of building a monastery. The king was unaware of owning the island and would not donate it without first having seen it. Rather than asking the king to journey to the island with him, Albeus granted the king the gift of long distance sight. The king could immediately see the island. These accounts associate supernatural knowledge with political advice; the saints use their divine insight to counsel kings. Stories such as these helped to reinforce notions that the kings' clerical advisors were gifted with magical knowledge.

b) Gerbert of Aurillac

Clerical training was often considered magical, especially if it included exotic or arcane knowledge. The hagiographers have shown how learning was often seen as the result of divine aid. Gerbert of Aurillac (c. 940-1003 A.D., Pope Sylvester II 999-1003 A.D.) is another figure embodying the equation of erudition and magic. Gerbert came from humble origins, but took orders and rose quickly in the ranks of the clergy. He spent three years in Spain at the Monastery of Santa Maria de Ripoll, where he studied the quadrivium. Although Europe at this time had little contact with the Arab world, Southern Spain was one point of interaction. In the monastery of Santa Maria, Gerbert was introduced to Arabic mathematics, which at that time were considerably more advanced than those in the West. His knowledge won him the favour of pope John XIII who introduced him to Emperor Otto I. A long association between Gerbert and the Ottonian emperors followed. As a result Otto III chose him as successor to Pope Gregory V in 999 A.D. Gerbert was known for his close ties and cooperation with the three Ottonian emperors. Emperor and pope appeared as intercessors for petitioners in each other's documents and participated in each other's councils.

Gerbert was successful not only as a papal politician, but also as a scientist. He constructed a time piece, several musical organs and a monochord for studying music theory. He also wrote several scientific treatises including works on rhetoric, the abacus, astronomy, the astrolabe, and geometry.

Gerbert embodied the qualities later found in the court magician: great erudition and practical skill, interest in natural sciences, a collection of inventions and a swift rise to high political/religious power. In the popular imagination, Gerbert's great learning and success could only have come about through supernatural means. Medieval popular conceptions already associated the Catholic church, its rites and members with magic. At the turn of the millenium, Arabic sciences were all but unknown in western Europe. The seemingly miraculous application of their exotic numerals in the production of marvellous inventions was equated with demonic aid. Gerbert's great erudition and success resulted in the formation of legends about him which sprang up shortly after his death. His first chroniclers, Hermann von Reichenau and Bernold, made no direct connections between the pope and magic in 1054, but they already cast suspicions on his piety. "Gerbert sei den weltlichen Wissenschaften allzusehr ergeben gewesen und deshalb in der Gunst des wißbegierigen Kaisers (Otto III.) so hoch gestanden".[1] In the following century, doubts about Gerbert's faith continued to grow. At the end of the eleventh century Cardinal Benno claimed that Gerbert had not only given himself over to the black arts, but had been the founder of a school for black magic which had existed in Rome throughout the eleventh century. Gerbert's pupil had been the bishop Laurentius of Amalfi, "der zuweilen Künftiges voraussagte, auch das Zwitschern der Vögel zu deuten wußte" (Döllinger, 186). Laurentius supposedly passed on Sylvester II's lessons to popes Benedict IX, Gregory VI and Gregory VII.

The legend of Sylvester II enjoyed great popularity in the twelfth century. Versions can be found in William of Malmesbury's *Chronicle of the Kings of England* (ca. 1142)[2] and in Walter Map's *De Nugis Curialium* (completed around 1193).[3] A Middle High German version (in which Gerbert is not named but simply called "des teuvels bâbest") is collected by Friedrich Heinrich von der Hagen in his *Gesamtabenteuer*.[4] The story in the three accounts varies somewhat, but the basic story is the same: a poor cleric signs a pact with the devil who helps him become pope. One might argue that the story is simply a *topos*, but Gerbert was a historical figure whose great erudi-

---
1 Ignaz von Döllinger, *Die Papstfabeln des Mittelalters*, p. 185.
2 Döllinger, p. 188.
3 Walter Map, *De Nugis Curialium. Courtiers' Trifles*, Dist. iv. c. 11.
4 Friedrich Heinrich von der Hagen, *Gesamtabenteuer: Hundert altdeutsche Erzählungen*, Band II, pp. 550-561.

tion and spectacular career were greeted with suspicion. Important for our understanding of the magical advisor is that in all three episodes, a cleric uses magic in order to gain the favour of the ecclesiastical court and rise to power. Magic was considered one avenue to success and those who were learned were thought to know how to use it.

These popular stories of saints and Pope Sylvester II present a portrait of magicians as learned sophisticates who have gained their magical skills through study. There is often no clear-cut distinction between magic and religion and clergymen are frequently considered to be practitioners of magic. It is now important to consider whether or not these stories were just empty *topoi*, or if they were literary reflections of actual medieval beliefs and and practices.

5. Historical Clerics and Magic

Although the majority of clergymen were undoubtedly not magicians, there seems to have been a surprising number who were indeed fascinated by the black arts. These clerics were not dissuaded by official church policy and apparently shared the laity's more pragmatic attitude to magic. An indication of such interests can be seen in the number of church declarations prohibiting clergymen from practicing magic: "Quod non oportet eos qui sunt sacrati, vel clerici, esse magos, vel incantatores ... ".[1] Gratian's *Concordia discordantium canonum*, (more commonly known as the *Decretum*, c. 1140) was the standard medieval text on church law. It contains theoretical legal cases and exemplary verdicts. In the twenty-sixth *causa* Gratian discusses the case of a priest who had been caught practicing magic. The appropriate sentence was excommunication.[2] Although this case was fictional, it shows that clerical magicians concerned church authorities enough to warrant discussion in the standard medieval law text.

An indication of some types of magic which clerics practiced can be found in the synod of Trier (1227). It decreed that holy water, oil and the host be

---

[1] Harmening, p. 223. For further information about prohibitions for priests see Harmening, pp. 223-24.
[2] Edward Peters, p. 72.

kept under lock and key in order to prevent them from being used in magical operations. The synod also forbade reading masses for the dead for anyone still alive. A monk from Corvey in the twelfth century was to have read masses daily for the purposes of harming his Abbot.[1] From these accounts we can deduce that popular notions equating clerics and magicians were not unfounded: some clerics did indeed practice magic.

a) Magic in the Schools

Where did these clerics find an opportunity to learn magic? One possibility was the schools. Whereas the monastic schools were primarily concerned with religious education, the cathedral schools also taught secular knowledge to prepare their students for state service. The political importance of clerical statesmen in the Middle Ages increased dramatically with the Ottonian and Salian kings who chose and installed bishops as political allies on the basis of their administrative skills. Otto I established the episcopal office as a means for his own political motives, as a buffer between emperor and feudal nobility.[2] Because of the numerous administrative activities now imposed on the bishops, they often spent more time at the court of the king than caring for the members of their diocese.[3]

The education of these clerical administrators came to reflect their secular responsibilities:

> As a result, the chapel became the training ground for higher office ... the set of values formed in the chapel, based as much on Ciceronian as on Christian notions of state service and the conduct of public life, might appropriately be called "courtly humanism". (Jaeger, "The Courtier Bishop", 292-293)

As the demand for trained administrators grew, the responsibility of training them passed from the chapels to the cathedral schools, which were big-

---

[1] Harmening, p. 223.
[2] C. Stephen Jaeger, "The Courtier Bishop," p. 293.
[3] Jaeger, "The Courtier Bishop", p. 293. Adam of Bremen in his *History of the Archbishops of Hamburg -Bremen* accuses Bishop Adalbert of neglecting his diocese for this same reason.

ger and better equipped to handle larger numbers of students. The cathedral schools began turning out large numbers of clerics trained as civil servants. Not only prelates but also a large number of educated men who had not taken orders moved from cathedral school to court. The courts provided a number of employment possibilities for these educated young men. They included court scribe, secretary, tutor, court chaplain or chancellor.[1]

Because of the secular nature of these duties, the courtly administrator did not necessarily have to be devout. We may expect this of the clerics who had not taken orders, but it was also true of the "courtier bishops":

> ... piety was not a requisite quality for the position in the same way that statesmanship and administrative skill were ... The orthodox ideal of the episcopate had next to nothing to do with the conception of the court chaplain and future bishop in the Ottonian-Salian imperial church. (Jaeger, "The Courtier Bishop", 294)

Thus many students attended these institutions without any intention of becoming priests. They required the rudiments of a clerical education but did not necessarily have pious interests. Nor did all of those who had been ordained as priests receive full-time positions. Some were privately employed as "chantry" priests, in order to say "advance" daily masses for the souls of their employers so as to shorten possible future stays in purgatory.[2] Once these masses had been read, the priest had a large amount of free time, in which he could find plenty of ways to get into trouble. As Richard Kieckhefer notes: "Necromancy was merely one of the forms this trouble might take: not the most common form, perhaps, but not the least interesting" (154).

Those clerics interested in magic could find occult manuscripts in their libraries. In the earlier Middle Ages there had been few texts which dealt with magic, but the situation changed in the course of the twelfth century. During this time there was a large influx of Arabic writings which were translated into Latin. The Islamic countries had a rich literature of learned magic, particularly alchemy and astrology, much of which they had gotten from an-

---
1 C. Stephen Jaeger, *Medieval Humanism in Gottfried von Straßburg's Tristan and Isolde*, p. 7.
2 Kieckhefer, p. 154

cient Greece. In response to Islamic criticisms of these arts, Arabic occultists like al-Kindi and Abu Ma'shar (both from the ninth century) had responded by establishing astrology as a scientific discipline, thus including it among the legitimate sciences. By the early twelfth century, a number of these Arabic astrological and alchemical works were being translated into Latin by inquisitive clerics. The *Greater Introduction* to Astrology by Ma'shar was translated in 1133 and Ptolomy's *Tetrabiblos* five years later. In the course of the twelfth century, well over one hundred Arabic works were translated into Latin.

These books circulated in school libraries in the late twelfth and early thirteenth century. William of Auvergne, in his *De legibus*, recalls that he had seen magical texts as a student in Paris "et haec omnia in libris judiciorum astronomiae, et in libris magorum atque maleficorum tempore adolescentiae nostrae nos meminimus inspexisse" (c. 25).[1] As both Edward Peters and Lynn Thorndike have noted,[2] the knowledge of magic which William relates is extensive and reflects first-hand knowledge of these books.

Many of these magic books contained spells of particular interest to the court. Clerics in possession of these books could offer valuable services to rulers or courtiers willing to use magic. One work containing spells for the court is the *Picatrix*,[3] supposedly compiled by Norbar the Arab in the twelfth century and translated from Arabic into Spanish in 1256 at the behest of Alfonso the Wise. With the aid of the *Picatrix*,[4] a courtier can direct the king's wrath at a rival. A ruler can use one spell to free troops captured by an enemy, or another one to sow discord among his opponents. He can also make his own subjects loyal. There is a spell to prevent dogs from barking at intruders, useful for a ruler's spies or saboteurs. A ruler can cast a spell to aid the construction of his own fortifications while hindering the erection of enemy castles. If his wrath is great enough, he can use the *Picatrix* to destroy his enemies and their cities.

---

1 quoted in Edward Peters, p. 89.
2 Edward Peters, p. 90; Thorndike *History of Magic and Experimental Science* II, p. 342.
3 Thorndike, "Picatrix," in: *History of Magic and Experimental Science* II, pp. 813-824.
4 Thorndike, *History of Magic and Experimental Science* II, p. 821.

Medieval magic books were often attributed to famous classical figures in order to increase their own authority. These classical figures were often associated with great erudition and political knowledge, and the books attributed to them often contained advice and magic formulae of particular relevance for rulers. King Solomon, because of his legendary wisdom, was considered in the Middle Ages to have been a master sorcerer. Several works of magic were attributed to him.[1] Some of the books associated with Solomon deal with the *Ars Notoria*. These notory arts employ magical figures and prayers to invoke angels in order to gain divine knowledge or commune with God. Of these works dealing with the notory arts, the most famous (or perhaps infamous) is the *Liber sacratus*, as William of Auvergne calls it. It is also known as the *Liber sacer* or *Liber juratus* or *The Sworn Book of Honorius*, since it was also associated with a magician named Honorius. The *Liber sacer*, like the *Picatrix*, contains several spells of specific interest to the court. Some of these operations allow a ruler to construct an indestructible castle and destroy enemy towns. He can also find information on waging war. There are incantations which enable a ruler to sow discord among his enemies and establish harmony among his own subjects. A courtier can find a spell to have a ruler grant a petition.

Aristotle was another figure from antiquity associated with occult learning and consequently also with occult treatises. These writings are nowadays referred to as books of the Pseudo-Aristotle. The most famous of all Pseudo-Aristotelian works was the *Secretum Secretorum*. The *Secretum Secretorum* is a king's mirror; a compilation of what was considered essential knowledge for rulers. It is in the form of a dialogue between Aristotle and his historical pupil, Alexander the Great, considered in the Middle Ages to have been the greatest ruler. It is thought that a Graeco-Persian treatise was the source for its discussion of kingship, and other parts from other sources were added to it before it reached its present form in the seventh or eighth century. The *Secretum Secretorum* was partially translated into Latin by John of Spain in the first half of the twelfth century and then fully translated in the twelfth or early thirteenth century by Philip of Tripoli for Guido of Valencia, the pontiff

---

1 Thorndike, "Solomon and the Ars Notoria," in: *History of Magic and Experimental Science* II, pp. 279-289.

Medieval Christian Responses to Magical Knowledge 59

of Tripoli. There are over two hundred extant Latin manuscripts and partial or complete translations exist in almost every European language. A Middle High German version was translated by Hiltgart of Hürnheim in 1282.[1]

The *Secretum secretorum* includes chapters on royal conduct, justice, court administrators, and war. In addition to advice on good rule, the *Secretum secretorum* also contains medical knowledge mixed with a good deal of astrological advice. Proper hours for blood-letting and giving or taking medicines are indicated.[2] The study of astrology is specifically mentioned as the art a good king should promote. Alexander is advised to seek the aid of astrologers before going into battle.[3] In another passage the author even forbids Alexander to get up, sit, eat, drink or in fact do anything else without consulting a qualified astrologer.[4] Other occult information in the *Secretum Secretorum* is also of specific interest to rulers. One chapter explains how to calculate the victor in a battle from the names of the commanders.[5] There are lists of stones whose properties will allow Alexander to conquer any army. Other stones can reveal the location of enemy soldiers by making their horses whinny.[6] These stones can also be used to keep one's own horses silent, a useful aid for surprise attacks.[7]

It would be possible to extend this list of occult books considerably, but the brief survey given here should suffice to indicate that a large number of magical works was available in the Middle Ages to anyone curious or unscrupulous enough to make use of them. Many of these books contained

---

1 *Hiltgart von Hürnheim: Mittelhochdeutsche Prosaübersetzung des "Secretum Secretorum,"* ed. Reinhold Möller. For English versions see *Secretum Secretorum: Nine English Versions*, ed. M.A. Manzalaoui.
2 Manzalaoui, p. 63.
3 Manzalaoui, p. 197.
4 Manzalaoui, p. 46.
5 Manzalaoui, pp. 14-17
6 Manzalaoui, p. 66.
7 Although the *Secretum Secretorum* was translated into Middle High German in 1282, the great majority of vernacular German translations on occult arts appeared only at the end of the Middle Ages. The most prolific translator was Hans Hartlieb, who translated a treatise on geomancy in the 1430's, a book on lunar divination between 1430-1435, a work on onomatomancy, or name divination, in 1440 and a book on chiromancy, or hand divination, in 1448. Wolfram Schmitt, *Hans Hartliebs mantische Schriften und seine Beeinflussung durch Nikolaus von Kues*; also Schmitt, *Magie und Mantik bei Hans Hartlieb*.

spells of particular interest to the court, and they were probably attempted by those curious readers not frightened off by the church's condemnations.

The possibilities for studying magic were present at the schools, but was it actually practiced? A first-hand account of magic practiced at the schools can be found in Book II, Chapter xxviii of John of Salisbury's *Policraticus*. John relates the story of how one of his teachers involved him in magical operations:

> Dum enim puer, ut psalmos addiscerem, sacerdoti traditus essem, qui forte speculariam magicam exercebat, contigit ut me et paulo grandiusculum puerum, praemissis quibusdam maleficiis, pro pedibus suis sedentes ad speculariae sacrilegium applicaret, ut in unguibus sacro nescio oleo aut crismate delibutis uel in exterso et leuigato corpore peluis quod quaerebat nostro manifestaretur indicio. Cum itaque praedictis nominibus, quae ipso horrore licet puerulus essem demonum uidebantur, et praemissis adiurationibus, quas Deo auctore nescio, sociusque meus se nescio quas imagines tenuiter tamen et nubilosas uidere indicasset, ego quidem ad illud ita cecus extiti, ut nichil michi appareret nisi ungues aut peluis et cetera quae antea noueram. Exinde ergo ad huiusmodi inutilis iudicatus sum, et quasi qui sacrilega haec impedirem, ne ad talia accederem condempnatus, et quotiens rem hanc exercere decreuerant, ego quasi totius diuinationis impedimentum arcebar. Sic michi in ea etate propitiatus est Dominus. (II. xxviii)

> During my boyhood I was placed under the direction of a priest, to teach me psalms. As he practiced the art of crystal gazing, it chanced that he after preliminary magical rites made use of me and a boy somewhat older, as we sat at his feet, for his sacrilegious art, in order that what he was seeking by means of finger nails moistened with some sort of sacred oil or crism, or of the smooth polished surface of a basin, might be made manifest to him by information imparted by us. And so after pronouncing names which by the horror they inspired seemed to me, child though I was, to belong to demons, and after administering oaths of which, at God's instance, I know nothing, my companion asserted that he saw certain misty figures, but dimly, while I was so blind to all this that nothing appeared to me except the nails or basin and the other objects I had seen there before. As a consequence I was adjudged useless for such purposes, and, as though I impeded the sacrilegious practices, I was

> condemned to have nothing to do with such things, and as often as they decided to practice their art I was banished as if an obstacle to the whole procedure. So propitious was God to me even at this early age. (II. xxviii)[1]

Was this incident simply concocted by John as a cautionary tale to frighten his audience? Evidence against such an interpretation can be found in a fifteenth century manuscript, Clm 849 in the Bavarian State Library in Munich.[2] The Munich manuscript is a necromancer's manual containing detailed instructions for magical operations. The method and purpose of one spell is identical to the ceremony John described. His clerical teacher was most probably a magician. John goes on to say:

> Cum uero paululum processissem, flagitium hoc magis et magis exhorrui, et eo fortius confirmatus est horror meus, quod, cum multos tunc nouerim, omnes antequam deficerent aut defectu naturae aut manu hostili beneficio luminis orbatos uidi, ut cetera incommoda taceam, quibus in conspectu meo a Domino aut prostrati aut perturbati sunt. (II. xxviii)

> But as I grew older more and more did I abominate this wickedness, and my horror of it was strengthened because, though at the time I made the acquaintance of many practitioners of the art, all of them before they died were deprived of their sight, either as the result of physical defect or by the hand of God, not to mention other miseries with which in my plain view they were inflicted. (II. xxviii)

Judging from the comments of William of Auvergne and the number of magic books in the libraries, John's accounts of magicians were not just empty warnings. Some clerics did indeed practice magic in the schools, and John felt it necessary to warn his readers of what was in all probability a real danger.

---

1 All translations of the *Policraticus* by Joseph Pike from: *Frivolities of Courtiers and Footprints of Philosophers (Policraticus)*.
2 Observed by Richard Kieckhefer, p. 151.

b) The Theoretical Legitimation of Magic

As a result of the increasing availability of manuscripts on magic and the growing interest in the subject, some clerics attempted to incorporate magic into the formal organization of knowledge.[1] Pedro Alfonso made one such attempt in his *Disciplina clericalis*, written in 1106. In this work Alfonso discusses whether necromancy is one of the seven liberal arts. He says:

> Philosophi qui prophecias non sectantur, aiunt nigromanciam esse septimam. Aliqui ex illis videlicet qui propheciis et philosophie credunt, uolunt esse scienciam que res naturales uel elementa mundana precellit. (11)
>
> The philosophers who do not believe in prognostication say that necromancy is the seventh [art]; others among them, namely those who believe in prognostication and in philosophy, think that it should be a science which encompasses all natural matters and mundane elements. (49)[2]

In his work *De divisione philosophiae* (1140), another Spanish cleric, Gundissalinus, the archdeacon of Toledo, considered magic as one of the worldly vanities which deserves neither praise nor condemnation. In a tree of knowledge from the school of St. Victor, the practical sciences were divided into the "mechanical" sciences (weaving, defence, navigation, agriculture, hunting, medicine and theatre) and "magic" (astrology, sorcery, divination, augury and illusion). A tree of knowledge from the school of Abelard had these same practical sciences as the counterpart of wisdom under the heading "means for salvation".[3]

Such scientific explanations of magic continued into the thirteenth century. Michael Scot said that there were two types of magic, one sort permissible and one to be condemned. *Ymaginaria astronomia, mathesis,* and *mathematica* were all legitimate forms of divination. The *magus sapiens* was a legitimate

---

[1] This is not to say that there were no attempts to justify magic before the end of the eleventh century. Julius Africanus (c. 160-c. 240 A.D.) wrote a magical tract including spells for love, good crops and healing. Africanus saw his methods as outside the realm of magic and religion, i.e. they were secular and thus not to be condemned. See Francis Thee, *Julius Africanus and the Early Christian View of Magic.*
[2] Translation from: *The Scholar's Guide*, by Joseph Ramon Jones and John Esten Keller.
[3] Plates I and II in *Medieval Humanism and Other Studies* by R.W. Southern.

sage. *Matesis* and *matematica* were diabolical sciences and were condemned along with the *maleficius* and the *praestigiosus*. The *Picatrix* defended the magician and tried to legitimize the profession by emphasising the years of learning and devotion the practitioner had to give to the art.[1]

The rise of Neo-Platonism in the 12th century[2] also helped contribute to the idea of magic as a legitimate science. The *Timaeus* of Plato, one of the most influential works for the Neo-Platonists, states: "then God, having decided to form the world in closest possible likeness to the most beautiful of intelligible beings and to a Being perfect in all things made it into a living being, one, visible, and having within itself all living beings of like nature with itself" (30d. 2-5)[3]. Connected to this thought was the idea of man as microcosm, a reflection of both God and Nature *in nuce*. Since the universe was a connected whole, it was only a small step to come to the conclusion that an action in one part of the universe would have its reverberations elsewhere, including on human beings. The magician could, by striking the right chords, influence people and objects in ways which would not be apparent to the average person.[4] This is not to suggest that Neo-Platonists were all magicians, but the theoretical groundwork for considering magic a legitimate branch of knowledge was there, and those who were interested in it could use these arguments to support the notion that the knowledge they were pursuing was scientific, and not magical. That such ideas were widespread can be seen from the church's efforts to exclude magic from the legitimate sphere of knowledge. An example of this is the condemnation issued by Hugo of St. Victor in his *Didascalicon*, written about 1141. Alongside Augustine's condemnation, Hugo's denouncement of magic was to influence the church's view of magic in the twelfth and thirteenth centuries.

> Magica in philosophiam non recipitur, sed est extrinsecus
> falsa professione, omnis iniquitatis et malitiae magistra, de

---

1 Edward Peters, p. 110.
2 For a good introduction to twelfth-century Neo-Platonism see M.-D. Chenu: *Nature, Man and Society in the Twelfth Century*, especially Chapter One, "Nature and Man: The Renaissance of the Twelfth Century".
3 Quoted in M.-D. Chenu: *Nature, Man and Society in the Twelfth Century*, p. 6, fn. 6.
4 This idea corresponds to the earlier mentioned folk idea of the world as an organism which had influences on humans. Here was one intersection point between popular and clerical cultures where both sought to legitimize magic.

vero mentiens, et veraciter laedens animos, seducit a religione divina, culturam daemonum suadet, morum corruptionem ingerit, et ad omne scelus ac nefas mentes sequacium impellit. (VI. XV)[1]

Magic is not accepted as part of philosophy, but stands with a false claim outside it; the mistress of every form of iniquity and malice, lying about the truth and truly infecting men's minds, it seduces them from divine religion, prompts them to the cult of demons, fosters corruption of morals, and impels the minds of its devotees to every wicked and criminal indulgence[2].

6. Conclusion

Although the church officially condemned magic, it was seen by many as an alternative source of supernatural power. The acceptance of magic in medieval culture was due in part to the laity's magical understanding of the universe which involved the supernatural in everyday life. Moreover, the church's sacramental view of religion made a qualitative distinction from magic difficult to establish. Because of the similarity of magic and religion, the laity often associated clerics and their learning with magic and some clerics did indeed practice it. The rediscovery of Arabic science and magic in the twelfth century fostered clerical interest in magic and gave it a scientific legitimacy which helped it to gain acceptance among many intellectuals.

---

1 Hugonis de Sancto Victore, *Didascalicon De Studio Legendi. A Critical Text*, edited by Charles Henry Buttimer.
2 *The Didascalicon of Hugo of St. Victor. A Medieval Guide to the Arts*. Translated by Jerome Taylor, pp. 154-55.

Chapter III

THE ADAPTATION AND TRANSFORMATION OF MAGICAL CONCEPTS IN MEDIEVAL COURT SOCIETY

1. High and Low Culture at the Medieval Courts

Magical beliefs influenced not only popular and academic spheres of medieval life, but the courtly sphere as well. Jacques Le Goff sees the lower nobility's attempt at self-assertion as the reason behind the increasing role of popular culture at court. According to Le Goff,[1] the lower nobility wished to

> oppose the culture of the Church and its ally, the aristocracy, by erecting not a counterculture but an alternative culture that was more its own, hence more amenable to its wishes ... *(The Medieval Imagination,* 29)

Le Goff believes the nobility turned to low or folkloric culture because it was "the only substitute culture that the lords could establish alongside - if not in opposition to - clerical culture" *(Time, Work and Culture in the Middle Ages,* p. 328, fn. 26). This alternative culture reflected the nobility's strong secular interests and dealt with such topics as chivalric combat and erotic love.[2] Although these interests were condemned by the church, the nobility was nevertheless successful in incorporating them into their lifestyle.

Another characteristic of the nobility's alternative culture was the large role which the supernatural played in it. When the nobility turned to folkloric culture, they chose a "culture of which the marvelous was an important component" (Le Goff, *The Medieval Imagination,* 29). The nobility's interest in the marvelous can be observed in the popularity of the Matière de Bretagne, which incorporated much Celtic mythology and folklore.

---

1 Le Goff takes up Erich Köhler's ideas on courtly literature. Köhler sees the rise of courtly literature connected with the interests of the rising knightly class. See Köhler, *Ideal und Wirklichkeit in der höfischen Epik.*
2 Rolf Sprandel has noted that the new erotic poetry was the clearest indicator of the general cultural emancipation of the lay nobility. Rolf Sprandel, *Gesellschaft und Literatur im Mittelalter,* p.137.

Of course the above examples do not mean that the church had no influence on court culture. In describing the literature of the nobility, Le Goff points out:

> ... der religiöse Anteil an dieser Literatur ist groß. Einmal weil die Herrn, die sie fördern und zugleich ihre Zuhörer sind, im allgemeinen glauben ... und auch, weil die Verfasser dieser Literaturwerke, wenn es auch unter ihnen Feudalherrn und professionelle Laien gibt, die oft Kleriker sind - und endlich auch, weil sich die Herausforderung an die christliche Ideologie in dieser Zeit nur in bestimmten Grenzen entwickeln kann. *(Das Hochmittelalter,* 176-77)

Paradoxically, however, the church itself contributed to a greater tolerance of magic and the marvelous in twelfth and thirteenth century culture. Le Goff finds that the church's success in establishing itself decreased its earlier opposition to the magical world-view of folkloric culture. "The marvelous had become less threatening, and the Church felt that it could tame it or turn it to advantage" (Le Goff, *The Medieval Imagination,* 29). Two aforementioned examples of the church's incorporation of the marvelous were its sacramental view of religion and its emphasis on miracles. Thus the church's greater tolerance of the marvelous and the nobility's attempts at self-assertion both helped to entrench the marvelous in court culture.[1]

The magical world-view of folkloric culture also influenced the medieval court's power structure. One example of its influence was the supernatural legitimation of rulers; another was the way in which power was disseminated at court. In this chapter I will examine how popular magical beliefs influenced the legitimation and dissemination of power at the medieval court and allowed a place for the court magician.

2. Charismatic Rule

The political structures of the Middle Ages were influenced by a charismatic view of kingship which invested rulers with supernatural authority. According to Edward Shils, the Christian formulation of charisma stems from the reference in II Corinthians, where the manifestations of divine

---
[1] Le Goff, *The Medieval Imagination,* p. 29.

grace are discussed.[1] Rudolf Sohm first used the term in his examination of the history of the Roman Catholic church,[2] which he considered to be a charismatic institution. Charisma and its relation to political leadership was further examined by Max Weber in his work *Wirtschaft und Gesellschaft*.[3] Weber defines charisma as:

> ... eine als außeralltäglich (ursprünglich sowohl bei Propheten wie bei therapeutischen wie bei Rechts-Weisen wie bei Jagdführern wie bei Kriegshelden: als magisch bedingt) geltende Qualität einer Persönlichkeit, ... um derentwillen sie als mit übernatürlichen oder übermenschlichen oder mindestens spezifisch außeralltäglichen, nicht mit jedem andern zugänglichen Kräften oder Eigenschaften [begabt] oder als gottgesandt oder als vorbildlich und deshalb als "Führer" gewertet wird. (140)

Weber finds the actual quality attributed to the ruler unimportant, because "darauf allein, wie sie tatsächlich von den charismatisch Beherrschten, den 'Anhängern' bewertet wird, kommt es an" (140). Charismatic people establish their power by disrupting established and rational systems of authority and setting up their own system. This system may be legitimized by supernatural authority or, on a more abstract level, by the individual's personality, which exhibits either a "commanding forcefulness or ... an exemplary inner state which is expressed in a bearing of serenity" (Shils, 129).

One of the manifestations of charismatic rule was the institution of sacral kingship. Sacral kingship was common to the Pre-Christian cultures of Western Europe and survived in many instances into Christian times. It was also found in pagan Germanic civilization. According to Walter Baetke, Germanic sacral kingship exhibited three major characteristics:[4]

---

1 Edward Shils, *Center and Periphery: Essays in Macrosociology*, p. 128.
2 Rudolf Sohm, *Kirchenrecht*.
3 Max Weber, *Wirtschaft und Gesellschaft*, 5. rev. Auflage, 1. Halbband.
4 Walter Baetke, *Das Heilige im Germanischen*, p. 138. Baetke later changed his mind about the existence of Sacral Kingship: *Yngvi und die Ynglinger. Eine quellenkritische Untersuchung über das nordische "Sakralkönigtum"*, Berlin: Sitzungsberichte der sächsischen Akademie der Wissenschaften Leipzig, 109/3, 1964. His revised opinion has met with little acceptance, being rejected by people like Folke Ström, "Kung Domalde i Svitjod och 'kungalyckan'," *Saga och Sed* 1967, pp. 52-66, and E. O. Turville-Petre,

1) The king possessed the gift of "Königsheil", i.e. the king was responsible for good weather and crops as well as domestic and external wellbeing.
2) The king served as intermediary between his people and the Gods, as a priest and offerer of sacrifices, including himself if need be.
3) The king was considered to be of divine origin, descended from Odin or one of the other Germanic gods.

Numerous examples of these three characteristics may be found throughout pagan Germanic Europe.[1] In Snorri Sturluson's *Ynglinga saga* (15) the Swedish king Dómaldi is held responsible for the welfare of his people. He is sacrificed by his people after a series of crop failures. *Halfdanssaga svarta* (IX) reports that Norway enjoyed years of fruitful crops under King Halfdan's rule. When the king died, his subjects argued over the burial site. Each community wanted Halfdan buried in their area, so that the body of the king could continue to provide good harvests. They finally solved their dispute by cutting up the corpse and burying the parts throughout Norway. Evidence of the king as intermediary between his people and the Gods can be found in Tacitus' *Germania* (X). Tacitus mentioned that the Germanic king had a special function among his people as prophet. Adam of Bremen *(Scholion,* 140) also noted that the kings of Uppsala are responsible for sacrifices. The Anglo-Saxon Kings began their genealogies with Woden and Geat, and even the family tree of King Henry II of England can be traced back to Woden.[2]

Although twelfth-century Europe was Christianized, the idea of supernatural royalty was far from forgotten. In fact, most of the examples of Germanic sacral kingship mentioned above were recorded in the eleventh and twelfth centuries. It would be incorrect, however, to assume that the Germanic concept of sacral kingship was simply adopted by the Christian rulers. A decidedly Christianized form of sacral kingship took the place of the pagan holy

---

"Fertility of Beast and Soil in Old Norse Literature," *Old Norse Literature and Mythology,* pp. 244-264.

1 For further documentation see Hans Naumann, "Die magische Seite des altgermanischen Königtums," pp. 1-12; W. A. Chaney, *The Cult of Kingship in Anglo-Saxon England;* Å. Ström & H. Biezais, *Germanische und Baltische Religion.*

2 Naumann, p. 3.

Adaptation and Transformation of Magical Concepts

kings. It drew on three traditions: the charismatic qualities of the Germanic kings, the cult of saints of late Antiquity and the divine attributes of Hellenistic and Roman rulers.[1] As such this sacral kingship was a creation of the early Middle Ages and reflected a continued interest in privileging the king as a bearer of supernatural powers. It was also a quick means of acquiring power from an indisputable source of authority. As Marc Bloch has pointed out, sacral legitimation was a valuable method for increasing the prestige and acceptance of newly established dynasties.[2]

The supernatural powers of sacral rulers were not identical. The kings often incorporated their own family history and the particular political circumstances in their countries into their sacral legitimation. Around 1000 A.D. the Capetians (and a century later the English kings) adopted the "royal touch", a dynastically-inherited supernatural power to heal the scrofulous, but only practiced on ritual occasions by consecrated kings. In England the Anglo-Saxon nobility used the notion of royal sainthood to further family members not directly in line for the throne.[3] Rulers in Norway and Kiev created royal cults around local martyrs like the Norwegian St. Olaf and the Russian saints Boris and Gleb.[4]

Christian adaptations of supernatural royalty were also taken up by German rulers. In 793 A.D. the cleric Alcuin wrote a letter to King Aethelred of Northumbria saying that the king's goodness was reflected in the welfare of his people, mild weather, fertility, enough male offspring and good health in general,[5] a clear reference to the Germanic *Königsheil*. When the excommunicated emperor Henry IV travelled through Tuscany in 1081 A.D., peas-

---

1 L. Taylor, *The Divinity of the Roman Emperor*; A. Alföldi, *Die monarchische Repräsentation im römischen Kaiserreich*; S.R.F. Price, *Rituals of Power. The Roman Imperial Cult in Asia Minor*; J. de Vries, "Das Königtum bei den Germanen", pp. 289-309; Peter Brown, *The Cult of Saints: Its Rise and Function in Latin Christianity*, noted in G. Klaniczay, *The Uses of Supernatural Power*, p. 80. See also K. Leyser, *Rule and Conflict in an Early Medieval Society*.
2 Marc Bloch, *The Royal Touch*, pp. 43-48.
3 Klaniczay, p. 82.
4 Klaniczay, pp. 84-86.
5 Alcuinus ad Aethelredum regem Northanhumbrorum, *Monumenta Germaniae Historica, Epistolae*, IV, Ep. 18.51, cited in Klaniczay, pp. 81-82.

ants followed him and tried to touch his clothes, thinking that this act would ensure them a good harvest.[1]

At the same time the ideas of royal unction were also beginning to play a role in sacral legitimation. The Carolingian and Ottonian emperors "revived the imperial [Roman] traditions of sacrality and added to them with the newly invented Christian rites for sanctifying a ruler - unction and coronation" (Klaniczay, 82). This ideology was further elaborated to view the king as the possessor of two "bodies", one personal and the other sacral-institutional.[2] In 1084 or 1085 A.D. Guy of Osnabrück wrote in his treatise *On the controversy between Hildebrand and the Emperor Henry* (IV) that the king, having been anointed with holy oil, was thus distinct from the general laity and participated in the priestly ministry.[3]

In twelfth-century Germany the idea of supernatural royalty was nowhere close to dying out. Since the eleventh century there had been a renewed interest in royal sainthood in the Holy Roman Empire.[4] Pope Gregory VII was apparently troubled by the number of rulers claiming supernatural legitimation. He wrote the Bishop of Metz that there were almost no holy Christian rulers but a large number of saintly monks and priests.[5] Renate Klauser sees the royal canonizations in the twelfth century as the Hohenstaufen's response to Gregory's assertions.[6] The emperor Henry II was elevated in 1146 A.D. by Pope Eugene III. In 1164 A.D. Rainald von Dassel, chancellor of Frederick I, and the anti-pope Pascal III transferred the relics of the three magi from Milan to Cologne to reinforce the imperial claims of royal sainthood.[7] A year later Rainald and Pascal canonized Charlemagne. Bernhardt Scholz has suggested that the English king Henry II, who was himself involved in conflicts with Rome, may have suggested

---

1 Rangerius, Vita Anselmi, *Monumenta Germaniae Historica, Scriptores.* XXX, 2, p. 1256, v. 4777 et seq.
2 E. Kantorowicz, *The King's Two Bodies: a Study in Medieval Political Theology.*
3 Marc Bloch, *The Royal Touch,* p. 110.
4 Klaniczay, p. 91.
5 *Monumenta Germania Historica, Ep. sel. ad usum scholarum,* 2, p. 558.
6 Renate Klauser, *Der Heinrichs- und Kunigundenkult im mittelalterlichen Bistum Bamberg,* pp. 48-52.
7 H. Hoffmann, *Die Heiligien drei Könige. Zur Heiligenverehrung im kirchlichen, gesellschaftlichen und politischen Leben des Mittelalters,* quoted in Klaniczay, p. 91.

the practice of royal canonization to Emperor Frederick I.[1] Henry II was well aware of the advantages of sacral kingship; he had Edward the Confessor canonized in 1163 A.D. and was responsible for popularizing the royal touch in England.

The exploitation of charisma was not limited to the formal institutionalization of sacral monarchy. Nor was the Christian religion the sole source of supernatural legitimacy. Although the holy kings of the twelfth century considered their supernatural power as originating from the Christian God, non-Christian forms of charisma could also be used to legitimize authority. The medieval nobility also claimed supernatural legitimization in an effort to tap into charismatic power. In this case, however, folk rather than Christian beliefs were used to justify supernatural power. In the twelfth and thirteenth century, the lesser nobility in France and Germany tapped into charismatic authority by claiming Melusina as a fairy ancestor.[2] Jacques Le Goff interprets this choice and appropriation of the folkloric Melusina motif for dynastic legitimacy as another example of the nobility's appropriation of folkloric culture. He thinks the nobility

> felt a certain distance from, and perhaps even a hostility toward the Church, if not Christianity itself. It refused to accept the Church's cultural models, preferring fairies to saints, entering into compacts with hell, toying with a suspect totemism. *(Time, Work and Culture in the Middle Ages,* 220)

Although it would be possible to examine further examples of sacral kingship in medieval Europe, the above examples show that medieval rulers throughout Europe were generally thought to be surrounded with an aura of supernatural power. Their powers could come from supernatural ancestors or the rituals associated with coronation. This supernatural concept of king-

---

[1] Bernhardt Scholz, "The Canonization of Edward the Confessor," *Speculum* 36 (1961), p. 53.
[2] Jacques Le Goff, "Melusina: Mother and Pioneer," in *Time, Work and Culture in the Middle Ages,* pp. 205-222. German versions of the Melusina legend have been collected and analyzed by Lutz Röhrich in *Erzählungen des späten Mittelalters und ihr Weiterleben in Literatur und Volksdichtung bis zur Gegenwart: Sagen, Märchen, Exempel und Schwänke,* vol. I, pp. 27-61 (summaries) and pp. 243-53 (commentary).

ship equated politics and magic and thereby helped to grant legitimacy to magical administrators.

3. The Dissemination of Power at Court

Supernatural powers were not limited to rulers and the nobility. Secondary members of the court could also have such powers attributed to them. In the first chapter, it was mentioned that there was a series of sorcery accusations in late Roman Antiquity. Peter Brown saw the existence of two systems of power, one "articulate" and the other "inarticulate" as the reason for these accusations.[1] The members of the court with articulate power had gained their influence by reason of their official duties and privileges. At the same time there were other people who enjoyed great esteem at court even though they had no official titles. They gained the ruler's favour because of intangible advantages like rhetorical skills, their relationship to important persons or their personality, which could also exude a charismatic charm. The success of those possessing inarticulate power over the bearers of official or articulate power could cause the latter group to level accusations of sorcery against the former group. Brown's concepts of articulate and inarticulate power have been applied to the medieval court by Edward Peters, who sees the parallel systems of articulate and inarticulate power begin to appear in Western European courts at the end of the twelfth century: "Although the thirteenth century witnessed the rise to power of great officers of state, the lords of courts just as frequently listened to individual favorites who often had no explicit authority" (113).

According to Peters, the continuing process of administrative centralization in Western Europe from the tenth century onwards resulted in considerable court entourages by the end of the twelfth century.[2] These entourages included official administrators: nobility and clerics whose rank or office had been formally conferred on them by the ruler, such as chancellors, ambassadors, and chamberlains.

---

[1] Peter Brown, "Sorcery, Demons and the Rise of Christianity: From Late Antiquity into the Middle Ages," pp. 119-146.
[2] Edward Peters, p. 113.

In addition to the official administrators, the court society included members who held no formal office, but could nevertheless still exercise a considerable amount of influence at court. In reference to Peter Brown, Edward Peters calls this group the *demimonde* of the court.[1] Such people included entertainers, physicians, astrologers, ladies and men in waiting, lovers, illegitimate offspring, holy men and clerics. Members from both official and inofficial groups could rise and fall rapidly in the ruler's esteem. As these courtiers rose in influence and power, they often aroused the envy and fear of their rivals, both among the official and the inofficial spheres of court. Just how great such animosities could become can be seen in the Wormser Hofrecht, written by Burchard of Worms (1024-1025) as a law for the government of the episcopal court. In writing down the punishment for murder, Burchard notes that in one year 35 clerics were murdered by their colleagues.[2] Burchard is aghast that the murderers were not remorseful but rather proud of their deeds. Intrigues at court were commonplace, and courtiers had to be constantly on their guard.

Magic, as in late Roman Antiquity, was one avenue to success at court. An unscrupulous courtier might resort to magic in order to rise in the ruler's esteem or to discredit or harm a rival. Conversely, courtiers could also attribute a rival's success or their own decline to the use of magic. Such accusations depended on the court's fear of malevolent occult powers to discredit an individual.

A courtier resorting to magic may have learned the arts while at a cathedral school. It was mentioned in the last chapter that magic had attracted the interest of inquisitive clerics at the cathedral schools, many of whom later found employment at the courts. Courtiers with no magic skills of their own could also find magicians among the court entourage. As Edward Peters notes:

> ... in an atmosphere of factionalism, struggles for favor, ambition, intense personal likes and dislikes, the demimonde of the court constituted the personnel at the disposal of those who wished to take advantage of the infor-

---

[1] Edward Peters, p. 115.
[2] Joachim Bumke, *Höfische Kultur*, vol. I, p. 11.

mal and devious means of acquiring power and favor. (115-116)

There was an outbreak of sorcery trials similar to those Brown describes in fourteenth century France and fifteenth century England.[1] These trials involved kings and the prominent politicians around them. They occurred at times when royal power was unstable and the fear of treason particularly prominent. In France origins of these sorcery trials lie in the feud between Philip IV and Boniface VIII, and in England in the dynastic rivalries during the reign of Henry V.[2] William R. Jones observes,

> the ambiguous dynastic and political roles of these men and women made them targets of accusations of practicing sorcery in ways which seemed to cast doubt on royal succession or connoted their reputations for intrigue. (687)

As in the case of the Roman sorcery trials, those influential but unofficial members of the court were conceived as threats by the established officials of the court. These established officials initiated plots to remove their rivals from power. In a culture which already gave credence to magic and charismatic power, charges of subversive sorcery were an effective means of dealing with unwanted rivals.

4. *Magicians in Court Writings*

The medieval court's interest in magicians is reflected in accounts of sorcerers in court literature. In the previous chapter it was mentioned that Pope Sylvester II was considered to have been a magician in the Middle Ages. Stories about Sylvester's magic were very popular at the twelfth-century courts and were collected in the writings of numerous court clerics including William of Malmesbury and Walter Map.

---

[1] William R. Jones, "Political Uses of Sorcery in Medieval Europe," pp. 670-687; H.A. Kelly, "English Kings and the Fear of Sorcery", pp. 206-38.
[2] Jones, pp. 670-87.

Adaptation and Transformation of Magical Concepts

The poet Virgil was another historical figure associated with magic in the Middle Ages.[1] In the medieval legends surrounding Virgil we see the same complex of ideas including knowledge, magic/religion and political activity which manisfested themselves in the Sylvester legends.

In these legends Virgil constructed a number of devices for the good of the citizens of Naples, where he spend a good deal of his life. These devices included a bronze fly which drove away real flies, a bronze horse which protected horses from disease and a butcher shop in which meat did not spoil. Virgil also created devices for the safety of the city, including a statue to keep Mt. Vesuvius dormant. Because of Virgil's connection to Naples, Domenico Comparetti has suggested that these tales began as local Neapolitan tales[2] but this theory has has been called into question by John Spargo.[3] Spargo notes that nearly all of the first accounts of Virgil's necromantic feats were recorded after 1194, when Naples was overrun by Henry IV of Germany, and then asks if "the Virgilian legends told during this period were travellers' tales told by clerics with not a little malicious satisfaction at the ultimate downfall of the popular faith in the sage's power of protecting the city?" (310-311). It is perhaps more appropriate to see the origin of the Virgil legends, as Otto Neudeck states, "eher im Bereich einer Übernationalen Gelehrtenkultur" ("Vergil im deutschsprachiger Literatur um 1300: Ein Zauberer und Magier in heilsgeschichtlicher Funktion", 43).

---

1 For two detailed studies of medieval treatments of Virgil, see Domenico Comparetti, *Virgil in the Middle Ages*, translated by E.F.M. Benecke, and John W. Spargo, *Virgil the Necromancer*.
2 Domenico Comparetti, *Virgil in the Middle Ages*.
3 Spargo observes:
   ...the legends first appeared in the *Policraticus*, a work written about 1159. Then during the next one hundred and seventy years, they were told pretty much all over Europe, by englishmen, Frenchmen, Germans, by a troubadour of Provence, in chronicles, encyclopaedias, romances, and in two of the greatest collections of stories known in the Middle Ages; but *never once* are the legends told by Italians during thhis period of one hundred and seventy years. (John W. Spargo, *Virgil the Necromancer*, 309)

Important for this study is not so much the origin of these legends as their equation of knowledge and sorcery. In the Middle Ages technologically sophisticated devices were considered to have magical powers.[1] Pope Sylvester's inventions had contributed to his reputation as a magician, and Virgil's performed benevolent magic reminiscent of the protection granted by patron saints. Indeed, Virgil's remains were also reputed to have magical protective powers similar to those ascribed to holy relics. According to Konrad von Querfurt, Naples would be safe as long as Virgil's bones remained undisturbed. But if anyone disturbed these bones, "it became suddenly dark, a noise as of a tempest was heard, and the waves of the sea became violently agitated" (Comparetti, 259). Konrad claims to have witnessed this himself.

Gervasius of Tilbury in his *Otia imperialia* (c. 1212) told of how a magician asked King Roger of Sicily for the poet's remains. The king agreed, "but the inhabitants of Naples, calling to mind the great affection which Vergil had shown their city, and fearing that if his bones were taken away some terrible calamity might befall them, preferred to disregard the king's command rather than by obeying it to bring about the ruin of so great a city" (Comparetti, 274). They forbade the magician to remove the bones and deposited them in the Castel di Mare, where they remained on display. In discussing medieval attitudes towards saints, Bob Scribner emphasized the "pragmatic efficacy" (25) of their supernatural power. Saints were venerated as long as appeals to them were successful. If these appeals went unanswered, the saints were mocked and non-Christian powers invoked.[2] The stories of Virgil's remains are another example of how Medieval Europeans saw magic as an alternative source of supernatural power. Although Virgil was not a saint nor even a Christian, the Neapolitans considered his protection helpful and effective.

There are other Virgil stories where the line between magic and Christianity is even more indistinct. In these accounts Virgil's magic is incorporated into Christian mythology; he was thought to have prophesied the coming of

---

[1] W. Eamon, "Technology as magic in the late Middle Ages and Renaissance", pp. 171-212; M. Sherwood, "Magic and Mechanics in Medieval Fiction", pp. 567-592.
[2] Scribner notes how weather bells were blessed in the name of the divinity, but if good weather did not follow, they were re-blessed in the name of the devil (p. 25).

Christ in his fourth eclogue.[1] In medieval mystery plays dating back to the eleventh century[2] Virgil often appeared at the side of the Sibyl. In a German epic, *Reinfried von Braunschweig*, Virgil has a much more important role in the Nativity. The story is as follows:

> A great magician named Zabulon (Savilon) lived on the Magnetberg. He was the inventor of astrology and necromancy and had written many books on the subject with the intent of hindering the birth of Christ. Shortly before Christ's birth, Virgil sailed to the mountain and, using magical assistance, tricked Zabulon out of his magic books and treasures. Because Virgil had diverted the sorcerer's attention away from the nativity, the Virgin was able to give birth to Christ.

In this story Virgil is presented as a benevolent sorcerer who not only conquers the evil magic of Zabulon, but even makes the birth of Christ possible: "Das zentrale Ereignis für das Heil der Menschheit, die Inkarnation Gottes, kann nur deshalb stattfinden, weil Virgilius als Handelnder in die Heilsgeschichte eingreift" (Neudeck, "Möglichkeiten der Dichter-Stilisierung in mittelhochdeutscher Literatur: Neidhart, Wolfram, Vergil", 351). Neudeck sees this interpretation of Virgil as dependent on the romance: "Die Grenzen des noch weisen, sogar zauberkundigen Menschen Savilon gegenüber der Allmacht Gottes werden auf der Folie der Heilsgeschichte dem Helden Reinfried und damit auch dem Leser/Hörer demonstriert" ("Vergil in Deutschsprachiger Literatur um 1300: Ein Zauberer und Magier in heilsgeschichtlicher Funktion", 47). Yet it is important not to underestimate the role of magic in this episode. It reveals several important ideas on this art held by people in the Middle Ages. First of all, magic is not in itself malevolent. A heathen may have invented it for evil purposes, but the virtuous Virgil also turns to it. Once Virgil has Savilon's books in his possession, he does not destroy them, but keeps them for his own (benevolent) purposes. Secondly, there is no clear distinction between magic and Christianity, since Virgil's magic plays a major role in the birth of Christ. Although Christianity is presented as the true religion, magic is needed to assist the coming of the

---

1 Comparetti, p. 99.
2 For example in the Latin Mystery of the Nativity performed in the Abbey of St. Martial at Limoges. For other examples of Virgil in mystery plays see Comparetti, pp. 309-317.

Saviour. In this case, magic is again an alternative form of supernatural power which can be used alongside Christianity.

The stories of Virgil's sorcery correspond to popular medieval notions of magic. Like Pope Sylvester, Virgil is learned and his magic an aspect of his erudition. His magic is benevolent and protects the citizens of his home town; Virgil functions as a supernatural guardian. There is no qualitative distinction between his deeds and those of Christian saints. The stories surrounding Virgil helped to reinforce medieval concepts associating magic, knowledge and religion; the large number of these tales indicates their popularity and influence at the court.

5. *Magicians at Historical Courts*

Magicians did not only appear in court writings. Historical accounts indicate that magical advisors were active at many medieval courts. We already find them at the Carolingian courts.[1] Charlemagne himself was greatly interested in astrology: he owned a silver table inscribed with the stars and the orbits of the planets. Charlemagne also included astrologers in his retinue. In 810 he had them draw up the various constellations in several manuscripts which are still preserved today.[2] Charlemagne also consulted the stars before embarking on campaigns. He asked his clerics Alcuin and Dungal to interpret the movement of Mars, the comets and the significance of an eclipse.[3]

Louis the Pious, in spite of his epithet, shared his father's interest in the occult. Paschasius Radbertus mentions that Louis' entourage was full of magicians and diviners and that political policies were carried out in accordance with their advice.[4] Louis' biographer Astronomus reports that the emperor asked Einhard and other clerics to interpret a comet which appeared in the skies in 837. Astronomus also mentions that a comet foretold the death of

---

[1] Pierre Riché, "La magie à l'époque Carolingienne", pp. 127-38.
[2] Pierre Riché, *Die Welt der Karolinger*, p. 225.
[3] Pierre Riché, *Die Welt der Karolinger*, p. 225.
[4] *Patrologia Latina* 120, columns 1616-17. Vita Walae, ed. G.H. Pertz, *Monumenta Germaniae Historica, Scriptores* ii, 553-554.

Pippin of Aquitaine and that an eclipse immediately preceded his death.[1] Empress Judith, the wife of the ninth-century Emperor Lothar, was accused by Lothar's supporters of having used magic to enchant her husband.[2]

Later courts also included magicians and diviners in their retinues. Adam of Bremen's *History of the Arch-Bishops of Hamburg-Bremen*[3] (c. 1080) relates the story of Archbishop Adalbert (c. 1000-1072). A man with high political ambitions, Adalbert spent much time at the court of Henry IV. The court nobility grew envious of Adalbert's success and accused the Archbishop of sorcery. As a result Adalbert was driven from the court (III. lxvii). Was Adalbert really a sorcerer? Adam goes to great pains to defend him from these charges:

> A quo crimine Iesum testor et angelos eius omnesque sanctos illum virum prorsus immunem et liberum esse, presertim cum maleficos et divinos et eiusmodi homines sepe iudicaret morte esse multandos. (III. lxiii)

> I call to witness Jesus and His angels and all His saints that the man was free and guiltless of this crime, especially since he himself often declared that magicians and fortune tellers and men of that sort must be punished with death. (III. lxiii)

Even if Adalbert was no magician, his biography indicates that he did rely on magical advisors. Adam speaks of an entourage which accompanied Adalbert and laments the amount of money the archbishop threw away on them:

> Pecuniam autem, quam recepit a suis sive ab amicis, porro seu ab his, qui frequentabant palatium vel qui regiae maiestati fuerunt obnoxii, illam, inquam, pecuniam, licet maxima esset, sine mora dispersit infamibus personis et ypocritis, medicis et histrionibus et id genus aliis. (III. xxxvi)

---

1 Riché, *Die Welt der Karolinger*, pp. 225-226.
2 Nithard, *Histoire des fils de Louis le Pieux*, I, 5; Paschius Radbertus, *Patrologia Latina* 120, col. 1617.
3 All quotes are taken from the following edition: *Adam von Bremen, Hamburgische Kirchengeschichte*, ed. Bernhard Schmeidler, 3d ed., *Monumenta Germaniae Historica, Scriptores rer. germ. in us. schol.*, vol. 2. English translations are taken from: Adam of Bremen, *History of the Archbishops of Hamburg-Bremen*, trans. Francis Tschan.

The money he received from his people or from friends or also from those who frequented the palace or who were answerable to his royal majesty, that money, I say, even though it amounted to a very large sum, he promptly dispersed to disreputable persons and hypocrites, healers and actors and others of that sort. (III. xxxvi)

Among this entourage were a number of diviners. "Erant autem cum pontifice alii pseudoprophetae longe alia promittentes, quibus maior fides habebatur" (III. lxiv) [But there were with the bishop others, false prophets, who made promises of a far different kind, and in them he had greater faith (III. lxiv)]. To Adam's dismay, these prophets promised Adalbert longevity even though he was on his deathbed. One of Adalbert's favourites was Notebald, who with his magic arts had won influence with the bishop.[1] Apparently Notebald's success rate was quite high, for even Adam grudgingly admits that the diviner was often correct in his predictions: "Familiarissimus omnium erat Notebaldus, qui multa pontifici sepe vera predicens uno et novissimo decepit verbo credentem" (III. lxiv) [The most intimate of all was Notebald who had often predicted for the archbishop many things that had turned true, but who from the first word to the last deceived his believer (III. lxiv)].

Adalbert's biography shows the important role magical advisors could have even at an episcopal court. Apparently Adalbert had no religious qualms about turning to magicians and diviners. Adam, in spite of his disapproval, exhibited an ambivalent attitude towards these advisors. He lamented the fact that Notebald had so much influence over Adalbert, but he disproved their false prophecies with the counter-prophecy of another fortune-teller: "In diebus illis supervenit quaedam mulier spiritum habens Phitonis; haec voce publica dixit omnibus celerem archiepiscopo transitum affore infra biennium, nisi forte converteretur" (III. lxiv) [In those days there came up a certain woman who had the power of divination. She publicly declared to all the people that the archbishop would pass away suddenly within two years unless, indeed, he was converted (III. lxiv)]. Thus Adam would also rely on diviners when it suited him. In the last chapter, it was mentioned

---

1 According to Adam, "Nothebaldus vir maleficus, adulator et mendax apertissimus" *Schol.* 88 (89) [Notebald was a magician, a flatter, and a most brazen liar *Schol.* 88 (89)].

Adaptation and Transformation of Magical Concepts 81

that clerical administrators did not have to be pious. Adalbert's interest in magic bears this observation out. The magicians in his retinue reflect the pragmatic attitude towards magic held by many of the laity and clergy.

Twelfth and thirteenth-century rulers also turned to magicians for advice. John of Salisbury's *Policraticus*, written c. 1159, gives an insight into the pervasiveness of magicians at court. The *Policraticus* was a handbook on proper government for court administrators and rulers. It is based on John's experiences at the courts of Theobald, Archbishop of Canterbury and King Henry II of England. In addition to describing proper conduct, John also warns his readers of the dangers and vices at the court. Among these frivolities John includes the court's excessive interest in hunting, gambling, actors, music, mimes, jugglers, and illusionists. In addition to these pastimes, John also concerns himself with more serious ones:

> Eos autem qui nocentiora praestigia artesque magicas et uarias species mathematicae reprobatae exercent, iam pridem sancti patres ab aula iusserunt, eo quod omnia haec artificia uel potius maleficia ex pestifera quadam familiaritate demonum et hominum nouerint profluxisse. (I. 9)

> Long ago the Christian Fathers condemned those who practiced the more demoralizing forms of legerdemain, the art of magic, and astrology because they realized that all these arts, or rather artifices, derive from unholy commerce between men and demons. (I. 9)

John's extensive description and catalogue of magical practices proceeds for several chapters. As an example, Chapter 12 of Book I is entitled "Qui sint incantatores, arioli, aruspices, phycii, uultiuoli, imaginarii, coniectores, chiromantici, specularii, mathematici, salissatores, sortilegi, augures" [Definitions of Enchanters, Wizards, Soothsayers, Prophets, 'Vultivoli,' 'Imaginarii,' Dream Interpreters, Palmists, Crystal-Seers, Astrologers, 'Salisatores,' Fortune Tellers, Augurs]. John's condemnation of these practices follows the earlier criticisms of Isidore of Seville, St. Augustine, and Hrabanus Maurus. Because of his use of classical and patristic authorities, some scholars have questioned whether or not John is making use of a topos, rather than describing actual contemporary events. Helen Waddell, in her book *The Wandering Scholars,* comments that it is never clear whether John is describing the court of Henry II or Augustus.[1] Waddell's objection has been countered by Edward Peters. Peters points out that in discussing magic, John must describe magic as it existed in the tradition of Christian literature.[2] Peters argues that John used the classical and patristic authorities to condemn such practices all the more forcefully.[3] The length and the vigor of John's condemnations of magic also indicate that the topic was a major concern for him.

John's descriptions are not limited, however, to paraphrasing classical and patristic sources. In the *Policraticus* it becomes apparent that John also speaks from his own experiences and is genuinely concerned about the popularity of magic at court. He gives examples of first-hand experiences with magical practitioners. John's experiences with his Latin teacher's divinatory operations were mentioned in the last chapter. According to John, courtiers were also fascinated in forecasting the future. He laments the high regard astrology enjoyed at court, and wished "Possit utinam tam facile mathematicorum error a praestantioribus animis amoueri quam leuiter in conspectu uerae fidei et sanae conscientiae istarum illusionum demonia conquiescunt (II. xviii) [Would that the errors of astrologers were as easily removed from superior minds as evil spirits are effectively stilled in the light of true faith and sound knowledge of these illusions (II. xviii)]. John also mentions his personal acquaintance with diviners, warning his readers that "Postremo plurimos eorum audiui, noui multos, sed neminem in hoc errore diutius fuisse recolo, in quo manus Domini condignam non exercuerit ultionem" (II. xxvi) [Finally, I have listened to many of them and am acquainted with many of them, but I recall not one who has persisted in this error on whom the Lord has not laid the heavy hand of condign punishment (II. xxvi)].

---

1 H. Waddell, *The Wandering Scholars*, reprint ed. London, 1968, p. xiii, noted in Edward Peters, p. 47.
2 Edward Peters, p. 47.
3 Edward Peters, p. 60, fn. 49.

Thomas Becket also listened to them; in 1157 Becket turned to soothsayers in order to foretell the outcome of Henry II's campaign against the Welsh. His efforts earned John's reprimand:

> Cum aduersus Niuicollinos Britones regia esset expeditio producenda, in quo te consultus aruspex praemonuit? ... Item chironomanticus adhibitus et consultus quid contulit? Nam sub eo articulo uterque, quisquis hoc egerit, consultus est. Tu quidem paucis diebus elapsis quasi stellam matutinam generis tui non praemonitus perdidisti. Cetera, quae melius nosti, scienter taceo; cum isti uanitate sua meruerint ne ulterius consulantur. (II. xxvii)

> When the King's army was preparing to advance against the Snowdon Welsh, in what respect did the soothsayers, when consulted, give you warning to advance ... Again, what has the palmist to offer when summoned and consulted? For at that crisis each, whoever he was, [soothsayer or palmist] who practiced either art was consulted. As a matter of fact after the lapse of a few days, without warning, you lost your brother-in-law, who was your star, the son of morning as it were. The rest of it, which you know better than I, I purposely pass in silence, since they, as a result of their lies, no longer deserve to be trusted. (II. xxvii)

Apparently Thomas Becket was not satisfied with relying on divine help and felt it necessary to turn to non-Christian supernatural advisors. John of Salisbury's warning to Becket seems to have gone unheeded. Lynn Thorndike notes that in 1170 John wrote a letter to Becket, again reproving him for his consultations with diviners. Acting on the advice of diviners, Thomas had delayed sending off important letters. John wrote his friend, rebuking him: "Nec dixeritis quae prouenerunt uobis non fuisse praedicta, sed potius quod, omnium auspicantium more, subtilitatem uestram uaticinia, quae non erant a Spiritu, deluserunt" (Letter 301[1]) "You cannot say that you were not told in advance the outcome in these cases: but rather that, as happens to all those who study the auguries, prophecies not inspired by the Holy Ghost deceived your wits" and asked him to renounce such prophecies in the future: "Vaticiniis ergo renuntiemus in posterum, quia nos in hac parte grauius infortunia perculerunt" (Letter 301) [From now on let us re-

---
[1] Latin and English translation taken from *The Letters of John of Salisbury* volume II, edited by W.J. Millor, S.J., and C.N.L. Brooke.

nounce prophecies, since on this account misfortunes have fallen on us the more heavily (Letter 301)]. Thomas Becket, like his fellow bishop Adalbert, was another cleric who pragmatically sought council from both diviners and Christian advisors.

A thirteenth-century occult advisor was Michael Scot, imperial astrologer and physician of Frederick II. The emperor employed Michael as his court astrologer in the early thirteenth century, from about 1220 until his death around 1235. While at the imperial court, he wrote the *Liber introductorius*, an introductory work on astrology dedicated to Frederick. Michael Scot must have been aware of the controversial nature of his book, for he assures his readers of his belief in God and Christianity. He condemns magic, since it was not a branch of philosophy, but the mistress of all iniquity and evil, and deceived and seduced those who practiced it.[1] He justifies his interest in the occult by differentiating between legitimate and illegitimate sciences. Michael separates superstitious astronomy from *ymaginaria astronomia*. The latter is a legitimate form of knowledge, used to discern concepts hidden to the eye such as mathematical lines and spiritual entities.[2] He gives an example of the astrological counsel he offered his emperor, saying that that this advice should be solicited when the moon is waxing and in a human sign, fiery or aerial.[3] Michael also believed in the occult forces in nature and the powers of words and numbers.[4] According to him, astrology is not for poor people, but rather an aid to physicians, kings, barons, alchemists, necromancers and practitioners of the *ars notoria*.[5] He gives specific applications of astrological precepts of special interest to the court. The hour of Saturn, for example, is not a good time for war, business or going to a ruler in order to gain favour from him.[6] In one manuscript of the *Liber introductorius*, the hour

---

1 Thorndike, *Michael Scot*, p. 116.
2 Thorndike, *Michael Scot*, p. 92.
3 Thorndike, *Michael Scot*, p. 94.
4 Throndike, *Michael Scot*, p. 116.
5 Munich, Staatsbibliothek, cod. lat. 10268, col. 15vb, 16ra. Quoted in Thorndike, *Michael Scot*, p. 92.
6 Munich, Staatsbibliothek, cod. lat. 10268, col. 10vb. Quoted in Thorndike, *Michael Scot*, p. 99.

of Saturn is mentioned as favourable for planning deception and fraud.[1] In another example Michael mentions a prince who had to put down a rebellion. The positions of the stars and planets were consulted to determine the prince's success in quelling the revolt.[2]

Michael Scot's writings also show a familiarity with contemporary magic books and operations. He mentions necromantic works ascribed to Solomon and describes their contents.[3] Michael held that demons, although malevolent and treacherous figures, could be invoked and made to obey conjurations. He also emphasized the importance of astrology in conjurations and provides his readers with long lists of suitable hours for such operations.[4]

Michael Scot may have not just been interested in magic but may have practiced it as well. A fifteenth-century manuscript of experiments includes the *Experimentum Michaelis Scoti Nigromantici*.[5] Although the extant manuscript postdates its author by two centuries, it was apparently copied from a much older manuscript. The work was dedicated to a certain Philip, who lay sick in the city of Cordova. Lynn Thorndike suggests that this dedication could support the authenticity of the document. According to Thorndike, this Philip might have been Philip of Tripoli, contemporary of Michael Scot and Latin translator of the *Secretum secretorum*.[6] If Thorndike is correct in his assumptions, then Michael Scot may have been not just Frederick's astrologer but his magician as well. Judging from the strong popularity and credence magic enjoyed at the court, Michael could well have found ample opportunity to apply his interests.

---

1 Paris, Bibliothèque Nationale, nouv. acq. latin 1401, col 119r. Quoted in Thorndike, *Michael Scot*, p. 99.
2 Paris, Bibliothèque Nationale, nouv. acq. latin 1401, 99v-100r. Quoted in Thorndike, *Michael Scot*, p. 104.
3 Thorndike, *Michael Scot*, p. 120.
4 Munich, Staatsbibliothek cod. lat. 10268, col.108va-b. Quoted in Thorndike, *Michael Scot*, p. 117.
5 Florence, Laurentian Library, Plut. 89 sup., cod. 38, for. 244v. Quoted in Thorndike, *Michael Scot*, p. 121.
6 Thorndike, *Michael Scot*, p. 121.

6. Conclusion

Magical beliefs played an important role in shaping the power structure of medieval courts. Rulers often claimed supernatural powers in order to gain metaphysical legitimation; therefore many kings were surrounded by a charismatic aura of supernatural authority. Magical beliefs also influenced the dissemination of power at the court. Because of the intrigues and constantly shifting alliances at court, courtiers often attributed the rapid and at times seemingly inexplicable changes in their standing to magic.

The court's interest in magic could be seen in accounts of historical "magicians" like Pope Sylvester II and Virgil. These erudite figures were perceived as great magicians in the Middle Ages and the stories surrounding them reinforced medieval notions equating magic and knowledge. Magicians did not only appear in medieval court writings, however. Rulers from Charlemagne to Frederick II actually employed magical advisors. These advisors could use their powers to counsel rulers and guide their campaigns; they could cast also spells to further or hinder the careers of courtiers. Whatever their duties, the court offered magicians ample opportunity to practice their skills.

Chapter IV

LANZELET

1. Introduction

Ulrich von Zatzikhoven's *Lanzelet*[1] deals with the education of its title hero as knight and ruler. In the course of his adventures, Lanzelet must face the powerful magician Malduc: King Arthur has enlisted Malduc's aid to rescue Guinevere from the evil Valerin. In return, Malduc asks that the knights Erec and Wâlwein be surrendered to him. It is up to Lanzelet to rescue his companions. I will begin my examination with a brief analysis of the Malduc episode in the context of the romance and then compare Malduc to historical magicians.

2. The Function of the Malduc Episode

In order to understand the function of the Malduc episode, it is important to situate it within the structure of *Lanzelet*. The structure of the romance has been a rich topic for recent discussion. Some critics like Kurt Ruh, Karl Bertau, Klaus Schmidt, Rene Perrenec, and Patrick McConeghy see the story as being composed of two parts, and Rodney Fisher even breaks it into four sections.[2] Other critics like James Schultz, Dieter Welz, and Barbara Thoran have seen *Lanzelet* as a single narrative unit.[3] Although the romance does not follow the "double course" of the classic Arthurian romances like *Erec*, *Iwein* and *Parzival*, there are nevertheless two distinct parts. The first part deals

---

1 All quotes are taken from: Ulrich von Zatzikhoven, *Lanzelet*. Ed. K.A. Hahn.
2 Kurt Ruh, *Höfische Epik des deutschen Mittelalters* Band II, p. 41; Karl Bertau, *Über Literaturgeschichte: literarischer Kunstcharakter und Geschichte in der höfischen Epik um 1200*, p. 36; Klaus Schmidt, "Frauenritter oder Artusritter? Über Struktur und Gehalt von Ulrichs von Zatzikhoven 'Lanzelet'", p. 10; Rene Perrenec, "Arthurroman und Familie: Daz welsche buoch von Lanzelete", p. 4; Patrick McConeghy, "Aventiure and Anti-Aventiure in Ulrich von Zatzikhoven's Lanzelet and Hartmann von Aue's Iwein", p. 60; Rodney Fisher, "Ulrich von Zatzikhoven's Lanzelet: In Search of 'Sens'", p. 283.
3 James Schultz, "'Lanzelet': A Flawless Hero in a Symmetrical World", p. 181; Dieter Welz, "Lanzelet im Schoenen Walde: Überlegungen zu Struktur und Sinn des Lanzelet Romans", p. 64, Barbara Thoran, "Zur Struktur des 'Lanzelet' Ulrichs von Zatzikhoven", p. 52.

with Lanzelet's education as knight. In this part Lanzelet learns about knighthood and is successful in a series of increasingly difficult duels.[1] It culminates with the revelation of his name and heritage in the middle of the romance (4706 ff.). These revelations introduce the second part, which deals with the education of Lanzelet as a ruler.

In addition to learning his name and heritage, Lanzelet also discovers that he is heir to a usurped kingdom. Lanzelet's father, King Pant, had been a very unjust ruler (61-65) and his tyranny had caused his nobles to commit regicide (97-188).

If Lanzelet is to regain his father's kingdom, he must first become a just ruler, and learn how to deal with threats to his rule. Lanzelet learns about good rule by working with the Arthurian court, at first as its helper and then as its leader: "Die Verteidigung der Artusgemeinschaft bereitet also den Helden stufenweise auf die Wahrnehmung von Schutz- und Schirmaufgaben, also von herrscherlichen Pflichten vor" (Perrenec, 20).[2] His education as ruler does teach him how to work on behalf of others and as leader of a team.[3] Yet it also teaches him how to deal with the most serious challenge a monarch must face - the threat of hostile magic.

The first threat of magic appears when King Valerin renews his claim to Guinevere and kidnaps her. In Lanzelet's previous adventures, he had been

---

[1] James Schultz finds Lanzelet to be perfect from the beginning on and sees his apparent development as merely a "compositional trick" (p. 170). Klaus Schmidt has a valid response to the view of Lanzelet as static: "Doch muß der mittelalterliche Entwicklungsbegriff eher mit einer Naturgesetzlichkeit verglichen werden, wo ein gegebener Kern sich seiner Anlage gemäß zur vollen Form entwickelt" (p. 6). Schultz' interpretation would also not explain Lanzelet's reluctance to rule before he has gained greater knowledge of kingship (8412-21).

[2] Klaus Schmidt also finds that the second half leads Lanzelet "zum exemplarischen Herrschertum" (p. 10). Although Barbara Thoran interprets the romance as following the scheme of loss and recovery (p. 76), she too sees the later adventures to prepare Lanzelet for the governance of his father's kingdom. "Zuerst gilt es also, sich als Helfer des Königs zu bewähren, bevor er selbst als König die Regentschaft in seinem Land antritt" (pp. 64-65).

[3] In the first adventure he jousts against King Valerin, who claims Guinevere as his betrothed. Here Lanzelet serves on behalf of the Arthurian community. In the second adventure at Plûrîs Lanzelet's knightly prowess results in a year of Minnehaft by the queen of Plûrîs. Arthur's knights must help him escape. This adventure shows him the importance of loyal friends and teamwork. After these two adventures he is ready to work as part of a team on behalf of the Arthurian court.

able to rely on his superior martial skills for success; now Arthur's enemies rely on a force more powerful than military strength - magic.[1] King Valerin's castle is surrounded by a thicket infested with magic snakes. Valerin can command these poisonous serpents to create a deadly barrier which not even his hardiest enemies can pass:

> die würme nement die mâze,
> daz si nimer koment dran,
> ê Valerîn der küene man
> in gebiutet daz si komen. (5050-5053)

After Lanzelet assesses the details of Guinevere's captivity, he quickly realizes that knightly prowess alone cannot win the queen back:

> nu ist aber sîn burc sô starc,
> daz nieman lebender ist sô karc,
> den sie umb ein hâr entsitzen. (6963-5)

Therefore he advises Arthur to seek out the help of more able counsellors:

> ich enkan nâch mînen witzen
> erdenken niht sô guotes
> sô daz ir iwers muotes
> gedultic sint unt nement rât
> von den fürsten umbe die getât,
> dâ von wir sîn unvrô. (6966-71)

Because of Lanzelet's inexperience with magical threats, he adopts at first a more passive role and waits for the advice of a more seasoned counselor. The council meets and recognizes its inability to counter Valerin's supernatural defenses. At the council Tristant, a knight known for his wisdom and craftiness,[2] suggests that they obtain magical help of their own:

> dâ von râte ich, daz besende
> mîn herre, der künic mære
> Malducken den zouberære

---

1 In the first part of the romance Lanzelet was captured by Mabuz' magic which turned all attackers into cowards (3570-3637). But the extent of Lanzelet's cowardice as a prisoner allows Mabuz to ascertain Lanzelet's bravery and release him to do battle with Iweret (3676-3777). The adventures in the second half of the romance exclude knightly prowess as a solution.
2 The narrator calls him "der listige Tristant" (6979).

> von dem Genibeleten sê.
> der kan zoubers michels mê
> dan ieman in den rîchen. (6988-93)

Malduc can use his sorcery to overcome Valerin's deadly defences. Yet the sorcerer has good reasons not to help Arthur and his knights. As Erec explains:

> sîm vater hân ich den lîp genomen:
> dô sluoc Wâlwein den bruoder sîn:
> ouch hat in der herre mîn
> der künic Artus vertriben
> vome lande dâ er was beliben
> mit sime galster manegen tac. (7006-11)

In spite of the animosity between Malduc and the Round Table, Erec finds the danger to Guinevere greater than any threats from Malduc:

> doch dês al ein, ob er uns mac
> ze disen dingen iht vervâhen,
> sô sulen wir gerne gâhen
> und süenen uns swie wir megen,
> daz wir daz laster nider gelegen. (7012-16)

The royal counsellors confer further and agree to enlist magical aid:

> si kômen alle dar an,
> daz der künic niht vermite
> wan daz er selbe vierde rite
> nach dem gougelære. (7020-23)

From this meeting, Lanzelet can infer the important role that magic plays at court. Powerful rulers rely on it to defend their kingdoms. Treacherous ones like Valerin can abuse sorcery to carry out injustices. The only response to these supernatural threats is stronger counter-magic. The entire council's willingness to seek Malduc's aid (si kômen alle dar an) shows Lanzelet the acceptability of magic as a political tool.

At the wizard's castle, Malduc's daughter agrees to act as an intermediary between Arthur and her father. She convinces her father to help his old enemies, but he stipulates his conditions: Erec and Wâlwein must be handed over to him as prisoners. When Arthur hears these severe terms, he acts as a responsible monarch: he refuses to allow his own men to sacrifice themselves for the sorcerer's help. Lanzelet, however, realizes that there is no practical alternative. At the same time he recognizes the bonds of loyalty between Arthur and his knights. Lanzelet knows that the knights regard their queen's safety as more important than their own and will accept Malduc's terms. He now steps in to offer Arthur advice, encouraging him to agree to the sorcerer's conditions. Lanzelet's suggestion receives the support of Tristant, the chief advisor at the previous princes' counsel:

> dem kûnege riet ouch Tristant,
> ein wortwîser wîgant,
> daz er albalde tæte
> als im gerâten hæte
> der tugenthafte Lanzelet. (7289-93)

Lanzelet's advice is further supported by all of Arthur's knights, including Erec and Wâlwein:

> "ir hætent anders getobet"
> sprâchens algelîche. (7330-31)

Lanzelet's assessment of the situation has been correct. The knights unanimously accept Malduc's conditions. They are still willing to use magical aid in spite of its great cost. This demonstration of support again emphasizes the important role magic can play in court affairs. In a situation where the court is threatened by hostile sorcery, the only appropriate defense is a supernatural response.

Upon Arthur's acquiescence, Malduc enchants the snakes and the castle's occupants, putting them into a deep sleep. Arthur's army can rescue the queen and kill Valerin. Although Guinevere is safe, Arthur must still fulfill his part of the agreement. He had agreed to Malduc's terms and is now bound by his word:

> swaz der künec Artûs gesprach,
> daz zerbræch er durch nieman. (7312-13)[1]

---

[1] Klaus Schmidt condemns Arthur's arrangement with Malduc and judges the ruler and his entire court severely:

In this precarious situation Lanzelet applies the lessons he has learned about leadership in order to resolve the crisis. At this point he has developed from a royal advisor to a leader of an independent military operation. His success will demonstrate his ability to deal with the threat of political magic.

Lanzelet selects a hundred loyal knights to accompany him on a rescue mission. In order not to compromise Arthur, Lanzelet keeps the mission secret from him. At the same time he realizes that he faces a potent wizard. Since Arthur's court magician is now the enemy, Lanzelet must find some other means of supernatural help. He does this by enlisting the aid of Esealt, a giant at Arthur's court. Esealt's size can assist the knights in overcoming Malduc's defenses:

> er was gewahsen alsô hôch,
> daz er verre langer schein
> danne türne dehein. (7548-50)

The giant helps the knights cross the deep lake surrounding Malduc's castle and then lifts them over the castle walls. Once inside they free the two prisoners and slay Malduc and his followers. Lanzelet saves only the magician's daughter,

> wan siu het berâten
> die helde güetlîche. (7634-35)

Acting as a good ruler, Lanzelet offers his helper a home at Arthur's court. Lanzelet's kindness also serves to protect Arthur from future magical threats, for Malduc's daughter shares her father's occult knowledge:

Zu keinem Zeitpunkt fungiert Artus und sein Hof als Leitbild für ideales Herrschertum und für eine Idealgesellschaft. Im Gegenteil, das tatsächliche Erscheinungsbild des Artushofes steht geradezu in kläglichem Widerspruch zu seinem Ruf und zur Erscheinung des Idealpaares Lanzelet und Iblis (p. 15).

Schmidt's judgement is too harsh. The knights of the Round Table are willing to risk their lives for Arthur because they can rely on him. Arthur had no desire to sacrifice his two knights, but they volunteered and his counsellors supported the idea. After Guinevere is freed, she and Arthur continue to act as responsible monarchs and do not abandon Erec and Wâlwein. Guinevere herself tries to convince Malduc to free the knights as soon as she hears of the situation (7430-41). When she does not succeed, Arthur himself tries to reach a compromise with the stubborn magician, but to no avail (7492-7495). My interpretation also shows how Lanzelet uses Arthur's actions as examples for his own behaviour.

> sô endorfte siu niht wîser wesen,
> wan siu hâte gelesen
> diu buoch von allem liste,
> dâ von siu wunder wiste. (7181-84)

Her skills are so great that they are second only to Fâmurgân's:

> âne Femurgân die rîchen
> so enkund sich ir gelîchen
> kein wîp, von der ich ie vernâm. (7185-87)

Fâmurgân was the most powerful sorceress in the Arthurian realm. Hartmann von Aue describes her magical abilities in his romances. She can make poultices capable of curing any wound within one day; they are used to cure Erec at first in Arthur's camp (*Erec*, 5132) and then in Guivrez' realm (*Erec*, 7230). In *Iwein* the Lady of Narison uses a magic salve prepared by Fâmurgân to heal Iwein's insanity (*Iwein*, 3420). If Malduc's daughter is second only to her then she must be a highly-skilled sorceress.

The great role magic plays in courtly affairs indicates that her supernatural skills will be of great help to Arthur and his knights. Now Arthur has his own court magician, he need no longer turn to ambivalent wizards like Malduc.

The Valerin-Malduc adventures have taught Lanzelet valuable lessons in leadership and have given him an opportunity to prove himself a capable leader. The final stage in Lanzelet's education as ruler was the challenge posed by Malduc's wizardry. By saving Erec and Wâlwein, Lanzelet demonstrates his ability to use supernatural forces as an effective response to hostile sorcery. He has now learned how to deal with the danger magic can pose to a kingdom.

3. *Malduc and Historical Magicians*

While Malduc is a fictional character, there are nevertheless a number of similarities between him and his historical counterparts. As in the case of our historical magicians, Malduc is associated with knowledge. The narrator describes him repeatedly as "wîs" (7535, 7364). Malduc is also literate, for he consults his "swarzen buochen" (7357) in order to find the appropriate sleeping spell. As mentioned previously, these "black books", written mostly in Latin, circulated in many court and clerical libraries. In order to read them Malduc must have learned Latin. While learning Latin he, like John of Salisbury, may have come into contact with clerics skilled in the arts of necromancy.

Malduc's social status also coincides with our historical descriptions. He is no simple village conjurer, but a man who often deals with the Arthurian circle. His name is well known to the princes' council, and members of his family have often been their adversaries. Erec slew his father and Wâlwein his brother. Arthur considered Malduc sufficiently dangerous to drive him out of his realm. The extent of these conflicts with Malduc indicate that he was a serious threat to the stability of the court. Malduc is no ragged *homo silvestris* either. He possesses a fortified castle and a large number of men loyal to him so that Lanzelet requires a hundred knights to storm his castle. Even with these knights Lanzelet must still rely on Esealt to pass the castle's defences.

Malduc's daughter also leads a life that reflects her priviliged social status:

> siu fuort ein sperwære,
> von maneger mûze wol getân.
> man sach ir pferit schône gân,
> mit dem selben stolzen kinde
> liefen zwêne winde
> wan siu durch baneken ûz reit. (7174-79)

This aristocratic lifestyle reflects the great power and wealth her family enjoys.

Another similarity between Malduc and historical magicians is the ambivalent attitude towards them and their magic. The narrator does not present the magician simply as an incarnation of evil, but as a complex character. Although Malduc is an enemy of Arthur's court, he is not treacherous. He does not avenge himself on the Round Table until Arthur seeks him out. Even then he gives the harsh terms of his assistance in advance. As in the case of *Parzival's* Clinschor, Malduc's anger reaches extreme proportions, yet his anger at the court is well-grounded. Arthur's men have killed his relatives and driven him into exile.

While Malduc participates in Guinevere's rescue, he keeps his promise and does not attack Arthur. He does not break his word to Arthur, as Valerin did, and in fact plays an essential role in the rescue of Guinevere. Malduc, like Clinschor, is a man of his word. Both are bound by the aristocratic code of the nobility and keep their word, even to their enemies. As a result, Arthur keeps his promise to Malduc.

The accommodation of magicians and their craft in court culture is also seen in The narrator's treatment of Malduc's daughter. The narrator presents her as a wholly positive character:

> ein schoeniu maget,
> hübsch und erbære. (7172-73)

Malduc's daughter does not share any of her father's negative traits. On the contrary, she conducts herself nobly throughout the adventure. When Arthur seeks her father's help, she unhesitatingly offers to act as intermediary between king and magician. Her efforts result in a successful rescue operation. Her ability to bring the two enemies into an alliance shows that she has considerable diplomatic skills as well, an indication of the subtlety and refinement a successful courtier possessed. Like her father, she also keeps her word. She remains true to Arthur; she, too, is bound by the honour code of the aristocracy. Her noble conduct is suitably rewarded when Lanzelet spares her life and brings her to Arthur's court.

The important role Malduc's daughter can play at Arthur's court is indicated by the court's reliance on magic in this romance. Rulers throughout the romance depend on it to stabilize their rule. In the first part of the romance, the cowardly prince Mabuz had used sorcery to remain in power. His castle was protected by a spell that robbed all his attackers of their courage (3542-3547). Like Mabuz, Valerin also uses wizardry to fend off adversaries and remain in power. He commanded supernatural snakes to guard his castle against intruders.

Arthur must also resort to magic in order to restore stability to his kingdom. Although he is at first hesitant to deal with Malduc, all of his counsellors fully support the idea, even after they learn the magician's terms.

Lanzelet himself makes use of supernatural aids. When the fairy queen reveals Lanzelet's name, she gives him a valuable magic tent which keeps its occupants healthy. This tent also serves as an important aid to Lanzelet: when he enters the tent he sees only "sin vriunt derm aller holdest was" (4771). This "vriunt" is his wife Iblis. The tent reveals her complete loyalty to Lanzelet. He now knows that she will be the proper wife and queen for him and any doubts he might previously have had are erased. The tent's magic thus serves to stabilize Lanzelet's marriage and, by extension, his rule. He will not suffer the pangs of jealousy and doubt which paralyzed Gottfried's King Marke.

As with magic at historical courts, the nature of magic in *Lanzelet* can help to explain its acceptance. The sorcery employed in the romance is not demonic. Malduc's sleeping spell has tragic consequences for its victims, but it does not in itself harm anyone. His magic is used to rescue Arthur's queen from a treacherous kidnapper. The magic used in making Lanzelet's tent is not demonic either, for the tent is described in very positive terms: "ez was ein irdisch paradîs" (4836).

The powers of Lanzelet's tent reflect the medieval notion of magic as part of other disciplines of knowledge. The tent has healing properties:

> swelch man ie sô sælic wârt,
> daz er drin getêt eine vârt,
> der was imer mê gesunt. (4767-4769)

Fâmurgân's sorcery was to a large degree medicinal. The tent's ability to heal illustrates the medieval equation of magic and medicine.

The tent is also a marvel of medieval engineering. A mechanical gold eagle sits atop the tent. It appears to float in the air (4786) and its mouth opens when a chain is pulled (4792-94). Various animals are embossed on a band which covers the tent joinings. They can be made to move:

> sô der wint kom drin gevlogen,
> sô begund ez allez sament brogen,
> als ez wolte an die vârt.
> ieglichez nach sîner ârt
> und half dem arn, der oben schrie. (4891-95)

Sylvester II and Virgil were also reported to have invented fantastic mechanical devices. Their interest in engineering fostered their reputations as magicians. Similar devices were actually built by medieval engineers; the technology for such automata originated in antiquity. Philo of Byzantium and Hero of Alexander had written treatises on mechanical devices. Their technology was preserved in the East and by the tenth-century reports of fantastic machines had made their way to Western Europe. Liutprand of Cremona visited the imperial court at Constantinople in 948 and again in 986. He was awestruck by the Throne of Solomon. A gilded tree with bronze birds that could sing in different pitches stood in front of the throne. Gilded lions with moving tails and frightful roars guarded the throne which itself could be raised or lowered.[1] The technology for constructing elaborate automatons had been brought from the Orient to Western Europe by the thirteenth century.[2] These fanciful machines naturally attracted the interest of the courts; rulers with sufficient finances could have such machines built for their amusement. Their constructors delighted in the amazement of their audiences and often took pride in having their stupendous engineering skills associated with magic. As late as the fifteenth-century engineers like Conrad Kyeser and Giovanni da Fontana devised mechanical inventions which they purposely associated with necromancy.[3]

The decorations on Lanzelet's tent are similar to the automatons at historical courts. Like the automatons, it also has mechanical figures which appear to move by themselves. Through its healing properties and mechanical ornaments the tent's magical qualities reflect popular medieval notions equating magic, medicine and mechanics.

---

[1] Eamon, p. 175.
[2] Kieckhefer, p. 101.
[3] Eamon, 186-191.

4. Conclusion

The concept of magic in *Lanzelet* corresponds to popular medieval notions of magic. It is not demonic, but a learned art which can be used for positive or negative purposes. It serves a vital role in political activities at the court and its practitioners move in the highest echelons of the aristocracy. Its important role at the court explains the integral function it serves in Lanzelet's education as ruler. The most potent threat he must overcome is hostile magic. A prospective ruler must know how to defend himself from it and use it to his advantage before he can become a successful monarch. Lanzelet's defeat of magical threats show that he has become a competent ruler, capable of ascending his father's throne.

Chapter V

PARZIVAL

1. Introduction

Although Clinschor and Cundrie only make brief appearances in Wolfram von Eschenbach's *Parzival*,[1] both of these magicians play important roles. Cundrie la surziere is the grail messenger who brings news of Parzival's failure at the grail castle to Arthur's court. Clinschor is a powerful duke who holds over 400 ladies prisoner. Gawan must overcome his magical defences in order to release these prisoners.

2. The Function of the Cundrie and Clinschor Episodes
a) Cundrie

Cundrie appears just twice in the story. She makes her first appearance at Arthur's court just after Parzival has been made a knight of the Round Table. After condemning Parzival's failure at Munsalvaesche she returns to the Grail castle. We see her again only when she meets Parzival on his second journey to the Grail castle.

Cundrie is a curious figure, a collection of incongruities. On the one hand, she is hideously grotesque:

> si was genaset als ein hunt:
> zwên ebers zene ir vür den munt
> giengen wol spannen lanc.
> ietweder wintbrâ sich dranc
> mit zöpfen vür die hârsnuor. (313, 21-25)

Her clothing is completely out of keeping with her appearance. She is stylishly attired in the latest foreign fashions:

---

[1] All quotes taken from: Wolfram von Eschenbach, *Parzival, Mittelhochdeutscher Text nach der Ausgabe von Karl Lachmann*, trans. and with an afterword by W. Spiewok.

> ein brûtlachen von Gent,
> noch blâwer denn ein lâsûr
> het an geleit der vröuden schûr:
> daz was ein kappe wol gesniten
> al nâch der Franzoyser siten:
> drunde an ir lîb was pfelle guot.
> von Lunders ein pfaewîn huot,
> gefurriert mit einem blîalt
> (der huot was niuwe, diu snuor niht alt). (313, 4-12)

Cundrie's mode of transportation reflects her own contradictory appearance. A pathetic mule which bears a noble saddle and bridle has brought her to Arthur (312, 6-13).

Yet Cundrie is not merely a hideous maiden who evokes wonder and amusement. She also has positive qualities. The narrator praises her integrity and calls her "ein magt gein triuwen wol gelobt (312, 3). Cundrie is also highly learned: she is fluent in several languages and has been educated in the seven liberal arts:

> der meide ir kunst des verjach,
> alle sprâche sî wol sprâch,
> latîn, heidensch, franzoys.
> sî was der witze curtoys,
> dîaletike und jeômetrî:
> ir wâren ouch die liste bî
> von astronomîe. (312,19-25)

Her knowledge of astronomy hints at another of her interests. She is also versed in the magic arts: "surziere was ir zuoname" (312,27).

Cundrie is primarily a product of the narrator's imagination. Although there is a similar character in Chretien's *Li Contes del Graal*, her character is not nearly as developed as Cundrie's. She has no name, no education and no magical abilities. She is simply an ugly maiden on a mule.[1]

The narrator's fanciful development of Chretien's ugly maid has led to much speculation about the sources of his additions. Ernst Martin and Eduard

---

1 D.D.R. Owen, *Arthurian Romances*, p. 435.

Hartl have suggested Celtic origins for Cundrie.[1] Franz Rolf Schröder has pointed out that an ugly but learned sorceress appears in the Tales of a Thousand and One Nights.[2] However, he prefers an Iranian origin: he sees a pair of Old Median gods called *Kunda-Kundi* as the source for Cundrie. Phyllis Ackermann has even proposed an old Egyptian goddess in the shape of a pregnant hippopotamus as Cundrie's origin.[3] Her interpretation, however, has not found much resonance among other Parzival scholars. Arthur Groos sees Cundrie and her brother as descendants of "the apocryphal daughters of Adam, who permanently disfigured their progeny by eating forbidden fruit".[4] The text supports Groos' interpretation. The narrator states that Cundrie's mother ate herbs which

> die menschen vruht verkêrten
> unt sîn geslähte unêrten. (518,19-20)

Cundrie's grotesque appearance becomes more understandable when seen in light of her function as grail messenger. Just before her arrival Parzival visits the Arthurian court a second time. His beauty bedazzles the Arthurian Society:

> Artûs mit den werden
> enpfieng in mineclîche,
> guotes willen wâren rîche
> alle die in gesâhen dâ.
> gein sîme lobe sprach niemen nein:
> sô rehte minneclîche er schein. (308, 4-10)

Yet Parzival's perfection is only illusory. His ethical shortcomings lead to his failure at the grail castle. Cundrie arrives at Arthur's court and harshly scolds the young knight in public:

> gein der helle ir sît benant
> ze himele vor der hôhsten hant:

---

1 Ernst Martin, *Wolfram von Eschenbach Parzival und Titurel, Teil II: Kommentar*, Halle, 1903, LXII; Eduard Hartl, "Wolfram von Eschenbach," in: *Verfasserlexikon*, Bd. IV, 1953, Col. 1068.
2 Franz Rolf Schröder, "Cundrîe", pp. 188-189.
3 Phyllis Ackerman, "Who is Kundrie - What is She?", pp. 458-468.
4 Arthur Groos, "Cundrie's Announcement ('Parzival' 781-782)", p. 403.

als sît ir ûf der erden,
versinnent sich die werden. (316,7-10)

Cundrie's appearance serves to emphasize her condemnation.[1] As a hideous creature she stands in marked contrast to the beautiful Parzival and the aesthetic ideal of courtly society. She herself points out the discrepancy between herself and Parzival:

ich dunke iuch ungehiure,
und bin gehiurer doch dann ir. (315, 24-25)

Her words are intended to make Parzival take a closer look at the person beneath his dazzling exterior. Cundrie points out Parzival's insensitivity in not inquiring about Anfortas' suffering. Although Parzival is physically perfect, he still lacks compassion and understanding. Cundrie, on the other hand, is learned, erudite and loyal, yet physically grotesque. These two figures thus embody opposite characteristics and make us aware of Parzival's shortcomings.

This interpretation has been taken up by a number of critics. As Andree Kahn Blumstein has pointed out, "Cundrie represents not the ideal, but an exaggeration in reverse of Parzival's strengths and weaknesses. She is ugly where he is beautiful and beautiful where he is ugly" (164-165). Fritz Peter Knapp interprets Cundrie's appearance along similar lines: "Der Sinn der Absonderlichkeit der beiden Wundermenschen [Cundrie and Malcreatiure] und insbesondere der Gralsbotin liegt zuvörderst darin, als Gegenmaßstab für Parzival zu dienen".[2] Knapp finds Cundrie's ugliness to have its roots in the Victorine doctrine of seeing the world as *imago mundi divini*:

---

1 Andree Kahn Blumstein finds that Cundrie's condemnation is a rejection of the Arthurian world and its chivalric code. "She comes to Arthur's Court to pass judgement upon courtly society and to curse Parzival for adhering to its superficial conventions" (161). Blumstein takes Cundrie's message too far. Cundrie does indeed condemn Parzival for his failure at the grail castle, yet that does not mean that Arthurian society is at fault. Gurnemanz' advice not to ask too many questions was improperly understood by the young and immature Parzival. A similar case of misunderstood chivalry can be found in Hartmann's *Iwein*, when Kalogrenant explains knighthood to the wild herdsman (531-537). Kalogrenant's simplistic explanation is not a critique of chivalry, but of superficial knights like himself who do not really understand the purpose of knighthood. Andree Kahn Blumstein, "The Structure and Function of the Cundrie Episodes in Wolfram's *Parzival*", pp. 160-169.
2 Fritz Peter Knapp, "Die hässliche Gralsbotin und die Victorinische Ästhetik", p. 7.

> Dann wäre der Anblick der häßlichen Gralsbotin ein schriller Anruf an Parzival, nicht in der selbstgenügsamen Anschauung des Schönen dieser Welt zu verharren, sondern vor allem das wahre und ewige Schöne zu suchen... Dann wäre nur die häßliche Kreatur wahrhaft tauglich, Parzival in jene Unruhe zu setzen, die ihn den steinigen Weg zum Gral gehen heißt. (10)

Arthur Groos uses Cundrie's role as an apocryphal daughter of Adam to explain the function of her appearance. He focuses on the "Adamic" motifs in the work, specifically Trevrizent's use of *ungenuht* to describe Cain's murder of Abel, and the parallel to Parzival's murder of his relative Ither.[1] In Cundrie's second meeting with Parzival, she warns him about *ungenuht* (782,23). Groos concludes:

> Adam's fall transmits an inner corruption to his daughters, and their subsequent fall externalizes that corruption in the faces of ensuing generations, destroying the outward appearance that originally reflected man's creation in the image of God. Cundrie's warning to Parzival not to compromise his achievement or his future by *ungenuht* is thus no impersonal message. (403-404)

Cundrie's second meeting with Parzival show that her words have served their purpose, for she comes to apologise for her earlier criticism and inform him that he has been chosen as the new grail king:

> wol dich des hôhen teiles,
> du crône menschen heiles!
> daz epitafjum ist gelesen:
> du solt des grâles hêrre wesen. (781,13-16)

Cundrie's second appearance structurally complements her first as a successful completion to Parzival's grail quest. Blumstein notes:

> The two scenes are thus reverse images of one another in function: the curse becomes the blessing; the search for intangible values, when fulfilled, results in tangible reward. The complementary functions of the initial woe-filled scene and the final, happy one are in turn reflected in an internal structural parallelism between the two scenes. (161)

---

1 Arthur Groos, "Cundrie's Announcement ('Parzival' 781-782)", p. 402-404.

Blumstein correctly recognizes Parzival's spiritual growth between the first and second meetings and the two scenes are indeed complementary.[1]

Cundrie's reprimands have indeed spurred Parzival on to atone for his previous sins and heal Anfortas. His success allows him to transcend the Arthurian court society and ascend the Grail throne. Parzival's search is finally at an end.

b) Clinschor

The Clinschor episode, which occurs in Book XI and carries over into Book XII, is one of adventures ascribed to Gawan. In his adventures, Gawan repeatedly encounters situations where the social order is awry and must be set right. As Heinz Rupp has pointed out, Gawan "ist eine Art Heiler und Strafer von Zuständen, die den Maßstäben des ritterlich-höfischen Daseins, wie es Wolfram versteht, nicht entsprechen"[2] (12). These situations usually (but not exclusively[3]) result from problematic love relationships. Friedrich Maurer finds "daß Minne und Frauendienst, ferner die ritterliche Bewährung

---

[1] She takes the parallels between Parzival and Cundrie too far, however, when she also tries to see a growth in Cundrie's character: "... both Parzival and Cundrie have grown as a result of their mutual encounters" (p. 167). Blumstein bases her interpretation on a change in Cundrie's appearance and bearing on the second visit: "Cundrie, at first outwardly hideous and lacking in courtesy, yet inwardly pure, comes for the second time with noble, dignified bearings and the best trappings of courtly society that she can muster" (p. 167). Wolfram points out that her clothing is just as out of place as before (780, 24-28). Blumstein feels Cundrie to have grown emotionally because she now displays *zuht*, a quality she did not exhibit when condemning Parzival (p. 165). Yet both the condemnations of the page at the Grail Castle (247,26-27) and Sigune (255, 13-16) support the validity of Cundrie's judgement. Their words are just as harsh as Cundrie's and they, too, are members of courtly society governed by *zuht*. The force of their words accurately reflect the grave consequences of Parzival's failure. Cundrie's display of *zuht* at the second meeting is now appropriate. It doesn't mean that Cundrie did not possess this quality previously. Strong words were required to jar Parzival out of his complacency. As Blumstein herself admits, "without her Parzival might still be quaffing mead at the Round Table" (p. 166). There is therefore neither motive nor indication for any development in Cundrie's character.

[2] Neil Thomas states that Gawan's mission "is not religious and solitary, but rather social" ("Sense and Structure in the Gawan Adventures of Wolfram's 'Parzival'", 848).

[3] On the other causes of conflict, see Heinz Rupp, "Die Bedeutung der Gawan-Bücher im *Parzival* Wolframs von Eschenbach", pp.1-16; Sidney M. Johnson, "Parzival und Gawan: Their Conflict of Duties", pp. 98-116.

[3] Neil Thomas even goes so far as to say that Gawan "rides into what appears to be a very *terre gaste* of blighted sexual relationships" ("Sense and Structure in the Gawan Adventures of Wolfram's 'Parzival'",p. 848).

überhaupt in *strît* und *triuwe* die zentralen Themen der Gawangeschichten sind" (79).[3]

Of the problematic love relationships, the one with the most serious consequences deals with the sorcerer Duke Clinschor. Clinschor was caught having an affair with Queen Iblis of Sicily and is castrated by King Ibert, her husband. In revenge, Clinschor uses magic to gain control over *Terre marveile*. He holds four queens and four hundred maidens captive in *Schastel marveile*. The knight who can survive the adventure in the castle will free the prisoners and rule over the land.

Most scholars see the Clinschor episode as the main adventure of the Gawan cycle of the romance,[1] because of its similarities to Parzival's grail adventure. There are indeed several striking parallels between them.[2] Some of the most obvious ones are: both Clinschor and Anfortas have a sexual wound caused by forbidden love adventures; both rule over enchanted castles which must be disenchanted by paragons of knighthood; the maternal relatives of these knights reside in the castle; each knight must release these relatives from their sorrowful situation; the knight successful in each adventure becomes the new lord of the castle and its inhabitants.

The relationship between grail castle and *Schastel marveile* are already hinted at when the two adventures are announced. Both quests are made known to the Arthurian society by Cundrie, the grail messenger. After having condemned Parzival's failure at the grail quest, she then describes the adventure of *Schastel marveile*:

"ist hie kein ritter wert,
des ellen prîses hât gegert,
unt dar zuo hôher minne?
ich weiz vier küneginne

---

1 Wolfgang Mohr, "Parzival und Gawan", p. 296; Marianne Wynn, "Parzival und Gâwân" - Hero and Counterpart", p. 154, reprinted in her book *Wolfram's Parzival. On the Genesis of its Poetry*, pp. 174-75; Sidney Johnson, "Parzival and Gawan: Their Conflict of Duties", p. 115; Joachim Bumke, *Wolfram von Eschenbach*, 6th edition, p. 148.
2 Wolfgang Mohr, "Parzival und Gawan", pp. 297 ff.; Marianne Wynn, "Parzival und Gâwân" - Hero and Counterpart", p. 154 (*Wolfram's Parzival. On the Genesis of its Poetry*, pp. 174-75); Norbert Wolf, "Die Gestalt Klingsors in der deutschen Literatur des Mittelalters", p. 7; Walter Blank, "Der Zauberer Clinschor in Wolframs 'Parzival'", pp. 330-331; Joachim Bumke, *Wolfram von Eschenbach*, 6th edition, p. 148.

> unt vier hundert juncvrouwen,
> die man gerne möhte schouwen.
> zu Schastel marveile die sint:
> al âventiure ist ein wint,
> wan die man dâ bezalen mac,
> hôher minne wert bejac". (318, 13-22)

It is also interesting to note that Parzival and Gawan do not attempt to undertake each other's adventures: Gawan never seriously searches for the grail castle[1] and Parzival did not ask about *Schastel marveile* when he was in its vicinity:

> "hêrre, ern hât es niht ervarn.
> ich kunde mich des wol bewarn
> daz ichs im zuo gewüege:
> unvuoge ich danne trüege". (559, 23-26)

The adventure is not to be Parzival's but Gawan's. The separation of these adventures thus defines the different realms in which each of the knights function; the Arthurian realm is Gawan's domain while the Grail world is to be Parzival's. Their successes reflect their supremacy in their respective realms.

Although the *Schastel marveile* adventure deals with the consequences of an illicit love relationship and also serves as an "Erlösungsaufgabe" (Mohr, 296), it is nevertheless important to take into account the important role which magic plays in the episode. The chief antagonist in Gawan's most difficult adventure is a sorcerer. The knight's task here is not only to rectify the grave consequences of Clinschor's illicit love; he must, like Lanzelet,[2] also demonstrate that he can deal with hostile political magic. His ability to do this not only ends Clinschor's usurpation of *Terre marveile*, but grants him rule over the land.

The important role of magic in the adventure can be seen in the narrator's additions to his literary source. Like Cundrie, Clinschor is largely Wolfram's

---

[1] As part of Gawan's negotiations with Vergulacht, he agrees to take over Vergulacht's promise to seek out the grail. But Wolfram never makes any mention of Gawan having any success in this quest, and after Gawan meets Orgeluse, at the beginning of Book X, the grail appears to be forgotten.

[2] And like the knights in the following chapters as well.

creation. There is an equivalent character in Chretien's *Li Contes del Graal*, but his description is limited to five lines: "a clerk, expert in astronomy, whom the queen brought with her, established such great marvels that you never heard their equal".[1] The cleric does not even have a name. The narrator goes a great deal beyond Chretien's sparse account, and invents a detailed history for Clinschor[2]. This history is more realistic than fantastic and gives the impression that the narrator wanted to create a life-like and believable character. Clinschor is given a necromantic family tree:

> von des nâchkomen er ist erborn,
> der ouch vil wunders het erkorn,
> von Nâpels Virgilîus.
> Clinschor des neve warp alsus. (656, 15-18)

Clinschor is not given a devil as a father, as Merlin was, but a historical figure associated with magic.

An actual place, Terre de Labur (Terra di Lavoro) near Naples becomes the magician's homeland. The narrator also explains how Clinschor received his magic training. The sorcerer traveled to Persida to learn these arts (657,28).

Clinschor then uses his newly acquired knowledge to amass political power. He forces King Irot into giving him a castle, *Schastel marveile,* and eight miles of land around it known as *Terre marveile.* Clinschor's hunger for power is not satiated by this action, for he then mounts a bold attack against the

---

1 Chretien de Troyes, *Arthurian Romances*, trans. D.D.R. Owen, p. 473.
   Uns clers sages d'astrenomie,
   Que la reine i amena,
   An dest grant palés qui est ça,
   A fet unes si granz mervoilles
   Qu'onques n'oistes lor paroilles (7548-7552).
   Quoted from Alfons Hilka, ed., *Der Percevalroman von Christian von Troyes*, Werke, Vol. V, Halle, Niemeyer, 1932.
2 Walter Blank tries to posit the existence of a lost French source from which Wolfram and Johann von Würzburg both gleaned their magicians (324). Wolfram shows his originality throughout the text. Why could he not be responsible for the additions to Chretien? However, I have shown in Chapter III that clerical magicians were a historical reality. It seems much more probable that Wolfram found his source of inspiration in real court magicians.

Arthurian court. He kidnaps Queen Arnive, Arthur's mother and Gawan's grandmother, along with three other queens: Gawan's mother and his two sisters. This mass abduction threatens the *vröude* of the court, and therefore poses a dangerous challenge to the stability of Arthur's rule.

Clinschor guards his prisoners with nearly omnipotent sorcery:

> er hât ouch aller der gewalt,
> mal unde bêâ schent,
> die zwischen dem firmament
> wonent unt der erden zil;
> niht wan die got beschermen wil. (658, 26-30)

No knight has survived the adventure. Gawan, too, is warned of the great difficulties lying in store for him:

> hêrre, ez wart versuochet nie
> ûf Schastel marveile diu nôt.
> iuwer leben wil in den tôt.
> ist iu âventiure bekant,
> swaz ie gestreit iuwer hant,
> daz was noch gar ein kindes spil. (557, 8-13)

The magnitude of Clinschor's magic already becomes apparent when Gawan enters the castle. The imprisoned women suddenly vanish from view and the building appears completely vacant. They will not reappear until the castle has been disenchanted:

> weder grôz noch cleine
> vint ir niht daz dâ lebe. (561,18-19)

The defences Gawan now encounters show the mechanical applications of Clinschor's occult skills. The first of these is the *Lit marveile*. When Gawan finally manages to jump on this bucking bed, his actions trigger the next phase of the enchantments. Five hundred stones followed by an equal number of arrows magically rain down upon him, and only his sturdy armor saves him. This onslaught is the last of Clinschor's supernatural trials. Gawan must still slay a lion, but there is no longer any hostile magic at work in the castle.[1] Now that Gawan has survived these tests, he need no longer fear Clinschor. The magician has stated that whoever disenchants the castle:

> ... solte ouch vride von im hân,
> des jach er offenbâre
> (er ist mit rede der wâre),
> swer diese âventiure erlite,
> daz dem sîn gâbe wonte mite. (659, 6-10)

The adventure reaffirms Gawan's knightly prowess and shows him to be the best Arthurian knight. But it also shows the dangers of political magic and the necessity of being able to deal with it. Through this magic, King Irot was forced to surrender *Terre marveile*, and Arthur and Gawan lost four members of their family. Gawan's victory over Clinschor's sorcery has important political consequences. Firstly he reintegrates the noble prisoners back into Arthurian society, thereby reestablishing the *vröude* integral to the well-being of the court. He also liberates the inhabitants of *Terre marveile* from a dangerous ruler. By showing that he can counter the threat which magic can pose to rule, Gawan is rewarded with his own castle and territory. His success in this adventure shows that he is capable of warding off any future hostile magic which might threaten his political stability.

4. Clinschor, Cundrie and Historical Magicians

In spite of their fantastic powers and appearances, Clinschor and Cundrie share many characteristics with their historical counterparts. Like Chretien's magician (a clerk, expert in astronomy), Clinschor and Cundrie are educated clerics. The narrator introduces Clinschor as a cleric: "ein pfaffe, der wol zouber las" (66, 4). Cundrie, too, is highly educated. She is fluent in French as well as Latin and Arabic, the literary languages of medieval academics. She has also been taught the seven liberal arts, the standard medieval school curriculum.

Clinschor does go to the fictional Persida to learn magic, but he does so as a cleric who culls his knowledge from books (zouber las). Wolfram does not

---
[1] The only remaining magical device is a pillar whose surface shows everything that happens within a six mile radius (592, 1-13). Yet Clinschor did not construct it and it cannot harm anyone.

state where Cundrie learned her sorcery - she might have learned it in her homeland; as a heathen she could have had access to Arabic scientific and occult knowledge. Her fluency in Arabic and Latin would have allowed her to read most magic manuscripts. Cundrie may also have acquired her supernatural training during her clerical education. As mentioned previously, clerics could have contact with necromancers like John of Salisbury's Latin teacher or access to magic works like those condemned by William of Auvergne.

Another similarity between the narrator's magicians and their historical counterparts is their social status. Both Clinschor and Cundrie are courtiers and move in the highest spheres of society. Clinschor was a duke and a greatly respected member of King Ibert's court. Even after his fall from grace, he is still a man of wealth and power. He can afford to travel abroad to study magic. When he returns, he becomes lord of *Schastel marveile* and the territory around it. The *Schastel marveile* is probably not Clinschor's only castle; as a duke he would also have his own residence. The magician's lengthy absence from *Schastel marveile* indicates that he has at least one other domicile. Clinschor can even afford to give the castle to the victor of the adventure, and he does not appear to suffer any hardship from this loss.

Cundrie, too, moves in courtly circles. Her home is Munsalvaesche; she is the messenger of the grail society and carries out important assignments on its behalf. In addition to announcing Parzival's failure and success in his grail quest, she brings Sigune food from the grail and often visits the captives of *Schastel marveile*. Her opulent clothing reflects her high social status.

The narrator's presentation of magic bears many similarities to popular medieval beliefs. Magic in *Parzival* intersects with other realms of knowledge. It was previously mentioned that clerics like Albertus Magnus and Michael Scot included certain magic operations in the realm of science. These operations were not considered demonic, however; they were seen as part of the natural occult world. Pope Sylvester's mathematical skills and inventions led people to consider him a sorcerer. Virgil's erudition contributed to his supernatural reputation and several fantastic inventions were attributed to him. The narrator plays on Virgil's reputation, when he makes Clinschor his "nephew".

The feats which Clinschor and Cundrie perform are in part similar to science and technology. Clinschor's magic, like Virgil's, manifests itself in the form of fantastic protective devices. In these devices magic and technology overlap. Although magic propels the *Lit marveile* around the room, the narrator also emphasizes the craftsmanship involved in its construction. It has special wheels to race around the room:

> ver schîben liefen drunder,
> von rubbîn lieht sinewel,
> daz der wint wart nie sô snel. (566, 16-18)

Clinschor has also constructed a unique floor which allows the bed to roll more quickly:

> von jaspis, von crisolte,
> von sardîn, als er wolte,
> Clinschor, der des erdâhte,
> ûz manegem lande brâhte
> sîn listeclîchiu wîsheit
> werc daz hier an was geleit. (566,21-26)

The bed and floor are in themselves not necessarily magical creations but rather masterpieces of construction. Similar non-magical objects could be built by anyone with sufficient resources.

The stones and arrows which rain down on the bed's occupant are akin to mechanical booby-traps. In Chretien's version, five hundred archers shot these projectiles; the castle's magic simply hid them from view.[1] The narrator automates these attacks by magic. Thus, the fantastic element of Clinschor's trap is not so much the nature of the device but the number of objects thrown: five hundred. Similar if more modest devices could have been built by medieval engineers. It was mentioned in the last chapter that medieval engineers constructed automatons for the amusement of the court. Although Clinschor's devices are more elaborate and serve a deadly purpose, they are not

---

1 Owen, p. 477.

qualitatively different from the mechanical inventions like the Throne of Solomon.

Cundrie, unlike her colleague Clinschor, does not actively work any magic during her appearances in the romance. This has led some critics to dismiss her epithet. Walter Blank, for example, sees the grail world as a "gesellschaftliche Realutopie" and finds, "in dieser [Welt] hat Magie keinen Platz" (10). Wilhelm Deinert[1] denies that Cundrie is a sorceress:

> Nirgendwo ist bei ihr von *nigrômanzî* die Rede, wie etwa bei Clinschor, denn sie wird ihrer wie Kyot auf Grund der Taufe nicht bedürfen (453,16f.). Alle heidnischen Züge, wie ihre Sprache und ihr Beiname, bezeichnen nur ihre Herkunft. (113-114)

Yet Deinert does not explain why the other heathens in the work are not also considered magicians or sorceresses. Chretien's hideous maiden was not a sorceress. Cundrie's brother Malcreatiure is never called a magician, and no magical abilities are associated with him. The narrator himself added the epithet "la surziere" or "sorceress" to Cundrie and uses it repeatedly; he therefore must have wanted to associate Cundrie with magic; that the narrator does not associate her with necromancy does not disassociate her from magic: necromancy is not the only form of magic available to a sorceress, nor was all magic necessarily malevolent.

Cundrie is indeed more than a sorceress in name. Her supernatural attributes can be seen in her visits to *Schastel marveile*. Cundrie is apparently impervious to Clinschor's magical defences. Unlike other people, she can freely enter and leave the castle. She also has contact with its prisoners, who are hidden from other people by Clinschor's enchantment.

During her visits she spends time with Queen Arnive, Arthur's mother. Cundrie's visits to Arnive are a key to understanding her magic skills: Cundrie's magic is not demonic, yet like Clinschor's it is connected with other formal disciplines of scientific knowledge. Cundrie imparts some of this knowledge to Arnive. Arnive explains:

---

[1] Wilhelm Deinert, *Ritter und Kosmos im Parzival. Eine Untersuchung der Sternkunde Wolframs von Eschenbach.*

> Cundrîe la surziere
> ruochet mich sô dicke sehen:
> swaz von erzênîe mac geschehen,
> des tuot si mich gewaltec wol. (579, 24-27)

According to Arnive, Cundrie's healing skills are very great. Cundrie uses her abilities to make a salve for the grail king:

> sît Anfortas in jâmers dol
> kom, daz man im helfe warp,
> diu salbe im half, daz er niht starp. (579, 28-30)

Medicines were often associated with magical powers in the Middle Ages. As mentioned in the last chapter, Hartmann's Fâmurgân made poultices capable of curing any wound within one day. In the same way, Cundrie uses her medicinal magic to heal. Her medicine is used to help Gawan (579,23-580,1) and members of the grail society.

Another branch of Cundrie's occult knowledge is hinted at when she announces Parzival's appointment as grail king. In her announcement she names the seven planets which forecast success for Parzival:

> si sprach "nu prüeve, Parzival.
> der hôhste plânête Zvâl,
> und der snelle Almustrî,
> Almaret, [und] der liehte Samsî,
> erzeigent saelekeit an dir.
> der vünfte heizet Alligafir,
> unde der sehste Alkitêr,
> und uns der naehste Alkamêr. (782, 5-12)

The above passage at first glance appears to hold an astrological message. Wilhelm Deinert finds Cundrie's message to announce the "Anfang eines neuen glücklichen Zeitalters" (42) with Parzival placed "in eine paradiesische, adamsgleiche Herrschaft" (55) as a new "Weltkaiser" (52).[1] Arthur Groos has compared the narrator's description of celestial movements with medie-

---

1 Deinert interprets the astrological passages strictly from a Christian perspective, and finds the stars to reflect "die von Gott gewollte Ordnung der Welt" (139). While Deinert's study is very thorough and painstakingly researched, Joachim Bumke is right when he comments: "Ich glaube allerdings, daß dieses Ergebnis Wolframs Darstellung in eine christliche Eindeutigkeit rückt, die so vom Dichter nicht beabsichtigt war" (*Die Wolfram von Eschenbach Forschung seit 1945*, p. 137).

val astronomical theories and their Christian interpretation. He concludes that Cundrie's message does not contain any astrological meaning.[1] Instead Groos finds that it draws Parzival's attention to the opposite movements of the firmament and the planets associating the "rational motion of the firmament with the turn toward God and the irrational motion of the planets with the turn toward the self" (399). Groos associates Parzival's earlier adventures with the "irrational" movements of the planets and his turn to God on Good Friday with the "rational" movements of the firmament: "the bipartite motion of the firmament and the planets, balancing or reconciling two contrary forces, stands as an exemplar for Parzival's achievement." (400)

Although Groos is correct in denying the passage any astrological meaning, his interpretation does not strip Cundrie of her magical abilities. Groos offers no explanation for Cundrie's epithet. She could well have used her astronomical knowledge for magical operations. Michael Scot pointed out the importance of astronomy for such purposes. Chretien emphasized the astronomical knowledge of his otherwise featureless clerical magician. Apparently Chretien thought it a sufficient explanation for his cleric's magical abilities.

As previously mentioned, magic in medieval Europe often overlapped or was confused with religion. Priests and clerics were sometimes seen as magicians by the laity. While Cundrie is not to be confused as a member of the clergy, she is closely connected to the Christian faith: she serves the grail king, the highest Christian ruler in the romance. Her curative skills keep him alive. In addition to her healing role, Cundrie also operates as a messenger on the grail's behalf.

It was also mentioned that the laity sometimes understood the Catholic mass as a magical operation in which wine and bread were miraculously transformed into blood and flesh. The narrator's sorceress also taps into the miracle of transsubstantiation. Signue explains that Cundrie supplies her with special food from the Grail:

> Cundrîe la surziere
> mir dannen bringet schiere
> alle samztage naht

---

[1] Groos, p. 388.

mîn spîse (des hât sie sich bedâht)
die ich ganze wochen haben sol. (439, 1-5)

A wafer brought down from heaven every Good Friday gives the Grail its ability to produce unlimited quantities of food (469, 29-470, 14). Thus the food the sorceress brings Sigune, like the wine and bread of a Catholic mass, is supernaturally transformed.

The intersection between magic and science, medicine and religion can help us to understand how the narrator presented his magicians. Critics have had difficulty reconciling Cundrie and Clinschor's magical activities with their benevolent qualities. Clinschor has often been seen solely as a negative character because of his animosity to the Arthurian society and his deadly traps. Therese Holländer describes him as the "Verkörperung des Bösen".[1] Walter Blank finds him to be an ambivalent character and explains this ambivalence in the following way: "Ist er einerseits noch der weltlich perfekte Fürst und Hofmann, galant gegen die Damen, so schlägt seine Rache letztlich um in Auflehnung gegen Gott, die sich als Menschenverachtung äußert" (331). In spite of recognizing Clinschor to be ambivalent, Blank ultimately reduces him to a diabolical antagonist. He sets up the opposition Anfortas-Clinschor which he defines as "sündhaft/bußfertig gegen sündhaft/verstockt, teuflisch" and finally concludes that the narrator developed Clinschor as "Negativfigur als Antipoden zu Amfortas" (331). Blank's evaluation is too one-sided: Norbert Wolf has pointed out that the reason "warum [Clinschor] nach dem Bösen trachtet wird ausführlich dargelegt" (7). Consequently, the magician's anger is justified, even if he goes to extremes in his revenge.

Clinschor also has positive characteristics. He is an educated courtier, who was highly regarded before his downfall. Arnive says:

> er trat in prîs sô hôhen pfat
> an prîse was er unbetrogen.
> von Clinschor dem herzogen
> sprâchen wîb unde man. (656,20-24)

Even once he does become a magician he is still a man of honour. He doesn't harm his female prisoners and offers the castle's disenchanter pos-

---
1 Therese Holländer, *Klingsor. Eine stoffgeschichtliche Untersuchung*, p. 18.

session of *Schastel marveile* and its inhabitants. This offer may at first appear to be overconfident arrogance, but he does keeps his word after he is defeated. Ernst Dick sees Clinschor's honour as a means of facilitating his disappearance from the story once the castle has been disenchanted. Because Clinschor keeps his word and leaves the castle to Gawan, Dick finds that he is "designed to be discarded again when he has outlived his narrative usefulness" (131). Walter Blank agrees, commenting that

> "während Amfortas erlöst wird, wird Clinschor mit dem Brechen seines Zaubers "vernichtet", d.h. er verschwindet aus der Erzählhandlung, und wir erfahren nichts über seine weitere Existenz. Dies läßt am deutlichsten erkennen, daß Wolfram´s Clinschor nicht als eigenständige Figur konzipiert ist, sondern nur als funktionaler Gegentyp zu Amfortas. (331)

Yet the narrator could have chosen less favorable ways of disposing of him, if he had wanted to. Gawan could have killed him, as Lanzelet had slain Malduc. Clinschor could already have been deceased like Fâmurgân *(Erec,* 5157), and his castle could have been a memorial to his history. The terms of the adventure give the magician the final say and then allow him to exit gracefully. That Clinschor continues to exercise his powers in other lands is hinted at by Arnive, who tells Gawan:

> "hêrre, sîniu wunder hie
> sint da engein cleiniu wunderlîn,
> wider den starken wundern sîn
> die er hât in manegen landen". (656, 6-9)

Arnive's description of his magic is free of moral condemnation. Although she is Clinschor's former prisoner, she still speaks in awe of his powers. Her tolerance may be seen in the fact that she herself learns medicinal magic from Cundrie.

Yet the narrator does not morally condemn his magicians either. Clinschor is ambivalent, but not diabolical. Hartmann, in contrast, demonizes Fâmurgân in spite of the positive application of her healing skills. He presents her magic as diabolical: "der tiuvel was ir geselle" *(Erec,* 5205) and states that she "lebete vaste wider gote" *(Erec,* 5190). He also laments that she conjures up demons:

> und daz mich daz meiste
> dunket, die übelen geiste,
> die da tiuvel sint genant,
> die waren alle under ir hant. *(Erec, 5194-5197)*

Cundrie, on the other hand, is presented as a very positive character. Although physically unattractive, she is nevertheless noble in heart. The narrator explicitly praises such women in his prologue:

> ich enhân daz niht vür lîhtiu dinc,
> swer in den cranken messinc
> verwurket edeln rubîn
> und al die âventiure sîn
> (dem glîche ich rehten wîbes muot).
> diu ir wîpheit rehte tuot,
> dane sol ich varwe prüeven niht
> noch ir herzen dach, daz man siht. (3, 15-22)

This description certainly applies to Cundrie. She embodies inner nobility, the highest quality the narrator requires in women. Her appearance does not offset her spiritual perfection; in fact her moral virtue is so great that she can be included in the grail society. Cundrie's magic can not be taken as a serious objection to her ethical worth.

5. Conclusion

The narrator's literary portraits of Clinschor and Cundrie bear many similarities to those of historical court magicians. Clinschor and Cundrie are educated clerics. They are courtiers and move in the highest social circles. Their magic is not simply demonic conjuration. To be sure, it can be used for malevolent purposes, but is in itself not innately evil. It is an acquired skill which intersects with other realms of knowledge and expertise, including medicine, engineering, and religion. Magic also plays an important role at court. It is useful to courtiers who use it to avenge intrigues against them or to help each other. Rulers must know how to respond to hostile magic, or they will suffer grave losses. As the greatest Arthurian knight, Gawan shows that he can counter political sorcery. His ability to defeat Clinschor's enchantments not only restores *vröude* to Arthur's court, but also demonstrates that he will be able to defend his newly won territory, even from magical attacks.

Chapter VI

WIGALOIS

1. Introduction

In Wirnt von Gravenberc's *Wigalois*,[1] the title hero must battle the treacherous magician Roaz. Roaz was a high-ranking courtier at the court of King Lar, until he used demonic magic to seize the throne. Larie, King Lar's daughter, has asked Wigalois to defeat the tyrant. If Wigalois is successful, he may marry Larie and rule over Korntin. Like Lanzelet and Gawan, Wigalois must learn how to deal with the danger magic poses to political rule. In order to become the successful ruler of Korntin, he must be able to counter Roaz' political sorcery with the benevolent supernatural forces available to him.

2. The Function of the Roaz Episode

The Roaz adventure occupies the majority of *Wigalois*[2] and consists of two sections.[3] In the first section, Wigalois follows Larie's messenger to Roimunt, defeating a number of giants and knights on the way. Most critics have in-

---

[1] All quotes are taken from: Wirnt von Gravenberg, *Wigalois, der Ritter mit dem Rade*, ed. J.M.N. Kapteyn.
[2] The adventure takes up lines 1717-9598 out of a total of 11708 lines. The first 1716 lines deal with the story of Wigalois' parents and his youth in the fairy realm, while the final section deals with the court's war on Lion and Wigalois' accession to the throne.
[3] Critics have generally divided the Korntin quest into these two sections: Joachim Heinzle, "Über den Aufbau des *Wigalois*", p. 263; Christoph Cormeau, *'Wigalois' und 'diu Crône'. Zwei Kapitel zur Gattungsgeschichte des nachklassischen Aventiureromans*, p. 23, chart pp. 247-248; Neil Thomas, "Literary Transformation and Narrative Organization in Wirnt von Gravenberg's *Wigalois*", p. 363; Ingeborg Henderson, "Dark Figures and Eschatological Imagery in Wirnt von Gravenberg's *Wigalois*", pp. 99-100. J.W. Thomas sees these adventures as divided up into three parts; the first part begins with the birth and childhood of Wigalois and continues up to his arrival at Roimunt; the second continues up to Wigalois' defeat of the dragon and the third part ends with the death of Roaz: *Wigalois, the Knight of Fortune's Wheel*, translated and with an introduction by J.W. Thomas, pp. 25-26.

terpreted this first series of battles as a means for Wigalois to prove himself as "geeigneter Kämpfer für Korntin" (Cormeau, 30).[1]

After Wigalois has proven his suitability as a warrior, he is ready to liberate Korntin from Roaz' tyranny. The Korntin adventure gives Wigalois the opportunity to gain a wife and a kingdom. Just as importantly, it also teaches him how to deal with political magic, the major threat to rule in the romance. If Wigalois is to rule Korntin well, he must learn how to deal effectively with magical attacks. In his first series of adventures, Wigalois' superior knightly prowess had allowed him to overcome his adversaries.[2] The Korntin adventure presents Wigalois with a series of supernatural opponents who will test his ability to deal with demonic threats.[3] These opponents can only be defeated with supernatural assistance. The forms of assistance at Wigalois' disposal are divine help and protective magic. In the course of the Korntin adventure, Wigalois learns to use both of these aids to counter Korntin's demonic threats as a preparation for his climactic encounter with the magician.

Wigalois must first face the dragon Pfetan, whose poisonous breath kills all opponents. In order to defeat him, Wigalois relies in part on divine assistance; before he entered Korntin, a priest had blessed him and bound a writ counteracting all magic around his sword (4415-29). But although Wigalois is a Christian knight, he also resorts to magical aid. He wears the belt which guaranteed him victory in all of his previous encounters. Lar's spirit gives him a special blossom to protect him from the dragon's breath (4742-46) and

---

[1] A survey of interpretations is listed by Cormeau, p. 30, fn. 18; see also Klaus Grubmüller, "Artusroman und Heilsbringerethos: zum 'Wigalois' des Wirnt von Gravenberg", p. 226.

[2] Admittedly Wigalois had always worn a magic belt given him by his mother (1362-77) which allowed him to defeat all other knights. Yet it only served to increase his physical prowess. The charms he now receives help him to survive the magical challenges of Korntin.

[3] Henderson, Cormeau and Knoll have observed that Wigalois' four monstrous opponents are all directly referred to as devils (Henderson, "Dark Figures and Eschatological Imagery in Wirnt von Gravenberg's *Wigalois*", 103 along with references to the text; Cormeau, 44, fn. 47; Hiltrud Knoll, *Studien zur realen und außerrealen Welt im deutschen Artusroman*, Diss. Bonn, 1966, p. 222).

also shows him a wondrous lance which can pierce the dragon's scales (4777-79).[1]

The blossom, belt and lance are not the only supernatural aids Wigalois relies on. He further prepares himself for the battle by eating some magic bread Larie had given him earlier:

> von wurzen hêt ez solhe kraft
> daz in lie diu hungers nôt
> als erz engegen dem munde bôt:
> ez gap im muot und solhe maht:
> er wære gewesen siben naht
> in einem walde âne maz
> als er sîn ein lützel gaz. (4472-78)

Thus equipped, Wigalois is able to kill the dragon. Wigalois' victory results in the loss of his belt, however, and he must now prove that he can carry on without his main magic aid. He shows that he is capable of utilizing other means of supernatural assistance by turning to God for help:[2]

> noch muoz mir gelingen
> zer selben âventiure;
> sin sit nie sô ungehiure
> ichn welle dâ tôt geligen,
> od mit der gotes kraft gesigen. (6001-05)

In spite of his increased reliance on God, Wigalois also continues to use magic as an alternative source of supernatural assistance. He receives another valuable weapon, a magic armour[3] which no weapon can penetrate.

In the following encounter, Wigalois is taught an important lesson about the danger of underestimating his supernatural opponents. He is attacked by the monstrous woman Ruel, who quickly overpowers and binds the knight. She

---

1 An angel had brought the lance from India and it now is buried in the castle wall. Like King Arthur's mythical sword Excalibur, the lance is also embedded in a stone and has a supernatural bearer. (The Lady of the Lake retrieved Excalibur after Arthur's death.)
2 Ingeborg Henderson has observed that the religious elements in *Wigalois* remain "total im Hintergrund" until the battle with Pfetan, "Selbstentfremdung im *Wigalois* Wirnts von Grafenberg", p. 43.
3 The armour has a history reminiscent of many mythical weapons: the narrator tells us that a dwarf living deep within a mountain spent thirty years making it.

is about to kill him when his horse frightens her away. Wigalois now realizes the dangers of overestimating his own abilities and sees that he cannot succeed by knightly prowess alone. He prays to God and his bonds are miraculously loosened. Wigalois is ready to continue his quest.

Roaz still has a number of supernatural guards and defences protecting his castle. If Wigalois is to reach the sorcerer's lair, he must prove himself capable of defeating the magic of these opponents. His first challenger is the dwarf Karrioz, whose marrowless bones give him superhuman strength: "einem man was er ein her" (6609). Wigalois' knightly prowess proves itself superior, however, and he kills the dwarf.

Roaz' next magical defence cannot be overcome by such earthly skills. This obstacle is a foul swamp and poisonous fog which surround his castle. The only means of crossing the swamp is a bridge, but Roaz has barred the way with a fantastic bronze wheel studded with sharp swords and deadly maces. Once again Wigalois can only proceed if he harnesses the supernatural forces available to him. Because his magical aids cannot deactivate the deadly wheel, he turns to God for assistance:

> den nebel [Gott] in daz wazzer treip,
> daz sîn niht vil dar obe beleip;
> dâ von ez sîn vliezen lie.
> daz rat dô nie mêr umbe gie;
> ez gestuont under dem bürgetor. (6885-6889)

Crossing the bridge, Wigalois must face Marrien, the next of the magician's monstrous guards. Marrien is a centaur-like creature with a canine head, a human torso and the body of a horse below. No sword can cut through its scales. Not only must Wigalois defeat this seemingly invincible adversary, he must also avoid the monster's supernatural weapon, a kettle filled with liquid fire:

> swaz ez wart geworfen an:
> bein, îsen unde stein.
> daz selbe viur mohte dehein
> wazzer niht erleschen sô
> ezn brünne drinne als ein strô. (6957-61)

Marrien throws this fire on the knight and his horse. Wigalois' horse and shield are consumed by the flames, but his magic armour saves him. He uses his consecrated sword to cut through Marrien's scales, and its blood quenches the flames. Wigalois' skillful use of magic and divine help has allowed him to defeat the last of Roaz' supernatural guardians.

Now Wigalois is ready for the next stage of the adventure, his confrontation with the wizard himself.[1] Although Wigalois has previously relied in part on magic to reach Roaz' castle, these aids cannot match the sorcerer's potent arts. Once again the knight resorts to divine help for success; he makes the sign of the cross and prays to God.

Roaz also relies on supernatural forces to assist him in this battle; the devil rides on a cloud before him.[2] Wigalois, however, is protected by the writ on his sword and the cross he made before entering the castle:

> dâ von getorste der tievel nie
> zuo im komen nâher baz. (7340-41)

These supernatural aids force Roaz to rely solely on his own knightly skills. After a difficult and drawn-out battle, Wigalois manages to slay the magician, whose soul is immediately seized by the devil:

> Rôaz der wart verstolen dan
> zehant von der tievel schar. (8136-37)

Now that Roaz is dead, the adventure is concluded. Wigalois can marry Larie and become ruler of Korntin.

The Korntin adventure has taught Wigalois one of the most important aspects of good rule.[3] In his encounters with the monsters of Korntin, Wigalois has had to prove himself capable of dealing with supernatural threats. His knightly skill alone was not sufficient to bring him victory. He also had to

---

1 There are two knights guarding the castle gate, but they have no supernatural weapons and Wigalois quickly defeats both.
2 Everyone except Wigalois can see the cloud. Apparently only heathens can see these devils, just as only Christians can see the Grail.
3 The Lion episode (9599-11284) teaches Wigalois leadership skills: he must learn to coordinate an army. Gawein also gives his son important advice on rule before Wigalois returns to Korntin (11531-11565).

harness the supernatural forces available to him: protective magic and divine help. Through his skillful combination of these forces with his own knightly prowess, Wigalois has proven that he can deal with the threat of political magic. The inability to deal with this threat caused King Lar to lose both his kingdom and life. By defeating Roaz and his treasonous sorcery, Wigalois has demonstrated that he will be able to keep his newly-won kingdom safe from magical usurpers.

3. *Roaz and Historical Magicians*

The narrator's portrait of Roaz reflects many popular medieval notions about magicians. Like his historical counterparts, Roaz is at home at the court. Before taking control of Korntin, he was a key advisor to King Lar and was so influential that Lar trusted him with everything:

> sîn hûs was im bereit
> und sîn guot unverseit;
> er hêt in in sîner pflege
> und beriet in alle wege. (3693-96)

In order for Roaz to have reached such a high position, he was likely a polished courtier, who used his artifice and refined manners to deceive his lord.

In addition to his influence with Lar, Roaz also enjoyed considerable influence with other members of the court. He was able to organize an army of four hundred knights to carry out his treachery (3712-13). This army is large enough to slay Lar's entire retinue:

> nieman mohte danne
> dem gâhen tôde enbresten. (3722-23)

Like historical magicians, Roaz is also associated with knowledge and learning. Although the narrator makes no mention of Roaz' formal education, the magician is a master engineer. He is responsible for the opulent construction of Castle Glois:

> des muoz man den heiden jehen
> grôzes listes ze Korntîn. (7081-82)

He has also constructed his wife's funeral casket (8242-43) and the vault in which it is to be laid (8317-18). In addition to these intricate stone structures, Roaz has designed the dangerous wheel which guarded the entrance to the castle:

> daz rat mit dreften umbe gie;
> durch daz tor ez niemen lie.
> daz hêt Rôaz gemeistert dar. (6780-82)

Ingeborg Henderson finds that Roaz' association with architecture "can best be understood in the light of literary tradition and especially biblical commentary, which held builders of great structures to be giants" (Henderson, "Dark Figures and Eschatological Imagery in Wirnt von Gravenberg's *Wigalois*", 107). While great structures were indeed associated with giants in the Middle Ages, engineering in *Wigalois* is also the dominion of another, less mythical social class. At the beginning of the romance, the narrator tells of a gold wheel of fortune in King Joram's castle. Although Joram rules over a magical fairy land, he did not employ a giant or other mythical figure to build the wheel:

> ez hêt ein pfaffe gemeistert dar;
> von rôtem golde was ez gar. (1048-49)

Engineering tasks in *Wigalois* are carried out by clerics whose education allows them to build elaborate mechanical devices. Since Roaz is the only other person in the romance who constructs an intricate wheel, it is not unlikely that he received training similar to the cleric who fashioned Joram's wheel.

Magic in *Wigalois* has more negative connotations than in *Lanzelet* or *Parzival*. Roaz made a pact with a devil in order to get his powers.

> er hât durch sînen zouberlist
> beidiu sêle unde leben
> einem tievel gegeben;
> der tuot durch in wunders vil;
> er vüeget im allez dazer wil. (3656-3660)

No such pact was required by the magicians in *Lanzelet* and *Parzival* for their powers. The narrator also mentions that the devil continuously hovers about

Roaz, offering him advice, but also waiting to collect his soul. He snatches it as soon as the wizard is killed. No mention was made in *Lanzelet* or *Parzival* that the magicians had forfeited their souls: on the contrary, Cundrie even served the grail king. The narrator's negative portrayal of magic is consistent with orthodox church policy. It reflects the teachings of Augustine, echoed by clergymen like John of Salisbury which saw all magic as demonic in origin.

The narrator also associates Roaz' sorcery with what was considered false religion, specifically the Islamic faith. When Nereja informs Wigalois of Korntin's fate, she immediately tells him that Roaz is a heathen (3652). Throughout the romance, Roaz' heathen beliefs are repeatedly emphasized (7081, 7342, 7480). Roaz' vassal Karrioz is also a heathen and even bears a shield with an image of Mohammed (6571). The narrator's equation of magic and religion is also seen in the final battle between Wigalois and Roaz. Although the confrontation is a contest of strength, it is given religious overtones. Max Wehrli finds that the battle shows "eigentümliche, fast zeremoniöse, ja liturgische Formen" (30) and also notes a similarity between the ritual pageantry at Glois and at Munsalvaesche (30). The narrator does present the battle as a ritualized ceremony. Before the battle begins, twelve pairs of young ladies bearing candles and accompanied by twelve minstrels enter the hall in a procession. They are followed by their lady. Once the women have entered the hall, they sit down to watch the battle. When Roaz makes his entrance, he does so in an elaborate fashion reminiscent of a solemn church procession. By giving Roaz' entrance and subsequent demise religious elements, the narrator reflects the orthodox church view of heathenism; it was a false religion propagated by Satan to win souls for Hell.[1]

The narrator's rejection of magic and heathenism is not as unequivocal, however, as his condemnation of Roaz may imply. Although Roaz confronts Wigalois as a demonic adversary, he is, like the magicians previously looked at, not just a negative character. Roaz' architectural achievements are praised, as is his knightly prowess. During the battle between Roaz and Wigalois, the narrator comments:

---

[1] *City of God*, most of Book VII and Book X. c. 10.

> ... der künic Rôaz, ir man,
> was ein helt ze sîner hant;
> sînen gelîchen niemen vant;
> über al die heidenschaft. 97533-7536)

After Roaz has been killed, the narrator even gives the magician a long eulogy of thirty-four lines (7801-34).

Although the narrator condemns Roaz as a heathen who has sold his soul to the devil, his view of Muslims in general is more ambivalent. Other Muslims are portrayed much more positively. Roaz' wife Japhite is described in very glowing terms:

> deheiner slahte gebreste,
> der ie an deheinem wîbe wart,
> des was ir lîp vil wol bewart
> wan daz si ungetoufet was. (7463-7465)

After her death, the narrator even prays to God for her salvation (8022-8030) and expresses hope that her steadfast devotion to her husband will gain her salvation:

> ir touf was diu riuwe
> die si dolte umb ir liep. (8031-32)[1]

The narrator not only displays a considerable tolerance towards heathens, he also shows a remarkable acceptance of magic. Although Roaz has been damned to Hell for his demonic pact, many of the romance's positive characters also resort to magic. King Joram uses a magic belt to defeat the knights of the Round Table, but the narrator at no point condemns him for it. On the contrary, Joram's magic is essential for the story. His supernatural

---

[1] The narrator also shows himself to be remarkedly tolerant of other heathens in the story. Count Adan, one of Roaz' gatekeepers, is portrayed as a completely loyal vassal and Wigalois can entrust his entire kingdom to him (8513-8525). Many other heathens are also friendly to Wigalois and a large number of them journey to Korntin to attend Wigalois and Larie's wedding (9235-37). The mood among Christians and Muslims is joyous and festive (92538-41). Kings Zaradech and Panschavar, Japhite's grieving brothers even help Wigalois in his campaign against Duke Lion of Namur (10074-10080). See also Henderson, "Dark Figures and Eschatological Imagery in Wirnt von Gravenberg's *Wigalois*", p. 113, fn. 19.

prowess allows him to take Gawein prisoner. While in captivity, Gawein marries Joram's daughter Florie and fathers Wigalois.

Wigalois himself repeatedly uses "magisch-christliche Hilfsmittel" (Grubmüller, 221) which exert a "direkten und massiven Einfluß auf seinen Erfolg" (Cormeau, 55). Joram's magic belt enables him to win all battles until it is stolen from him. Throughout the Korntin adventure, Wigalois relies repeatedly on supernatural assistance: he receives magic food, herbs and armour; his sword is charmed to counteract sorcery. Although he also relies on divine assistance, magic continues to be a potent source of alternative supernatural help.

Wigalois' divine help often seems to be rather magical itself. Max Wehrli has commented that "Märchenzauber und Legendenwunder sind hier schwer zu unterscheiden" (33). The narrator's presentation of divine help is indeed reminiscent of the beneficial magic practiced by saints in popular legends: consecrated swords cut through impenetrable scales; prayers drive evil demons away; prayers loosen ropes. As mentioned previously, there was often no qualitative difference in medieval society between the miracles of saints and the magic of sorcerers, and the border the narrator draws between miracle and magic is often indistinct.

Magic in *Wigalois* is not only associated with miracle, but also with legitimate disciplines of knowledge. As a constructor of buildings and mechanical devices, Roaz is a master of science and engineering. Other medieval wizards were also thought to have scientific skills, as noted earlier (cf. Virgil and Sylvester II.) Magicians in *Parzival* and *Lanzelet* were skilled in medicine and engineering.

Unclear borders between magic, miracle and science may help to explain the acceptability of Wigalois' magic. The narrator never mentions that Wigalois' use of it angers God, nor does he find it necessary to explain why a Christian knight should use any at all. The narrator's criterion for Wigalois' supernatural help appears to be its potency. This acceptance of magic is similar to the attitudes of the Archbishops Thomas Becket and Adalbert of Bremen: Becket had consulted diviners to determine the outcome of battles; Archbishop Adalbert had condemned magic but employed sorcerers in his retinue.

Becket's and Adalbert's ambivalence stems from their pragmatic conception of magic, and such is the narrator's presentation of magic. Wigalois uses any kind of non-demonic supernatural help which proves effective. Divine help is the most powerful and ethically acceptable form of supernatural aid, but magic is a potent and credible alternative. Wigalois must master it in order to defeat Roaz and liberate Korntin.

4. Conclusion

The presentation of magic in *Wigalois* reflects many popular medieval notions. Magicians are educated members of the nobility who circulate in the highest social circles and they use their sorcery for political purposes. Some forms of it are demonic, but others are associated with science and can serve beneficial purposes. There is at times no qualitative difference between magic and religion, and it is often difficult to discern the borders between magic and miracle. Magic can pose a grave threat to the stability of rule and a successful monarch must know how to deal with the danger it poses. He can only counter it with other supernatural forces, either divine or magic; the Korntin adventure plays a valuable role in teaching Wigalois about this important aspect of rule. By defeating Roaz, Wigalois demonstrates that he has learned how to harness benevolent supernatural forces in order to protect his kingdom from future threats of malevolent magic.

Chapter VII

DIU CRÔNE

1. Introduction

The magician Gansguoter plays a leading role in Heinrich von dem Türlin's *Diu Crône*.[1] Gansguoter is Gawein's uncle and Arthur's stepfather, and appears repeatedly in Gawein's adventures. Twice he serves as a magical tester of Gawein's abilities. In addition to this role as tester, Gansguoter also proves himself an invaluable ally of the Round Table. After the evil goddess Giramphiel has stolen magic treasures which assure Arthur good fortune, the court is threatened with disintegration. Only Gansguoter can help Gawein recover the objects. His magical aid proves crucial in saving the Round Table and ensuring Arthur's continued rule.

2. The Function of the Gansguoter Episodes

The great length (over 30,000 lines) and large number of adventures in *Diu Crône* has made it difficult for critics to discern a clear structure. Some critics have divided the work into two separate books,[2] the first ending with the wedding of Gawein and Amurfina (13,901). Others have seen the work as a whole being divided up into four adventure sequences (Cormeau), into sections ending in court feasts (Heller), into alternating trûren and vröude sections (Mentzel-Reuters) or into various interlacing adventures (Jillings, Thomas).[3] It has been generally recognized, though, that a first series of adventures ends with the marriage of Gawein and Amurfina and a second begins thereafter. Gansguoter appears in both series of adventures, and serves

---

1 All quotes taken from: Heinrich von dem Türlin, *Diu Crône*. Ed. G.H.F. Scholl.
2 S. Singer, *Allgemeine deutsche Biographie*, p. 21; Rosemary Wallbank, "The composition of 'Diu Krone': Heinrich's von dem Türlin narrative technique", pp. 317 ff.
3 E. K. Heller, "A Vindication of Heinrich von dem Türlin, based on a Survey of his Sources" p. 70; C. Cormeau, pp. 155-56; L. Jillings, *Diu Crône of Heinrich von dem Türlein: The Attempted Emancipation of Secular Narrative*, pp. 231,244-46; A. Mentzel-Reuters, *Vröude: Artusbild, Fortuna- und Gralkonzeption in der "Crône" des Heinrich von dem Türlin als Verteidigung des höfischen Lebensideals*, pp. 44-51; J.W. Thomas, *The Crown: A Tale of Sir Gawein and King Arthur's Court*, pp. XIII-XV.

as one of many structural links between the two sections. The magician's repeated appearances have not escaped the attention of the critics; Ernst S. Dick observes that the three episodes "represent three distinct stages in the hero-magician relationship" (144) and Arno Mentzel-Reuters finds the disenchantment of Gansguoter's magical castles to serve as a structural chain in the romance (42-43).

Oddly enough, Gansguoter has received little attention from scholars. In addition to the structure of the romance, the other main focus of research has been the relation of Heinrich to his sources.[1] Even Lewis Jillings' and Arno Mentzel-Reuters' recent monographs on *Diu Crône* pay little attention to the magician beyond his role within the romance and in relation to earlier sources. Jillings observes that "Heinrich specifically vindicates magic in a manner which must appear provocative when compared to the valuation placed upon the magician by Wolfram and the generally acknowledged perils of 'nigromantie' in this period" (206), but he does not examine the historical elements which provide the background to the Gansguoter figure. Mentzel-Reuters also sees the importance of the magician, noting that one could consider Gansguoter "fast den Regisseur der Handlung" (179). Yet his analysis of Gansguoter's magic does not go beyond the observation that "die gemeinsame Verwissenschaftlichung des Zauberwesen, das ohne Dämonen und Teufel, rein in der Auseinandersetzung mit der *natûre* auskommt, muß auffallen" (252).[2] I would now like to turn to the Gansguoter episodes in order to determine their role and function in the romance.

---

[1] Jessie Weston, *The Legend of Sir Gawain: Studies Upon its Original Scope and Significance*, Chapter 5, "The Magic Castle", pp. 32-43; Therese Holländer's chapter on Gansguoter in: *Klingsor. Eine stoffgeschichtliche Untersuchung*, pp. 11-18; Wolfgang Golther, *Parzival und der Gral in der Dichtung des Mittelalters und der Neuzeit,*; L.L. Boll, *The Relation of Diu Krone of Heinrich von dem Türlin to La Mule sanz Frain: A Study in Sources*; Irma Klarmann, Heinrich von dem Türlin: *"Diu Crône". Untersuchung der Quellen*, Diss. Tübingen 1944; M. O'C. Walshe "Heinrich von dem Türlin, Chretien and Wolfram"; Ralph Read, "Heinrich von dem Türlin's *Diu Krône* and Wolfram's *Parzival*", pp. 129-139; Ernst Dick, "The Hero and the Magician: On the Proliferation of Dark Figures from *Li Contes del Graal* and *Parzival* to *Diu Crône*", pp. 128-150.

[2] The association of magic with technology is, as we shall see later on, one of several important factors necessary for understanding Gansguoter's sorcery, and it is unfortunate that Mentzel-Reuters does not follow up this observation.

a) The Adventures at the Bridle Castle and Castle Salie

The first two times Gansguoter appears, he provides magical challenges for Gawein. Each adventure takes place in an enchanted castle and both times, Gawein must overcome its supernatural defenses. The adventures are designed to affirm Gawein's worth as the best knight of the Round Table. The first of these episodes is the "Bridle Adventure". Here Gawein must regain a magic bridle which assures its owner sovereignty over his lands.

The bridle is kept in a castle whose walls spin continuously, making entry all but impossible. But this is not the only sorcery at work. After Gawein arrives at the castle, Gansguoter challenges him to take part in a "beheading game". Gawein is to strike off the sorcerer's head, who may then return the blow.[1] Gawein does so, but Gansguoter miraculously heals. When it is the sorcerer's turn, he purposely misses. This part of the adventure is not designed to hurt Gawein, but to test his bravery (13170-73).

In the following encounters, Gawein is not only required to demonstrate his bravery, but also his combat skills. He must defeat two savage lions, an enchanted knight, and finally two dragons. His victory over them wins him the bridle. Gawein has successfully passed the first of Gansguoter's challenges: he has proven himself to be the best Arthurian warrior.[2]

The next adventure takes place in Gansguoter's Castle Salie. Like the castle in the bridle adventure, it is also defended by magic. Salie is protected by 500 arrows, which can be automatically shot at attackers. The castle also has a magical bed. If anyone other than the most virtuous knight sits on this bed, arrows will rain down and kill him (20441-51). Gawein passes the bed's test: all of the arrows are caught in the bed's canopy. Now Gawein must battle a

---

[1] This adventure has a direct parallel in the Old French romance, *La Mule sanz Frain*. For a detailed study of the two works, see Lawrence Leo Boll, *The Relation of Diu Krône of Heinrich von dem Türlin to La Mule sanz Frain*.

[2] In addition to testing Gawein's knightly prowess and restoring harmony between Sgoidamur and Amurfina, the adventure serves as a link to adventures in the second part of the romance. It prefigures Gansguoter's castle of marvels adventure, which also serves as another magical test for Gawein. The reconciliation between the sisters and subsequent double wedding is a parallel to the family reunions of Salie when Gawein and Arthur are reunited with their mothers, Igern and Orcades.

lion, but he is successful here as well.[1] By surviving the adventure, Gawein shows that he is the most virtuous Arthurian knight.[2]

This episode was the last of Gansguoter's tests.[3] Now that Gawein has successfully affirmed both his knightly prowess and his virtue, he is ready to undertake the most dangerous adventure in the romance, the recovery of Arthur's trophies from Fimbeus, archenemy of the Round Table. In this adventure, the very existence of Arthur's court is threatened. If the court is to survive, it must turn to Gansguoter's magic.

b)   The Recovery of Arthur's Treasures

The crisis has its origins in an earlier battle between Gawein and Fimbeus, lover of the goddess Giramphiel. Giramphiel had given Fimbeus a magic stone which made him undefeatable. Gawein had taken the stone from Fimbeus in a joust. The stone repeatedly aids Gawein in his chivalric adventures and helps him to maintain his status as the best Arthurian knight. Giramphiel, angered by the loss of the stone, plots a scheme to ruin Arthur's court. One of her courtiers tricks Arthur out of his ring and Gawein's stone.

---

1 From the description of this adventure it becomes apparent that there are parallels to both Chretien and Wolfram's marvellous castle episodes. Here, too, Gawein must disenchant a magic castle with a perilous bed. The parallels between the romances were already observed by nineteenth-century scholars and subsequent critics have also followed up the comparison: Jessie Weston, *The Legend of Sir Gawain: Studies Upon its Original Scope and Significance*, Chapter 5 "The Magic Castle" pp. 32-43. Therese Holländer's chapter on Gansguoter in: *Klingsor. Eine stoffgeschichtliche Untersuchung.* pp. 11-18; Wolfgang Golther, *Parzival und der Gral in der Dichtung des Mittelalters und der Neuzeit*, p. 219 f; Irma Klarmann, Heinrich von dem Türlin: *"Diu Crône"*. *Untersuchung der Quellen*, pp. 63-73; M. O'C. Walshe "Heinrich von dem Türlin, Chretien and Wolfram", pp. 204-218; Jillings, pp. 76-86; Ernst Dick, "The Hero and the Magician: On the Proliferation of Dark Figures from *Li Contes del Graal* and *Parzival* to *Diu Crône*".
2 Ernst Dick sees Gawein's new role here as "a liberator with almost religious overtones" (144). Although Gawein is described here as such (20948-51), he also liberated the maidens from the dragons in the Bridle Adventure. Dick is on the mark when he observes that the adventure is a test of virtue (144).
3 Like the Bridle adventure, the adventure at Salie also serves to reunite and expand the Arthurian circle. Gawein sees his mother Orcades and his sister Clarisanz for the first time in years. Gawein also uses the adventure to bring about another reunion. He invites Arthur and the court to Salie, thereby rejoining Arthur with his family. Arthur sees Igern, his mother; Orcades, his sister; and Clarisanz, his niece. New alliances are also formed, for Clarisanz marries Girmelanz.

Before he escapes, he explains the disastrous consequences of his actions for Arthur:

> Iuwer hof muoz zergên;
> Der mac niht langer gestên,
> Der iemer êwic wære gewesen;
> Ouch mac Gâwein niht genesen,
> Wil er nâch dem grâle varn
> (Daz enmac er nimmer bewarn,
> Wan er hât sîn gesworn)
> Sit er nû den stein hât verlorn,
> Die hantschuoch und daz vingerlîn,
> Daz sîn behelfe solte sîn,
> Und in solte haben widerbrâht:
> Daz ist nû gar widerdâht:
> Ez muoz belîben underwegen. (25452-64)

The calamitous effect that Gawein's supposed death had on the Arthurian court (16893-17313) indicates that his real failure in the Grail Quest will have incalculable consequences on the Arthurian society.

The welfare of the court cannot be saved by knightly endeavor. Giramphiel's lands are protected by magical defenses more potent than any forces Arthur can muster. In this episode the crucial role magic plays at the Arthurian court becomes apparent. If the court is to survive, it must resort to supernatural help. Only Gansguoter's magic aid can save the Round Table.

Arthur need not have any reservations about seeking out this sorcerer. In contrast to the ambivalent Malduc or the treacherous Roaz, Gansguoter can be considered a reliable ally of the Arthurian court. There is no feud between him and the Round Table. On the contrary, he has integrated himself into the Arthurian circle by marrying Arthur's mother and therefore has strong reasons to support his stepson.

Gansguoter's benevolence towards Arthur becomes apparent in his treatment of the rescue party. When Gawein, Keii, Kalogrenant and Lanzelet arrive at his castle, the sorcerer generously provides them with horses, armour and weapons. Gawein himself is outfitted with a magic hauberk that will protect him against Giramphiel's magic stone:

> Swer sie truoc, daz er niht was
> Überwunden und genas
> Vor allem zouber, und ob er
> Ieman bestüende, des gewer
> Er muoste sîn an ritterschaft;
> Ob er von deheines zoubers kraft
> Sigehaft muoste wesen,
> Der mohte dâ von niht genesen,
> Ez enwære an sîner manheit. (27348-56)

Ernst Dick sees this present as a "strategy of disenchantment" (137), and Lewis Jillings states that "the duel between Gawein and Fimbeus is the decisive confrontation of two concepts of chivalry, one which seeks by magic a life of ease, and one which endures travail in self-reliant application of prowess and endeavour" (100). While the hauberk does indeed neutralize hostile magic and forces Gawein's opponents to rely on their own prowess, it will not suffice in saving Gawein from Fimbeus' magic in the course of the adventure. Gansguoter must also accompany them, for only his supernatural knowledge and skill will allow them to survive.[1]

The knights require Gansguoter's magic almost immediately. Traveling through a forest, Gawein and his companions are confronted by a group of fiery knights. Gawein is prepared to attack them, but

> Gansguoter hiez in des enbern
> Und seit in, er wære tôt. (27447-48)

Gawein's magic hauberk is useless against these demonic adversaries. Unable to battle their opponents, the knights cannot continue; the sorcerer must rescue the knights from their predicament. He rides towards the flaming adversaries and disperses them.

Having gotten past the burning knights, Gawein and his friends are confronted with another supernatural obstacle. Here too, Gawein's hauberk cannot protect him from Giramphiel's magical threats. The party arrives at a bridge, and begins to cross it, but a portcullis blocks their path. While they are on the bridge, a giant appears and lowers himself into the water. The

---

[1] Dick is correct, however, when he says that Gansguoter's role seems to be increasingly that of a mentor (146). As we shall see, Gansguoter is vital in leading the knights safely to their adversaries. The knights survive only because of Gansguoter's help.

water level rises so greatly that the knights are in danger of being swept away. Gawein is again ready to press on, but Gansguoter bids him to wait.

> Gansguoter kêrte vür in sâ
> Gein der brücken durch den wâc:
> daz schuztor er ûf wac
> (Daz hât er geringe getân),
> Und hiez sie nâch ime dan
> âne alle vorht rîten. (27571-76)

Again Gansguoter's superior understanding of the situation saves the knights and allows them to continue their quest.

Once Gawein and his companions have entered Giramphiel's homeland, Gansguoter takes his leave. He has brought the knights past Giramphiel's magical defenses. Yet Gansguoter continues to help them:

> Er tet aber vor gar bekant
> gâweine, wie er solte varn
> Und sich an allen sachen warn. (27689-91)

In addition to his valuable advice, he also gives Gawein a small box, along with precise instructions on what to do with it (27692-94). This box will enable Gawein to recover the treasures from Fimbeus.

When Gawein arrives at the castle with his friends, he opens Gansguoter's box and shows it to the assembled company:

> Es was von golde ein kleiniu lade
> Dar inne ein solch bilde lac,
> Daz einer âventiure pflac:
> Swer ez niuwan an sach,
> Daz dem ze slâfen nôt geschach. (27851-55)

With the help of this sleeping spell, Gawein disables Fimbeus' army. He can defeat Fimbeus and recover the magic treasures. The stability of Arthur's kingdom is reestablished. Gansguoter's sorcery has saved the Round Table.

3. Gansguoter and Historical Magicians

Gansguoter, like the literary magicians previously examined, shares a great number of characteristics with his historical counterparts. He moves in the same social circles as they do. Gansguoter is a member of the nobility: the narrator calls him at one point "ein vil guot kneht" (20381) and "der hövesch Gansguoter" (13035), emphasizing his courtly refinement. After the death of Uther Pendragon, Queen Igern found Gansguoter to be a suitable husband. As Arthur's stepfather, he belongs to the inner circle of the Arthurian court.

Gansguoter's privileged social status is reflected by his material wealth. He possesses three castles. The first is the one in which the magic bridle is kept. Gansguoter was wealthy enough to make a present of it to his nieces Sgoidamur and Amurfina (13040-42). The bridle castle is not the only one he gives away. Gansguoter built Castle Salîe for his new wife Igern. It is large enough to accommodate her daughter Orcades and granddaughter Clarisanz, along with five hundred noble maidens. In addition to these castles, Gansguoter still has his third castle, Madarp (27205), in which he himself resides. The magician is also lord over his own territory surrounding Madarp, a land so desirable that he must constantly defend it from hostile neighbours (27322-25).

Gansguoter also shares the erudition of historical and literary magicians. The narrator introduces him as "ein pfaffe wol gelêrt" (13025). Like Clinschor and Cundrie, Gansguoter has been formally educated as a cleric. Other examples in the text also emphasize his (especially occult) knowledge. Gansguoter's great wizardry allows him to protect his lands from his neighbours (27317). When he accompanies Gawein and his accomplices in search of the magic treasures, he must constantly counsel the knights on how to conduct themselves. Only his superior familiarity with magic saves them from death. The narrator states:

> Daz ditz gesinde dâ genaz,
> Von Gansguotern daz kam,
> Der sie von dem kumber nam
> Mit sîner vil grôzen kunst. (27600-03)

Gansguoter himself is aware that his great occult wisdom is essential for Gawein's success. He tells the knight:

> Ez enmöhte ouch nieman hân getân,
> Wan der den list künde. (27647-48)

Magic in *Diu Crône* is associated not only with knowledge and learning in general, but with specific scientific disciplines as well. At the beginning of the romance, a messenger visits Arthur's court with a magic tankard. Although the messenger is himself a fantastic creature from a mythical land, he explains that the tankard was not constructed by supernatural beings but by a master magician educated in Toledo (1090-95). As we have already seen in *Parzival*, Toledo, with its contacts to the Arabic world, was considered one of the centers of occult knowledge in the Medieval West. This wizard was able to construct the tankard using the knowledge found in scientific books:

> Die steine und die feitûre
> Diu wart kûme vunden
> Von listen unkunden,
> Die man ûz den buochen
> Muoz mit kunsten suochen
> Von geômetrîe
> Und von astronomîe,
> Die habent in ir künde
> Himel und abgründe
> Mit listen gemezzen,
> Swaz die hân besezzen,
> Des ist niht vergezzen. (1114-1124)

Geometry and astronomy are two subjects from the quadrivium. Heinrich, like Chretien and Wolfram, considers an education in the liberal arts a prerequisite for magical operations.

Gansguoter is another magician educated in the sciences. Like Clinschor and Roaz, he is a master engineer. He is the architect of his three castles. The bridle castle is not simply a fortification, but an extraordinary example of engineering. The narrator himself calls it a "wunder" (12967) and describes its architectural features in detail. A stone moat "der immer wol tûret" (12957) surrounds it and it has walls smooth and shiny "als ein glas" (12947) which make it impenetrable (12946). The castle is also a masterpiece of construction. Its smooth walls rotate continuously, making entry into the castle all but impossible (12961-62). Gansguoter uses his knowledge of engineering to propel the walls. They are driven by a deep stream which flows underneath the castle (12958-61). The narrator likens its movements to a mechanical device: "reht als ein mül, diu dâ melt" (12965).

Gansguoter's castle Salie also owes its magnificence to the sorcerer's occult skills:

> Von nigromancîe
> Hât er ez gemachet
> Und mit listen sô besachet,
> Daz ez nieman wol gewinnen kan. (20404-07)

Like the bridle castle, Salie is equipped with fantastic mechanical defenses. A special system of five hundred bows and crossbows protects it from intruders:

> Sô man diu venster zuo tet
> Sô liezen sie nider ze stet
> Beidiu senewen unde strâle;
> Wenne man sie ze keinem mâle
> Wolte wider ûf tuon,
> Es wære urliuge oder suon,
> Sie spienen sich aber sâ ze hant. (20141-47)

Moreover, Gansguoter has constructed the magical bed inside the castle:

> Einem bette, daz ze Salîe
> Hete von nigromantîe
> Ein pfaffe gemachet. (8306-08)

Madarp, the third of Gansguoter's castles, is not specifically described as being built by necromancy, but it is also defended by magic:

> Er hâte an sîn selbes lant
> Sô grôzen zouber gewant
> Mit alsolhen listen,
> Dâ vor sich gevristen
> Nimmer mohte dehein man,
> Obe er des hete wân,
> Daz er dar durch wolte varn. (27315-21)

The magic is powerful enough to keep these giants at bay, even though they had already conquered ten other kingdoms (27327-31).

Yet Gansguoter is not the only person in the romance who turns to magical engineering. Other lords, too, rely on sorcery to defend their castles. When Gawein campaigns against the giant Assiles, he stops at Blandukors' castle. Blandukors is a vassal of Assiles and is constantly subject to his lord's vigilance. In order to find out who is at Blandukors' castle, Assiles resorts to a supernatural surveillance system. "Ein guoter nigromanticus" (7012)[1] has constructed a device which would inform the giant of any newcomers at the castle. This device, like Gansguoter's creations, is a mechanical object. In the courtyard stands an iron tree, on top of which is mounted a black iron figure with a horn.

> Dar umbe was ez sô gewant:
> Als ein ritter in daz hûs kam
> Und nahtselde dâ genam,
> Sô blies ez das grôz horn,
> Daz man ez wol mohte bekorn
> Von dannen vier mîle. (7000-7005)

The narrator's scientific understanding of magic can help to explain the favorable presentation of magic in *Diu Crône*. Gansguoter, the chief magician in the work is described in very positive terms. His benevolence is already indicated in his name. Arno Mentzel-Reuters has pointed out that although the interpretation of Gansguoter as "der gänzliche Gute" is linguistically problematic (none of the manuscripts use the variant "Ganzguoter or Gantzguoter"),[2] his surname Micholde "ist einwandfrei zu deuten als *michel holde*" (180). The narrator's descriptions and Gansguoter's conduct bear out this interpretation. As mentioned previously, he is "courtly" an "excellent knight", and "wise"; characteristics of a model noble. When Gawein seeks him out to recover the treasures, the narrator states that Gansguoter was

---

1 Could this magician be Gansguoter? Although the magician is not named, his engineering skills are similar to Gansguoter's. If they are one and the same, then this is yet another example of Gansguoter's technical mastery.
2 Mentzel-Reuters, pp. 179-180. This interpretation is narrow and pedantic. The name does not have to follow the rules of linguistic change. Its anomalous form comes from a poet's imagination, not natural development.

> ... ein ritter êrbære
> Edel und gewizzen,
> Und der sich gevlizzen
> Hât an aller tugende
> In daz alter von der jugende,
> Und der sîn hât guot stat. (27223-28)

Gawein can go to Gansguoter and receive the advice of a good friend (27264-65).

Gansguoter's court shares its lord's benevolence. When Gawein explains Arthur's situation to them, they all voice their support for the Round Table:

> Diu rede in allen misseviel
> Und begunden alle sprechen,
> Daz sie ir herze rechen
> Solten, daz wær michel reht;
> Und jach dâ manic guot kneht,
> Daz er dar umbe wolte
> Gern wâgen, obe er solte,
> Den lîp dar umbe dâ mit in. (27287-94)

Like their lord, they are virtuous and will be reliable allies of the Arthurian court.

Gansguoter's magic is no more diabolical than he is. Although potent and formidable, it is primarily used for defensive purposes. The sorcerer uses it to protect his territories from attack, and to defeat the hostile magic of Fimbeus. Admittedly, the supernatural defences in the first two castles result in the deaths of many knights who have attempted the adventures, but they are designed to protect the bridle and the maiden of the castle Salie. Only a brave and virtuous knight has the right to gain the lands. Gawein, because he possesses both these qualities completely, is able to succeed in disenchanting the castles.

Indeed, much of the magic in the romance is used to test virtue. There are several episodes in the romance where the virtue of the Arthurian society is placed under scrutiny. These include the tankard episode mentioned above, and also the glove probe (22990-24719). While the glove is sent by Giramphiel in order to bring ruin to Arthur's court, its powers are in itself not malevolent. It reveals the virtue (or lack thereof) of its bearer, but that has been determined by the bearer's previous conduct. The glove does not in itself do any harm.

Other examples of magic are also value-neutral in themselves. The stone which guaranteed Fimbeus invincibility is perhaps the best example thereof. Although Fimbeus is Gawein's archenemy, his magic is purely protective. It does not have any demonic influence on its owner. Giramphiel gave Fimbeus the magic stone so that he could not be injured in combat. Once Gawein wrests it from him, he has no qualms about using it himself. Until Giramphiel's knight steals it back, Gawein carries it with him on his adventures. At no point does the narrator or any of the characters in the romance criticise Gawein for using it. Magic is an accepted and often necessary form of supernatural help which characters in the romance repeatedly fall back upon.[1]

The acceptability of magic can help to explain its important role in *Diu Crône*. Most of the characters in the romance repeatedly rely on it. Although it would go beyond the scope of this study to examine all the instances of magic, it is helpful and pertinent to examine how it is used by the nobility. For magic in *Diu Crône* also plays a vital role in politics: rulers throughout the romance utilize it to stabilize their rule and defend their territories from the attacks of their enemies. The following examples will show how important and pervasive its political applications are.

It has already been mentioned that Gansguoter uses sorcery to defend his castles from unvirtuous knights and evil giants. But supernatural defenses are not options restricted to wizards. The knight Laamorz of Janfrüege also uses magic to protect his lands. Lady Siamerac warns Gawein of Laamorz' potent sorcery:

> Und ist ein hûs starke guot
> Und von zouber sô behuot,
> Mit starken listen sô gevrumt,
> Daz kein ritter dar kumt
> In einem jâre zallen zîten,

---

[1] The narrator's use of the miraculous reflects a very liberal understanding of supernatural powers. Unlike Wirnt's mixture of Christian miracle and magic, there is almost no Christian influence in the romance. For a detailed examination of the narrator's religious views see Jilling's chapter "Secularism in *Diu Crône*" in *Diu Crône of Heinrich von dem Türlin*, pp. 185-221.

er müeze dâ strîten
Mit Laamorz dem helde. (155300-06)

Gawein can only defeat him by fighting in front of the castle, beyond the range of its supernatural protection.

In the bridle episode, a fight between Sgoidamur and Amurfina arises from the seduction of magical legitimation. The allure of such power seduces Amurfina into robbing her sister of her rightful inheritance. The bridle is not the only magical aid Amurfina uses to maintain control of her lands. Once she has the bridle, she uses a number of potent supernatural devices in order to keep it in her possession.[1] After Gawein visits her, she repeatedly uses sorcery in order to gain his undying devotion. She arranges that a "slâftrinken" (8469) be brought to the knight. Having drunk the potion, Gawein is completely enamored of Amurfina:[2]

> Wan sîn lîp und sîn gedanc
> Wart im vil gar verkêret
> Und sô herzeclîche gesêret
> Daz im al solhe wunden
> Niht alle erzte kunden
> Geheilen mit erznîe. (8474-79)[3]

Through magic, Amurfina has secured the best knight as her husband, tested his feelings towards her and bound him inextricably to her. With Gawein on her side the stability of her rule and its continuation seem guaranteed.[4]

---

[1] Since the narrator never calls Amurfina a sorceress or says that she worked any of the magic herself, it is not unreasonable to assume that she received the potions and sword from Gansguoter, her uncle.

[2] Gawein was already in love with Amurfina before he drank the potion. Yet Amurfina's use of the potion as a safeguard shows her calculating nature. Having found Gawein, she is not content to let her natural charms work. She therefore turns to magic to assure herself of his love.

[3] Although Gawein is now hopelessly smitten with Amurfina, she still has more supernatural devices which will determine Gawein's suitability as husband. When Gawein is in bed with her, a magic sword tests his intentions towards her (8524-30). After he swears his fidelity, she gives him yet another love potion to finally bind him to her (8654-58).

[4] If Amurfina had told him of her bridle before Sgoidamurs enlisted his help, Gawein would never have entered into Sgoidamur's service. Amurfina's secrecy caused her to lose the bridle.

Although she in the end loses the bridle to her sister, she still has Gawein as a husband.

King Arthur is yet another ruler who resorts to magic to maintain his power. Gawein, Arthur's best knight, uses Fimbeus' stone to help him win battles.

> Den stein hât er allewege
> Bî ime in gewisser pflege,
> Vür daz er in im an gewan
> und solher krefte dar an
> Von der wârheit enpfant. (14976-80)

Gawein's victories bring great glory to Arthur's court.[1]

Arthur also has other magical devices which protect his court. Lady Fortune has favoured Arthur with a magic ring:

> ... Daz sol ein zeichen sîn
> Aller dinge sælekeit:
> Die wîle ez hât unde treit
> Artûs, sô mac niht zergên
> Sîn hof und muoz iemer stên
> Ganz von allen dingen. (15912-17)

Although Arthur's court rose to success through knightly prowess rather than supernatural means, once Arthur has the ring he indeed comes to rely on its powers. When Giramphiel's knight captures the stone, ring and gloves from the Round Table, he tells the bewildered court that the loss of these objects will doom them. Once Gawein has recovered the treasures, he immediately sends the gloves and the ring back to Arthur. After the Grail Quest Gawein and Arthur keep their supernatural aids, thus perpetuating the court's dependence on magic.

Now we can reconsider Ernst S. Dick's theory of disenchantment. Dick has stated that "the hero's way is consequently a progression from involvement in magic towards emancipation from magic" (137) and that in the final quest Gawein proves "himself superior to the forces of evil, not as a trickster-hero in possession of a lucky stone or magic arms, but as a (1) courageous, (2)

---

1 Examples include the rescue of Guinevere and the recovery of Arthur's treasures.

virtuous, and above all, (3) self reliant protagonist of (almost) real world knighthood" (145). A close examination of the final adventure has shown Gawein's dependence on magic throughout. Were it not for Gansguoter's constant advice and supernatural assistance, Gawein and his fellow knights would have perished before they reached the border of Fimbeus' land. Gansguoter's wizardry continues to play a vital role, even after he leaves the knights. His sleeping spell allows Gawein to reduce the enemy's ranks to a manageable size. The weakness of Dick's argument lies in his rationalistic conception of magic. He sees the magic in the romance as negative and feels that it must be overcome by virtue:

> the essence of [Gansguoter's] assistance relies on the ideal of self reliance. The neglect of this ideal in favor of a continued reliance on the seductive promises of magic has been largely responsible for Giramphiel's hostility and hence for the crisis itself. (146)

While Giramphiel's hostility is due to her desire to retrieve her magic stone, it is her abuse of magic that makes her a negative character. Gawein used the same stone after he won it from Fimbeus and did not "succumb to the seduction of magic". Magic can be abused for evil purposes, but it can always be defeated by benevolent sorcery. Magic and virtue are not mutually exclusive but intertwined. Indeed, its benevolent form is an integral instrument of rule in *Diu Crône*. Like his fellow rulers, Arthur relies constantly on magic in order to maintain rule and shows no inclination of abandoning it. Ignoring or rejecting magic can only have disastrous effects on a ruler's reign.

4. Conclusion

As in *Lanzelet*, *Parzival*, and *Wigalois*, the presentation of magic in *Diu Crône* is consistent with many popular medieval notions. Sorcerers are educated clerics, members of the nobility and at home in the highest circles of the aristocracy. Their art is not diabolical, but is associated with science and technology and plays an important role at court. Magicians can construct devices to test a warrior's prowess or the virtue of lords and ladies. Wizards are also invaluable to rulers, for they can set up elaborate defences to protect a ruler's territories and work magic to ensure his prosperity. Magic is in fact an integral part of political power, for a ruler must be able to defend his realm from hostile sorcery, while at the same time he must be able to use protective magic to maintain power. The ability to defeat hostile magic and use magic for their own success grants Gawein and the Arthurian court lasting prosperity.

Chapter VIII

WILHELM VON ÖSTERREICH

1. Introduction

In Johann von Würzburg's *Wilhelm von Österreich*,[1] written in 1314, the griffin-riding sorceress Parklise plays a small but important role. Parklise is a courtier in the service of Queen Crispin of Belgagan. She saves Wilhelm, the romance's hero, from death and then enlists his aid to rid her queen of Merlin, a diabolical magician who has besieged Belgagan. Wilhelm battles Merlin and liberates Queen Crispin's lands. After Wilhelm's victory Queen Crispin returns the favour by uniting Wilhelm with his beloved Agly. In concluding my study with *Wilhelm von Österreich*, written a century after the romances examined in the previous chapters, I will attempt to determine to what degree popular medieval notions of magic and knowledge continued to be reflected in this early fourteenth century romance and to what degree historical developments had influenced these notions.

2. The Function of the Merlin/Parklise Episode

The Merlin/Parklise episode occurs at approximately the middle of the work (lines 10861 ff.).[2] Of the two magicians in this adventure, it is Merlin who has received the most attention from scholars. Because he is an evil sorcerer who holds Queen Crispin and her court prisoner, critics have seen a functional similarity between Merlin and the sorcerer Clinschor from Al-

---

[1] All quotes taken from the following edition: *Johanns von Würzburg Wilhelm von Österreich*, Hrsg. Ernst Riegel.
[2] The unity of *Wilhelm von Österreich*, unlike that of *Lanzelet*, *Wigalois*, or *Diu Crône*, has not been a subject for critical debate. Interest has instead centered on the genre of the romance and its relationship to the development of the New High German prose novel; Renee Scheremeta, "Historical, Hagiographic Romances? Late Courtly Hybrids", pp. 93-102; Dietrich Huschenbett, "Tradition und Theorie im Minne-Roman Zum 'Wilhelm von Österreich' des Johann von Würzburg,", pp. 238-261; Veronika Straub, *Entstehung und Entwicklung des frühneuhochdeutschen Prosaromans*.

brecht von Scharffenburg's *Seifrid de Ardemont*.[1] In this romance Clinschor has kidnapped four women and has a giant guard them. As Adelaide Marie Weiss observes, "both [Clinschor and Merlin] aim at the ruin and destruction of women" (46). Eugen Mayser finds Merlin to be a fusion of Clinschor and the wild giant: "Johann läßt nun den Zauberer selbst der 'awentewr pflegen', d.h. die Frauen bewachen und mit den Helden kämpfen; so verschmilzt er mit dem wildem Riesen" (63). While there are similarities between Johann's Merlin and Albrecht's Clinschor episodes, the adventure also serves other purposes. Mayser has correctly pointed out that it serves to purge Wilhelm of his guilt in Wildomis' murder. Thus Wilhelm's service on Crispin's behalf can be interpreted "als Sühne für seinen Mord an Wildomis um Aglyes willen" (20). The encounter between Wilhelm and Queen Crispin is also vital for the happy outcome of Wilhelm's relationship with Agly. The queen rewards Wilhelm's service by devising a scheme to unite him with Agly (13281-16014). As the result of her efforts, the two lovers can finally marry.

But it is important to keep in mind the magical context of the episode. In this adventure, Wilhelm, like the knights in the romances previously discussed, confronts the threat of hostile political magic. He too, must demonstrate that he is capable of defeating the dangers it poses. At the beginning of the episode, Wilhelm finds himself in dire straits: he has been sentenced to death by King Melchinor for having killed Wildomis, the king's son. Only Parklise's magic can save him.

The sorceress is the most important courtier at Queen Crispin's court. She is the sole contact between Crispin's besieged kingdom and the outside world, and as such, the only one capable of finding a warrior to liberate Belgagan. Once she has chosen Wilhelm as Crispin's champion, her magic is instrumental in gaining him for her political purposes. She summons a devil to learn the details of an intimate conversation between King Melchinor and his wife. Claiming that she is bringing Melchinor a divine message, the sorceress then uses this information to gain the king's confidence:

---

[1] P.E.A. Schiprowski, *Merlin in der deutschen Dichtung*, p. 30; Adelaide Marie Weiss, *Merlin in German Literature*, p. 46; Eugen Mayser, *Studien zur Dichtung Johanns von Würzburg*, p. 63.

> ez is Mahmet, der werde got,
> der iu die botschaft hat gesant,
> als iu wol tut der brief erkant
> mit manigem worzaichen. (11023-27)

Parklise's letter deceives the king, and, empowered by this illusion, she can make her request. Melchinor is to give her custody of Wilhelm, for Mohammed has devised a fitting punishment for Wildomis' murderer:

> in sol tôten des tiuvels sun,
> sus hat ey sin almæhtic tun
> bedaht, er ist Merlin genant,
> sus blibt din ere ungeschant
> sit just gein tjost murdet niht:
> ietwederm ist kunftig diu geschiht,
> sus hat er din ere bedaht. (11063-68)

Melchinor consents to placing Wilhelm in her custody. Parklise's magic has freed Wilhelm and obtained Crispin her champion.

Parklise then explains the true purpose of her mission to Wilhelm and warns him of the dangers facing him. It is up to Wilhelm to defeat the political magic which has wreaked havoc in Queen Crispin's lands.

The first of Merlin's monsters he must face is a terrible *Mischwesen*:

> vornan waz ez ain stier
> und lief uf zwelf füzzen,
> sin ungehiures grüzzen
> dem armen da was wilde.
> ez truog ains menschen bilde
> obn uf dem rugk,
> do was daz zagel stugk
> der ungehurste wurm. (11718-25)

After Wilhelm has slain the dragon, he must defeat the other supernatural dangers which terrorize Queen Crispin's kingdom. Merlin has barred the only road to her castle with a fantastic construction. Two iron dragons stand on either side of the road and spew fire at anyone who tries to pass.

> ieglichem uz dem munde sluog
> ain viur gelich alsam ain berch. (11876-77)

These dragons, however, are not the only adversaries now facing Wilhelm. Merlin has sensed Wilhelm's presence and comes out to meet him. The magician is a frightening and dangerous opponent; Merlin's armour and club are fashioned from the hide and bones of mythical beasts[1] and the magician himself is no less monstrous than his weaponry:

> arm und bain diu baide
> warn dick und kurtz,
> da zwischen der lip ainn schurtz
> het in witer lenge:
> do was im daz gewenge
> me braiter denne ain wanne,
> noch swertzer denne ain pfanne
> was sin varwe, da diu schain. (11972-79)

After a fierce battle, Wilhelm finally manages to throw the sorcerer to his own mechanical dragons:

> dem tiuvel uf in was so not
> daz er in bi dem schilt begraif,
> er sloz in in der arme raif
> und schoz in in der wuerme fiur. (12172-75)

Now the evil magician has been destroyed and his reign of terror ended. Once the queen has received and honored her hero, she sends out her servants to destroy the mechanical dragons:

> diu kuenginne keren
> hiez da uf die strazzen,
> die aventuer verwazzen
> si hiez zer zerren ueber al:
> sus wart Merlines des tiuvels schal
> zerstoert und zerbrochen. (12957-63)

The final remains of Merlin's magic have now been destroyed. Queen Crispin's country is free again. Parklise's magic and Wilhelm's prowess have enabled her to defeat the wizard's tyranny.

---

1 The armour is made from the hide of a "fortaspinaht" (11967) and the club from the bone of a "cotantil" (11944).

Like the magic episodes in the previous romances, this one also shows the importance of magic at court. As part of his adventures, Wilhelm is shown its applications, as well as its dangers. Beneficial magic saved his life, and allowed Queen Crispin to find a champion. By defeating Merlin, Wilhelm has proven that he can defeat hostile magic. His lands will not succumb to the tyranny of such an evil sorcerer.

3. *Magicians in Wilhelm von Österreich and Historical Concepts of Magic*

The mentality equating knowledge, politics and magic was still active in the fourteenth century.[1] Studies by Robert Scribner, Robert Muchembled and Keith Thomas have shown that the magical world-view continued to exert its influence in Europe well into the seventeenth century.[2] The previously discussed phenomenon of the Royal Touch, for example, continued into the eighteenth century and the learned magic practiced by medieval clerics enjoyed its greatest popularity among the Renaissance magi of the fifteenth century.[3]

Magic also continued to enjoy great interest at the courts and concerns about its growing influence were reflected in the increasing theological and legal condemnations of magic which appeared in the course of the thirteenth century.[4] Fears of political sorcery manifested themselves in a series of trials involving high-ranking officials at the early fourteenth century royal French

---

[1] Jacques Le Goff has shown that mentalities often remain active for centuries. In his essay "For an extended Middle Ages" (pp. 18-23 in *The Medieval Imagination*), Le Goff even argues that "certain fundamental structures persisted in European society from the fourth to the nineteenth centuries, bestowing a coherent character on a period of some fifteen centuries" (21).
[2] Robert Scribner, "Magie und Aberglaube. Zur volkstümlichen sakramentalischen Denkart in Deutschland am Ausgang des Mittelalters," in: *Volksreligion im hohen und späten Mittelalter*, Hrsg. Peter Dinzelbacher & Dieter Bauer, pp. 253-273; Robert Muchembled, *Kultur des Volks - Kultur der Eliten. Die Geschichte einer erfolgreichen Verdrängung*; Keith Thomas, *Religion and the Decline of Magic*.
[3] D.P. Walker, *Spiritual and Demonic Magic, from Ficino to Campanella*; Frances Yates, *Giordano Bruno and the Hermetic Tradition*.
[4] See Edward Peters, "The Systematic Condemnation of Magic in the Thirteenth Century", pp. 85-109.

court: in 1303 King Philip IV accused Pope Boniface VIII of demonolatry;[1] five years later Bishop Guichard of Troyes was accused of having murdered Queen Joan with image-magic, and after Philip IV's death in 1314, charges of magical homicide were levelled against the family of the king's chamberlain, Enguerrand de Marigny.[2] Philip IV's campaign against the Templars (1307 to 1314) used accusations of sorcery to destroy the order.[3] Pope Alexander IV had allowed the Inquisition to prosecute magicians for divination or sorcery if these were overtly heretical practices, but had left the decision as to what was heretical to the bishops.[4] In 1320, William, cardinal of Santa Sabina, with Pope John XXII's permission, urged the inquisitors of Carcassone and Toulouse to investigate sorcerers in their jurisdictions.[5] Prosecution intensified after John XXII issued the decretal entitled *Super illius specula* in 1326. This decretal sentenced anyone who entered into a diabolical pact to excommunication and allowed the inquisitors themselves to determine what was heretical. The zeal with which John condemned heretical sorcerey has led Edward Peters to comment:

> The letters of William of Santa Sabina and John XXII draw to a close the noose left open by Alexander IV, although they do not exceed the injunctions of the earlier pope ... These letters simply mobilized a permission that was implicit in the earlier papal letter, and by the mid-fourteenth century, inquisitors, bishops, popes and secular magistrates alike knew very well in what ways sorcery and magic could automatically become heretical. (132-33)

These trials and condemnations indicate just how great a threat magic was thought to be at the early fourteenth century courts.

This growing fear of magic at court can also be seen in the portrait of it and its practitioners in *Wilhelm von Österreich*. Because of its late authorship the romance has generally been considered (and sometimes dismissed) as the

---

1 Jones, p. 673.
2 Jones, pp. 677-78.
3 Edward Peters, pp. 125-129.
4 Habiger-Tuczay, 94.
5 Edward Peters, 131.

work of an epigone.[1] Although the imitative aspects of the work cannot be denied, it is more than just a collection of earlier literary themes and topics. As a product of the fourteenth century, the romance also reflects later medieval concerns and interests, among them popular notions of magic and magicians. The narrator's portrait of it is in many ways similar to those in previously discussed romances, but it also reflects the growing apprehension that all magic, even when benevolent, is demonic. I will first examine to what degree the presentation of magic in *Wilhelm von Österreich* continues to reflect earlier popular notions and then determine how it was influenced by these new concerns.

One of the resemblances between the narrator's magicians and the literary and historical magicians previously discussed is their privileged social status. The beautiful sorceress Parklise has entered the service of Queen Crispin:

> von einer kuenginne ich las,
> diu hiez Crispin von Belgalgan,
> der was [Parklise's] dienst undertan,
> und was ir ingesinde. (10880-83)

In addition to her duties as royal messenger, she also plays a vital role in the affairs of state. Parklise undertakes the responsibility of eliminating Merlin's threats, a danger grave enough to threaten the existence of Crispin's kingdom. Her high social standing is reflected in her splendid attire:

> ir gewant was nach kuenclicher art
> geworht uz aim larikant:
> manic richer stain dar uz bekant
> tet siner tugent schin.
> sus kam Parklise phin
> gevarn gegen Frigia. (10916-21)

These fine garments indicate her privileged rank at Crispin's court.

---

1 For a comprehensive survey of Johann von Würzburg as an epigone see Albrecht Juergen's *"Wilhelm von Österreich", Johann von Würzburg's "Historica Poetica" von 1314 und Aufgabenstellungen einer narrativen Fürstenlehre*, especially Part III, "Johann von Würzburg als epigonischer Dichter", pp. 207-310.

Like the historical and fictional magicians previously discussed, magicians in *Wilhelm von Österreich* are also associated with knowledge. Parklise comes from an educated family; her father was an erudite scholar:

> Hie vor ain wiser maister was
> an ainem alten buoch ich las
> er was gehaizzen Dedelus. (10861-63)

Dedelus' academic pursuits have not only brought him a Master's title. The narrator tells us:

> daz er in nigramanci was
> der best, (fuer war wizzet daz!)
> der ainer uf erden wart. (10865-67)

The learned aspect of his occult knowledge becomes apparent in the narrator's description of it. He calls it "swartze buoche kunst" (10877). Like the historical and literary magicians previously discussed, Dedelus also learns his sorcery from occult books. Dedelus is another example of an educated cleric whose scholarly pursuits gained him access to occult knowledge. The narrator of *Wilhelm von Österreich*, like those in the romances previously discussed, considers magical knowledge the dominion of clerics.

Dedelus has passed on his erudition to his daughter Parklise. Like her father, Parklise is highly intelligent. The narrator refers to her as "wise" (10910) and "die cluegen Parclysen" (11358-59). As a result of her father's occult instruction she, too, has become a powerful sorceress:

> Dedelus si niht betrogen
> het mit der swartzen buoche kunst
> auch het si von ir schon die gunst
> daz man si minnet, swa si was. (10876-79)

Her powers are so great that:

> si was zu der selben stunde
> von nigramanci diu best erkant
> die man under dem hymel vant. (10906-08)

Parklise's actions reflect her intelligence. She rescues Wilhelm from death with cunning and superior knowledge. She conjures up a devil to learn the details of an intimate conversation between Melchinor and his wife. This knowledge gives her the authority to negotiate Wilhelm's release. Parklise herself points out to Wilhelm the role her intelligence plays in his rescue: "so han ich dich mit witzen erlost" (11233).

Magic in *Wilhelm von Österreich* is not only associated with knowledge in general, but particularly with the science of engineering. Magicians in the romance construct complex mechanical devices. King Melchinor possesses a magical chair upon which only the most worthy man may sit:

> ain man der nie geswachet
> sich selb an kainen orten
> mit werken noch mit worten,
> an manigen tugenden uzerwelt,
> an degenhait ain mannes helt,
> der maister was in eren schuol. (4980-85)

The chair will affirm the man's virtue by raising him high up into the air:

> so der gesezzen uf den stuol
> was von dem ich sait vor,
> do gieng er uober sich enbor
> durch die linden este
> in daz gewelb veste. (4986-90)

It was fashioned long ago by none other than Virgil, the most famous of ancient magicians:

> Virgilius, niht ein kristen,
> der het in so gemachet. (4978-79)

The narrator's presentation of Virgil's chair is consistent with that of other fabulous mechanical creations in the previous romances. He emphasizes the craft and workmanship that went into its construction (4936-43). The vault over the chair is also ornately crafted and detailed astronomical images have been engraved on its underside:

> da zunten inne sunn und man,
> Mars und Mercurius,
> Jovis und Venus,
> Saturnus der planet
> auch do geschoenet het

> daz gewelbe wunnesam.
> daz gestirne fuor sich bran
> die naht in schoenem glast
> des tages lieht es last. (4992-5000)

Although the planets and constellations can be seen as an intricate example of Virgil's great skills, they also serve another function: magical operations were dependent on the positions of the stars and planets. Chretien's cleric, Cundrie and the constructor of the tankard in *Diu Crône* were other magicians versed in astronomy.

Virgil is not the only magician in the romance associated with engineering skills. Merlin is also a master engineer. His wild appearance and hostile nature have led critics to see him primarily as a wild man. P.E.A. Schiprowski describes him as "dieser wilde Riese" (30). Adelaide Marie Weiss states that "there is a close resemblance in this version of Johann between Merlin and the Giant Herdsman in the *Livre d'Artus*. This Giant Herdsman, as we have already noted, may be no other than a transformed Merlin" (45). While Merlin undeniably does reflect the influence of medieval wild man legends and the narrator repeatedly emphasizes the diabolical origin of Merlin's powers,[1] his feats also reflect the learned aspect of magic. His great knowledge of mechanics allows him to construct the metal dragons which have sealed off all land routes to Queen Crispin's castle. As with Virgil's magical chair, the narrator also provides a detailed description of the construction of these devices, from which it becomes apparent that the dragons have been built in accordance with mechanical principles. The dragons have been made of iron, so that their fiery breath will not cause them to melt (11873). The fires are fanned by giant bellows driven by windmills:

> wintmueln vier
> stuonden uf der ecken,
> gæn des windes strecken
> sah man si laufen snelle:
> uz mangem wilden velle
> si blaspalge triben,
> grozzer roerrn siben

---
[1] The narrator repeatedly refers to Merlin as "des tiuvels sun" (11063, 11140, 11250, 11878-79).

> giengen von ieglichen,
> von listen wunderlichen
> warn do gegozzen,
> und wær ez niht verdrozzen,
> ich sagt iu wunder da von:
> in sie gie maniges luftes don. (11852-64)

As with Clinschor's and Gansguoter's magic castles, it is the complexity of the mechanical devices rather than their nature which constitutes their fantastic aspect. Mastery in magic is reflected by skill in engineering.

Magicians in *Wilhelm von Österreich*, like those previously discussed, work largely benevolent magic. The notable exception is Merlin, whose magic causes great pain and suffering to Crispin's people:

> [Merlin] do mit grozen pinen
> daz lant so het besluotzt;
> des wart dor inne genuotzt
> maniges hertzen swære
> von vrawen clagbære. (11880-84)

Yet Merlin's malevolence is not shared by the romance's other magicians. None of his colleagues engage in evil deeds. Virgil has created his chair as a virtue test. Far from harming anyone, the chair's purpose is to reveal the most noble person in the world. Wilhelm's virtue is affirmed by it. The narrator makes no mention of any malevolent acts committed by Dedelus; he uses his occult knowledge to instruct his daughter Parklise, who serves Queen Crispin as a valuable messenger and confidante. Parklise's magic allows her to find a hero to defeat Merlin and save her queen. The narrator, moreover, describes the sorceress in very positive terms; in addition to her intelligence, she is also a very beautiful woman:

> si was schoen und wise,
> daz har was ir geflohten
> guldin gevar: ir mohten
> die winde ez wol zefuern,
> swenne sich der griffe ruern
> mit sim gevider in lueften wart. (10910-15)

Parklise's beauty is so great that the king of Sorbrait has a portrait of her on his shield (10870-71). When king Melchinor and his court see Parklise, her appearance leads them to think that she is a divine creature:

> si schrirn alle: 'warta wart!
> ist dizz ain engel oder ain wip?
> oder ist ez ain goetinne?'
> ir schoen in manigem sinne
> sich want biz uf des hertzen grunt. (11004-09)

Parklise's conduct is as pleasing as her appearance. It is her magic which allows her to save Wilhelm's life and and Queen Crispin's kingdom. By acquiring Wilhelm's aid for Crispin, she even paves the way for Wilhelm's reunion with Agly, made possible by the grateful queen.

Although the majority of the narrator's magicians are positive characters, his presentation of their magic reflects the growing criticism of it in the fourteenth century. When wizards in the romances previously discussed had exhibited negative characteristics, their hostility had been explained and complementary portraits of positive sorcerers had shown the acceptance of benevolent magic. In *Lanzelet*, Malduc's hostility had been motivated by his long feud with Arthur and his knights. His daughter, however, was a virtuous sorceress and found a home at the Arthurian court. Clinschor's anger was rationalized and he (and certainly Cundrie) exhibited positive qualities as well. Although Roaz had made a pact with the devil, many other characters in *Wigalois*, including the title hero, used non-demonic magic without condemnation. Gansguoter was a very positive magician and invaluable member of the Arthurian court.

The portrait of magic in *Wilhelm von Österreich*, on the other hand, is more negative: Merlin's fantastic powers come from his infernal father; Virgil, Dedelus and Parklise's operations are all described as necromancy.[1] Of these benevolent sorcerers, Parklise is the only one who actually works magic during the romance.[2] Her operations are accomplished only with the help of demons. She has summoned a demon to guide her griffin (10894-

---

1 Virgil, 4908; Dedelus, 10865; Parklise, 10907.
2 Virgil's chair was constructed long before the story takes place and Johann makes no mention of any spells that Dedelus cast.

903) and she conjures another one to find out the details of King Melchinor's conversation:

> ain insigel stempfen,
> si balde hiez den tiuvel da
> und gebot im iesa
> daz er ir sait mit warheit,
> do der von Marroch von huse rait
> und ze naht bi sinem wibe lac,
> was er mit ir biz an den tac
> begienc ... (10946-10953)

As previously mentioned, Augustine and other church fathers had condemned all magic as the illusions of demons. Parklise also uses demons to delude others. A demon has deceived her griffin into obedience:

> ir grifen der tiuvel vor swanc
> in aines grifen gestalt:
> er schain als ain zuhter alt,
> da von der grif nah im vlog;
> an der zugt er in betrog;
> er wand er het in uz gebruot
> er tet als noch manic vogel tuot
> der sinem vater vliuget nach. (10894-901)

She deceives Melchinor into believing that she bears a message from Mohammed. Her knowledge of Melchinor's conversation, however, does not come from the prophet, but a demon. The concept of natural or non-demonic magic has no place in the narrator's portrait of Parklise's magic; all magic is demonology.

Because this magic is demonic, the narrator emphatically warns his readers about it. This concern can be seen in Wilhelm's reaction when he learns that Parklise practices demonology:

> ez is mins hertzen swær
> daz mit iu vert der tiuvel:
> soelt ich den von iu schiuvel
> mit wer, daz wær min girde.
> ez zimt niht wibes wirde,
> der rainikait is also groz:
> ain engel schoelt sin iur genoz,
> ir sit so wol gestellet. (11406-13)

Parklise must reassure Wilhelm that she is not in danger:

> du werder ritter, ungemach
> muezz dir sin ymmer wilde!
> min wipliches bilde
> den tiuvel niender rueret:
> der grife der mich fueret,
> den han ich von jgent erzogen,
> doch han ich in also betrogen
> als ich dir ietz ze wizzen tet. (11426-31)

None of the positive magicians in romances previously discussed had to defend their art. Their benevolent results were sufficient proof of the positive aspects of their activities. This is no longer the case in *Wilhelm von Österreich*: although Parklise is a benevolent character and had only used her magic to save Wilhelm and end Merlin's tyranny, it is still suspect. Even after the positive results of Parklise's sorcery are evident, the narrator again finds it necessary to warn of its dangers:

> helf uns an dem ende
> daz diu sel wol gevar,
> daz wir niht werden tiuvel par!
> Swer hie Got getruwet,
> wizzet, der niht buwet
> uf den regen bogen,
> er ist unbetrogen. (12222-12228)

The narrator's repeated warnings show his uneasiness about all magic. Necromancy had gained enough negative connotations by the early fourteenth century that even its appearance in a literary work merited a warning. The church's opposition to magic was clearly on the rise.

4. Conclusion

Although *Wilhelm von Österreich* was written a century after the romances discussed before, the narrator's presentation of magic still reflects many popular medieval notions. Magicians in this romance also enjoy a high social status and enter the service of rulers. They are erudite and their magic is associated with scientific disciplines, specifically engineering. Fantastic mechanical devices are the products of their art. Magic continues to play an important role in the affairs of court; malevolent magicians can pose great problems to rulers and their kingdoms, and the only answer to magical attacks is stronger counter-magic. Yet the narrator's portrait of sorcerers not only reflects medieval society's fascination with magic, but also the growing uneasiness with their presence at court. In this portrait, even benevolent magic involves demons and medieval readers are warned not to succumb to its temptations. The narrator's concern with its demonic aspects reflects the growing fear of and hostility to magic in late medieval society which would ultimately culminate in the witch hysteria of the fifteenth and sixteenth centuries.

CONCLUSION

In this study of court magicians in Middle High German romances, I have focused on the medieval attitudes equating magic and knowledge and the crystallization of these attitudes in the figure of the fictional sorcerer. I began by showing that court magicians not only filled the pages of medieval romance but also played an important role at historical medieval courts. They already influenced the politics of Latin, Celtic and Germanic cultures, where the concept of the magical administrator manifested itself in their mythologies and social organization. In the Middle Ages, the laity's magical understanding of the universe and the church's sacramental view of religion allowed magic to remain a credible source of supernatural power, while the introduction of Arabic science gave magic a theoretical basis that attracted the interest of many educated clerics.

Magic influenced the power structure of the medieval courts: rulers claimed supernatural powers to gain metaphysical legitimation while courtiers saw magic as the reason for a rival's success or their own misfortune. The constant atmosphere of crisis at the court and the practical need to foresee the unforeseeable helped to fuel the desire for magical aid. Indeed, magicians could find ample opportunities to work magic at court; there were spells to divine the outcome of important events or influence anything from military campaigns to a ruler's disposition toward a particular courtier. Magicians could be found at courts throughout the Middle Ages, from those of Charlemagne to those of Frederick II.

After examining the presence and activities of historical magicians, I turned my attention to their presentation in literature. Although they are fictional creations, they bear a number of similarities to their historical counterparts. Like the historical magicians, the fictional sorcerers enjoy a privileged social status and make the court their home; most of them, like Malduc, Clinschor, Roaz and Gansguoter own castles. Duke Clinschor is even a member of the aristocracy and Gansguoter has married into King Arthur's family. Others, like Cundrie, Roaz, and Parklise, are important courtiers who play major roles in the affairs of the court.

Fictional magicians are associated with knowledge and learning and reflect the medieval equation of knowledge and magic. Clinschor, Cundrie, Gansguoter and Dedelus are educated clerics and their sorcery is often close to science. Most of the magicians, including Clinschor, Roaz, Gansguoter, Merlin and Virgil, are skilled engineers, capable of constructing elaborate castles and complex mechanical devices. Cundrie is versed in medical knowledge and uses her magic to heal. In these literary portraits, just as in medieval society, the lines between magic and legitimate sciences are often indistinct.

Political sorcery plays an important role at fictional courts. Enemies of the court often use magic to carry out intrigues. Valerin and Malduc hold members of Arthurian society prisoner in castles protected by magic. Roaz uses demonic assistance to overthrow King Lar. Giramphiel turns to magic aids to rob King Arthur of his treasures and Merlin uses supernatural means to terrorize Queen Crispin's kingdom. But magic is not just an instrument of evil which can be overcome by the strength and virtue of Arthurian knights. Malevolent political sorcery can only be defeated by a supernatural response: Malduc overcomes Valerin's magic defenses with a sleeping spell, Wigalois uses a combination of magic and miracle to defeat Roaz' tyranny, Gansguoter's magic helps Gawein to defeat Fimbeus, and Parklise's aid allows Queen Crispin to free herself from Merlin's terror. A ruler must know how to use magic in order to safeguard his kingdom: the adventures which prepare Lanzelet and Wigalois for kingship serve primarily to teach them how to defeat political sorcery. Arthur and Crispin rely on Gansguoter's and Parklise's wizardry to bring their rule lasting stability. These literary portraits reflect the importance of magic as a political tool. While historical rulers were not as dependent on magic as King Arthur, they did grant the occult arts considerable influence at their courts, as seen for example in the accounts of Bishop Adalbert, Thomas Becket and Frederick II.

The influence of magic was not welcomed by all members of medieval society. Many were frightened by its growing importance, especially in politics. During the thirteenth century the church increased its condemnation and persecution of magicians. This increased persecution was also felt at the court. As hostility towards magic grew, many courtiers suspected of practicing magic found themselves facing charges of demonology or political sorcery. The portrait of Parklise shows how even benevolent magic was often equated with demonology by the early fourteenth century. As the church's campaign against magic gathered force, The literary condemnation of Parklise's magic was finally echoed in similar charges against actual witches. The church's demonization of magic ultimately drove the magical advisor from court, thus helping to end the mentality equating politics, knowledge and magic.

* * *

In tracing the history of the court magician I have often turned to non-literary sources to document the importance of magic at court. Had my choice of sources been restricted to literary works, this study might have relegated the fictional magician to a literary topos. While the study of topoi by Ernst Curtius and other scholars has without question brought many valuable insights to the field of literary studies, it pays short shrift to the socio-historical influences which often play just as important a role in shaping literary works. As Alois Kircher pointed out in *Dichter und Konvention*, his 1973 study of courtly lyric,

> das Aufspüren gemeinsamer Topoi, der bloße Nachweis literarischer Übereinstimmung - wobei die Vermittlung meist unerklärt bleibt - vermag bestenfalls die Außenseite von Literatur, das Handwerkliche zu erhellen, ist jedoch ungeeignet für das Verständnis dichterischer Motivation. (9)

Although the possibility of determining authorial intention has become a matter of debate for many literary scholars, Kircher is certainly correct in pointing out the importance of seeing literature as "geistiger Spiegel und Interpretation des Zustandes der Gesellschaft einer spezifischen historischen Situation" (10). All too often, we disregard the "alterity"[1] of the Middle Ages, allowing our judgement of it to be distorted by the viewpoint of orthodox Christianity and our own twentieth-century "modern" concepts. This study has sought to illuminate one aspect of the "otherness" of the Middle Ages. It focused on a specific historical situation - the one found at the medieval

---

1 Hans Robert Jauß, *Alterität und Modernität in der mittelalterlichen Literatur*.

European court - and also on the literature written and received there. Its purpose was to show the influence of a magical world-view on this society and its literature, and how this view crystallized in the figure of the court magician. For it is the social reality specific to the medieval court which forces us to revise our "modern", rationalistic view of the magician. Magicians were not just fringe figures, representatives of superstition and low culture, but elegant, learned and powerful courtiers, whose services were valued in the center of power. This view of magicians not only circulated at the court, but also found its way into court literature, a literature which is not simply fantastical, but an accurate reflection of these ideas and attitudes. The border between fiction and reality, which can be clearly drawn between fabulous and historical events, is more difficult to determine when seeking the lines between the mentalities active in a society and those presented in its romances. If this study has brought its readers new insights into the importance of magical beliefs in medieval court society, and the value of literature in illuminating such beliefs, then it will have accomplished its purpose.

BIBLIOGRAPHY

I. Primary Sources

Adam of Bremen. *Adam von Bremen, Hamburgische Kirchengeschichte.* Ed. Bernhard Schmeidler, 3d ed., *MGH, SS rer. germ. in us. schol.*, vol. 2 1917; rpr. Hannover and Leipzig; Hahn, 1977.

Adam of Bremen. *History of the Archbishops of Hamburg-Bremen.* Trans. Francis Tschan. New York: Columbia University Press, 1959.

Ammianus, Marcellinus. *Res gestae.* 3 vols. Trans. John C. Rolfe. Cambridge: Harvard University Press, 1956-1958.

Augustine. *City of God.* Trans. Henry Bettenson. Harmondsworth: Penguin, 1984.

Augustine. *On Christian Doctrine.* Trans. D.W. Robertson. Indianapolis, 1958.

Beowulf. A Dual Language Edition. Trans. with an Introduction and Commentary by Howell D. Chickering, Jr. New York: Anchor Books, Doubleday, 1977.

Caesar. *The Conquest of Gaul.* Trans. S.A. Handford. 1951. Harmondsworth: Penguin, 1965.

Caesar. *The Gallic War.* Dual Language Edition. Trans. H. J. Edwards, C.B. 1917. Cambridge: Harvard University Press, 1970.

Cassius Dio. *Roman History.* 9 vols. Trans. Earnest Cary. Cambridge: Harvard University Press, 1960-1961.

Chrétien de Troyes. *Arthurian Romances.* Trans. D.D.R. Owen. London & Melbourne: Dent, 1987.

Chrétien de Troyes. *Der Percevalroman von Christian von Troyes.* Ed. Alfons Hilka. Werke, Vol. V. Halle: Niemeyer, 1932.

Diodorus. *The Library of History*. 12 vols. Trans. C.H. Oldfather. Cambridge: Harvard University Press, 1957-1967.

Die Papstfabeln des Mittelalters. 1895. Ed. Ignaz von Döllinger. Reprinted Darmstadt: Wissenschaftliche Buchgesellschaft, 1970.

Early Irish Myths and Sagas. Trans. and Introd. by Jeffrey Gantz. Harmondsworth: Penguin, 1981.

Egils saga. Trans. Hermann Pálsson and Paul Edwards. Harmondsworth: Penguin, 1976.

Eirik the Red and other Icelandic Sagas. Trans Gwyn Jones. 1961. Oxford: Oxford University Press, 1988.

Eiríks saga rauda. In: *Eirik the Red and other Icelandic Sagas*. Trans. Gwyn Jones. 1961. Oxford: Oxford University Press, 1988. 126-157.

Eyrbyggja saga. Trans. Hermann Pálsson and Paul Edwards. Harmondsworth: Penguin, 1972.

Gautreks saga. In: *Seven Viking Romances*. Ed. Hermann Pálsson, & Paul Edwards. Harmondsworth: Penguin, 1985. 138-170.

Gesamtabenteuer: Hundert altdeutsche Erzählungen. Ed. Friedrich Heinrich von der Hagen. 3 vols. 1850. Darmstadt: Wissenschaftliche Buchgesellschaft, 1961.

Grettis saga. Trans. Paul Herrmann. Düsseldorf: Eugen Diederichs Verlag, 1963 (Thule V).

Hartmann von Aue. *Erec*. Ed. Albert Leitzmann, Ludwig Wolff. 6th Edition: Christoph Cormeau, Kurt Gärtner. Tübingen: Max Niemeyer Verlag, 1985.

Hartmann von Aue. *Iwein*. Ed. G.F. Benecke & Karl Lachmann. 7th Edition: Ludwig Wolff. Berlin: Walter De Gruyter & Co., 1968.

Heinrich von dem Türlin. *Diu Crône*. Ed. G.H.F. Scholl. Stuttgart, 1852. Reprinted Amsterdam: Rodopi N.V., 1966.

Heinrich von dem Türlin. *The Crown: a Tale of Sir Gawein and King Arthur's Court*. Trans. J.W. Thomas. Lincoln: University of Nebraska Press, 1989.

Hiltgart von Hürnheim: *Mittelhochdeutsche Prosaübersetzung des "Secretum Secretorum"*. Ed. Reinhold Möller. Berlin: Akademie Verlag, 1963. (DTM 56).

Hoensna-Thóris saga. In: *Eirik the Red and other Icelandic Sagas*. Trans. Gwyn Jones. 1961. Oxford: Oxford University Press, 1988. 3-38.

Hrafnkel's Saga and other Icelandic Stories. Trans. Hermann Pálsson. Harmondsworth: Penguin, 1971.

Hrólfs Saga Kraka. In: *Eirik the Red and other Icelandic Sagas*. Trans. Gwyn Jones. 1961. Oxford: Oxford University Press, 1988. 221-318.

Hugonis de Sancto Victore. *Didascalicon De Studio Legendi*. Ed. Charles Henry Buttimer. Washington: Catholic University Press, 1939.

Hugo of St. Victor. *The Didascalicon of Hugo of St. Victor. A Medieval Guide to the Arts*. Trans. Jerome Taylor. New York: Columbia University Press, 1961.

Johann von Würzburg. *Wilhelm von Österreich*. Ed. Ernst Regel. Berlin: Weidmannsche Buchhandlung, 1906 (DTM III).

Johannis Saresberiensis. Episcopi Carnotensis policratici sive de nugis curialium et vestigiis philosophorum libri VIII. Ed. C. C. I. Webb. 2 vols. Oxford: Clarendon, 1909.

John of Salisbury. *Frivolities of Courtiers and Footprints of Philosophers (Policraticus)*. Trans. Joseph B. Pike. Minneapolis: University of Minnesota Press, 1938.

John of Salisbury. *The Letters of John of Salisbury*. vol. II Ed. W.J. Millor S.J. & C.N.L. Brooke. Oxford: Clarendon, 1979.

Laxdoela saga. Trans. Rudolf Meißner. Düsseldorf: Eugen Diederichs Verlag, 1963 (Thule VI).

Lucan. *The Civil War (Pharsalia)*. Trans. J.A. Duff. Cambridge: Harvard University Press, 1962.

Map, Walter. *De Nugis Curialium. Courtiers' Trifles*. Trans. M.R. James. Oxford: Clarendon Press, 1983.

Medieval Handbooks of Penance. Eds. John T. McNeill and Helena M. Gamer. New York: Columbia University Press, 1938.

Pedro Alfonso. *Die Disciplina Clericalis des Petrus Alfonsi*. Eds. Alfons Hilka & Werner Söderhjelm. Heidelberg: Carl Winter, 1911.

Pedro Alfonso. *The Scholar's Guide*. Trans. Joseph Ramon Jones & John Esten Keller. Toronto: Pontifical Institute of Medieaval Studies, 1969.

Philostratus, Flavius. *The Life of Apollonius of Tyana*. Trans. F.C. Conybeare. Cambridge: Harvard University Press, 1960.

Pliny. *Natural History*. Trans. D. E. Eichholz. Cambridge, Mass.: Harvard University Press, 1926.

Poems of the Vikings: The Elder Edda. Trans. Patricia Terry. Intro. Charles W. Dunn. Indianopilis: The Bobbs-Merrill Co., Inc., 1969.

Saxo Grammaticus. *Gesta Danorum*. 2 vols. Trans. H.R. Ellis Davidson. Cambridge: D.S. Brewer, 1979.

Secretum Secretorum: Nine English Versions. Ed. M.A. Manzalaoui. Oxford: Oxford University Press, 1977 (EETS 276).

Seven Viking Romances. Trans. Hermann Pálsson and Paul Edwards. Harmondsworth: Penguin, 1985.

Snorri Sturluson. *Edda*. Trans. Anthony Faulkes. London: J.M. Dent & Sons Ltd., 1992.

Snorri Sturluson. *Snorris Königsbuch (Heimskringla)*. 3 vols. Trans. Felix Niedner. Jena: Eugen Diedrichs, 1922.

Strabo. *The Geography*. 8 vols. Trans. H. L. Jones. Cambridge: Harvard University Press, 1959-1967.

Tacitus. *Agricola. Germania*. Trans. M. Hutton. Cambridge: Harvard University Press, 1914.

Tacitus. *The Histories. The Annals.* 4 vols. Trans. J. Jackson and C.H. Moore. Cambridge: Harvard University Press, 1925-1937.

Ulrich von Zatzikhoven. *Lanzelet.* Ed. K.A. Hahn. Berlin: de Gruyter, 1965.

Ulrich von Zatzikhoven. *Lanzelet.* Trans. Kenneth Webster. Introduction R.S. Loomis. New York: Columbia University Press, 1951.

Wirnt von Gravenberg. *Wigalois, der Ritter mit dem Rade.* Ed. J.M.N. Kapteyn. Bonn: Klopp, 1926.

Wirnt von Gravenberg. *Wigalois, the Knight of Fortune's Wheel.* Translated and with an introduction by J.W. Thomas. Lincoln: University of Nebraska Press, 1977.

Wolfram von Eschenbach. *Parzival. Mittelhochdeutscher Text nach der Ausgabe von Karl Lachmann.* Trans. and with an afterword by W. Spiewok. Stuttgart: Reclam, 1981.

II. Secondary Literature

Ackermann, Phyllis. "Who is Kundrie - What is She?" *The Literary Review* 2 (1958-59). 458-468.

Alföldi, A. *Die monarchische Repräsentation im römischen Kaiserreich.* Darmstadt: Wissenschaftliche Buchgesellschaft, 1970.

Baetke, Walter. *Das Heilige im Germanischen.* Tübingen: J.C.B. Mohr, 1942.

Baetke, Walter. *Yngvi und die Ynglinger. Eine quellenkritische Untersuchung über das nordische "Sakralkönigtum".* Berlin, 1964 (= Sitzungsberichte der sächsischen Akademie der Wissenschaften Leipzig 109/3).

Baird, Joseph. "Unferth the Thyle." *Medium Aevum* XXXIX (1970). 1-12.

Barb, A.A. "The Survival of Magic Arts." *The Conflict Between Paganism and Christianity in the Fourth Century.* Ed. A. Momigliano. Oxford: Clarendon Press, 1963. 100-125.

Bayerschmidt, Carl. "The Element of the Supernatural in the Sagas of the Icelanders." *Scandinavian Studies*. Ed. Carl Bayerschmidt and Erik Friis. Seattle: University of Washington Press, 1965. 39-53.

Bertau, Karl. *Über Literaturgeschichte: literarischer Kunstcharakter und Geschichte in der höfischen Epik um 1200*. München: Beck, 1983.

Blank, Walter. "Der Zauberer Clinschor in Wolframs 'Parzival'." *Studien zu Wolfram von Eschenbach. Festschrift für Werner Schröder*. Ed. Kurt Gärtner and Joachim Heinzle. Tübingen: Max Niemeyer Verlag, 1989. 321-332.

Bloch, Marc. *The Royal Touch*. Trans. J.E. Anderson. 1961. New York: Dorset Press, 1989.

Blumstein, Andree Kahn. "The Structure and Function of the Cundrie Episodes in Wolfram's Parzival." *German Quarterly* 51 (1978). 160-169.

Boll, L.L. *The Relation of Diu Krone of Heinrich von dem Türlin to La Mule sanz Frain: A Study in Sources*. 1929, reprinted New York: AMS Press, 1970.

Brown, Peter. "Sorcery, Demons and the Rise of Christianity: From Late Antiquity into the Middle Ages." *Religion and Society in the Age of Saint Augustine*. Ed. Peter Brown. London: Faber and Faber, 1972. 119-146.

Brown, Peter. *The Cult of Saints: Its Rise and Function in Latin Christianity*. Chicago: Chicago University Press, 1981.

Bumke, Joachim. *Die Wolfram von Eschenbach Forschung seit 1945*. München: Wilhelm Fink Verlag, 1970.

Bumke, Joachim. *Höfische Kultur*. 2 Bde. München: Deutscher Taschenbuch Verlag, 1986.

Chaney, W.A. *The Cult of Kingship in Anglo-Saxon England*. Manchester: Manchester University Press, 1970.

Chenu, M.-D. *Nature, Man and Society in the Twelfth Century*. Trans. J. Taylor and L. Little. Chicago: University of Chicago Press, 1968.

Comparetti, Domenico. *Virgil in the Middle Ages*. Trans. E.F.M. Benecke. London: Sonnenschein, 1895.

Cormeau, Christoph. *'Wigalois' und 'die Crône'. Zwei Kapitel zur Gattungsgeschichte des nachklassischen Aventiureromans.* München: Artemis, 1977.

Deinert, Wilhelm. *Ritter und Kosmos im Parzival. Eine Untersuchung der Sternkunde Wolframs von Eschenbach.* München: C.H. Beck'sche Verlagsbuchhandlung, 1960.

Dick, Ernst. "The Hero and the Magician. On the Proliferation of Dark Figures from Li Contes del Graal and Parzival to Diu Crône." *The Dark Figure in Medieval German and Germanic Literature.* Ed. E.R. Haymes & S.C. Van D'Elden. Göppingen: GAG 448, 1986. 128-150.

Dobozy, Maria. "The Function of Knowledge and Magic in *Salman und Morolf*". *The Dark Figure in Medieval German and Germanic Literature.* Ed. E.R. Haymes & S.C. Van D'Elden. Göppingen: GAG 448, 1986. 27-41.

Dumézil, Georges. *Archaic Roman Religion.* 2 vols. Trans. Philip Krapp. Foreword Mircea Eliade. Chicago: University of Chicago Press, 1970.

Eamon, William. "Technology as Magic in the Late Middle Ages and Renaissance." *Janus* 70 (1983). 171-212.

Ellis-Davidson, H.R. "Hostile Magic in the Icelandic Sagas." *The Witch Figure.* Ed. Venetia Newall. London: Routledge & Kegan Paul, 1973. 20-41.

Fisher, Rodney. "Ulrich von Zatzikhoven's Lanzelet: In Search of 'Sens'." *Archiv für das Studium der neueren Sprachen und Literaturen* 217 (1980). 277-292.

Flint, Valierie I.J. *The Rise of Magic in Early Medieval Europe.* Princeton: Princeton University Press, 1991.

Golther, Wolfgang. *Parzival und der Gral in der Dichtung des Mittelalters und der Neuzeit.* Stuttgart: J.B. Metzlersche Verlagsbuchhandlung, 1925.

Goltra, Robert J. Jr. *Five Ceremonial Magicians of Tudor-Stuart Drama.* Emporia State Research Studies XXXIII (Fall 1984).

Goodrich, Norma Lorre. *Merlin.* New York: Franklin Watts, 1987.

Groos, Arthur. "Cundrie's Announcement ('Parzival' 781-782)." *Beiträge zur Geschichte der deutschen Sprache und Literatur* (Tübingen) 113 (1991). 384-414.

Grubmüller, Klaus. "Artusroman und Heilsbringerethos: zum 'Wigalois' des Wirnt von Gravenberg." *Beiträge zur Geschichte der deutschen Sprache und Literatur* (Tübingen) 107 (1985). 218-239.

Gurevich, Aaron J. *Das Weltbild des mittelalterlichen Menschen*. Trans. Gabriele Loßack. München: C.H. Beck, 1980.

Gurevich, Aaron J. "Medieval Culture and Mentality According to the New French Historiography." *Archives européennes de sociologie* 24 (1983). 167-195.

Gurevich, Aaron J. *Medieval Popular Culture*. Trans. János Bak and Paul Hollingsworth. Cambridge: Cambridge University Press, 1988.

Habiger-Tuczay, Christa. *Magie und Magier im Mittelalter*. Munich: Diederichs, 1992.

Harmening, Dieter. *Superstitio: Überlieferungs- und theoriegeschichtliche Untersuchungen zur kirchlich-theologischen Aberglaubensliteratur des Mittelalters*. Berlin: Erich Schmidt Verlag, 1979.

Hartl, Eduard. "Wolfram von Eschenbach." *Die deutsche Literatur des Mittelalters. Verfasserlexikon*. Ed. Karl Langosch. Berlin: de Gruyter, 1953. Vol. IV, Col. 1068.

Heinzle, Joachim. "Über den Aufbau des Wigalois." *Euphorion* 67 (1973). 261-271.

Heller, E.K. "A Vindication of Heinrich von dem Türlin, Based on a Survey of his Sources." *Modern Language Quarterly* 3 (1942). 67-82.

Henderson, Ingeborg. "Selbstentfremdung im Wigalois Wirnts von Gravenberg." *Colloquia Germanica* 13 (1980). 35-46.

Henderson, Ingeborg. "Dark Figures and Eschatological Imagery in Wirnt von Gravenberg's Wigalois." *The Dark Figure in Medieval German and Germanic Literature*. Ed. E.R. Haymes & S.C. Van D'Elden. Göppingen, 1986. 99-113.

Bibliography

Hoffmann, H. *Die Heiligen Drei Könige. Zur Heiligenverehrung im kirchlichem, gesellschaftlichen und politischen Leben des Mittelalters.* Bonn, 1975.

Holländer, Therese. *Klinsgor. Eine stoffgeschichtliche Untersuchung.* Diss. Vienna 1927.

Huschenbett, Dietrich. "Tradition und Theorie im Minne-Roman. Zum 'Wilhelm von Österreich' des Johann von Würzburg." *Zur deutschen Literatur und Sprache des 14. Jahrhunderts.* Ed. W. Haug, T.R. Jackson, J. Janota. Heidelberg: Carl Winter Verlag, 1983. 238-261.

Jaeger, C. Stephen. *Medieval Humanism in Gottfried von Straßburg's Tristan and Isolde.* Heidelberg: Carl Winter Verlag, 1977.

Jaeger, C. Stephen. "The Courtier Bishop." *Speculum* 58 (1983). 291-325.

Jauss, Hans Robert. *Alterität und Modernität der mittelalterlichen Literatur.* Munich: Wilhelm Fink Verlag, 1977.

Jillings, Lewis. *Diu Crône of Heinrich von dem Türlein: The Attempted Emancipation of Secular Narrative.* Göppingen: Kümmerle, 1980.

Johnson, Sidney. "Parzival and Gawan: Their Conflicts of Duties". *Wolfram Studien.* Ed. Werner Schröder. Berlin: Erich Schmidt Verlag, 1970. 86-116.

Jones, William R. "Political Uses of Sorcery in Medieval Europe." *The Historian* 34 (1972). 670-687.

Juergens, Albrecht. *'Wilhelm von Österreich.' Johann von Würzburg's 'Historica Poetica' von 1314 und Aufgabenstellungen einer narrativen Fürstenlehre.* Frankfurt: Peter Lang, 1990.

Kantorowicz, E. *The King's Two Bodies: a Study in Medieval Political Theology.* Princeton: Princeton University Press, 1957.

Kee, Howard Clark. *Medicine, Miracle and Magic in New Testament Times.* Cambridge: Cambridge University Press, 1986.

Kelly, H.A. "English Kings and the Fear of Sorcery." *Medieval Studies* 39 (1977). 206-238.

Kieckhefer, Richard. *Magic in the Middle Ages*. Cambridge: Cambridge University Press, 1990.

Kircher, Alois. *Dichter und Konvention*. Düsseldorf: Bertelsmann Universitätsverlag, 1973.

Klaniczay, Gabor. *The Uses of Supernatural Power*. Trans. Susan Singerman. Princeton: Princeton University Press, 1990.

Klarmann, Irma. *Heinrich von dem Türlin: "Diu Crône". Untersuchung der Quellen*. Diss. Tübingen 1944.

Klauser, Renate. *Der Heinrichs- und Kunigundenkult im mittelalterlichen Bistum Bamberg*. Bamberg: Historischer Verein, 1957.

Knapp, Fritz Peter. "Die hässliche Gralsbotin und die Victorinische Ästhetik." *Sprachkunst* 3 (1972). 1-10.

Knoll, Hiltrud. *Studien zur realen und außerrealen Welt im deutschen Artusroman*. Diss. Bonn 1966.

Köhler, Erich. *Ideal und Wirklichkeit in der höfischen Epik*. Tübingen: Niemeyer, 1970.

Le Goff, Jacques. *Das Hochmittelalter*. Trans. Sigrid Metken. Frankfurt: Fischer, 1965.

Le Goff, Jacques. "Mentalities: a History of Ambiguities." Trans. David Denby. *Constructing the Past*. Ed. Jacques le Goff and Pierre Nora. Cambridge: Cambridge University Press, 1974. 166-180.

Le Goff, Jacques. *Time, Work and Culture in the Middle Ages*. Trans. Arthur Goldhammer. Chicago: University of Chicago Press, 1980.

Le Goff, Jacques. *The Medieval Imagination*. Trans. Arthur Goldhammer. Chicago and London: University of Chicago Press, 1988.

Leyser, Karl. *Rule and Conflict in an Early Medieval Society*. Bloomington: University of Indiana Press, 1979

Littleton, C. Scott. *The New Comparative Mythology*. 1966. Berkeley: University of California Press, 1973.

Loomis, C. Grant. *White Magic: An Introduction to the Folklore of Christian Legend.* Cambridge (Mass.): Medieval Academy of America, 1948.

Luck, Georg. *Magie und andere Geheimlehren in der Antike.* Stuttgart: Alfred Kröner Verlag, 1990.

Mac Cana, Proinsias. *Celtic Mythology.* London: Hamlyn, 1970.

Maksymiuk, Stephan. Rev. of *Magie und Magier im Mittelalter,* by Christa Habiger-Tuczay, and *Magie im Mittelalter,* by Richard Kieckhefer, trans. by Peter Knecht. *Arbitrium* 1/94: 27-30.

Maksymiuk, Stephan. "Knowledge, Politics and Magic: The Magician Gansguoter in Heinrich von dem Türlin's *Crône.*" *The German Quarterly* 67 (1994). 470-83.

Martin, Ernst. *Wolfram von Eschenbach. Parzival und Titurel. Teil II: Kommentar.* Halle, 1903.

Maurer, Friedrich. "Die Gawangeschichten und die Buch-Einteilung in Wolframs Parzival". *Der Deutschunterricht* Heft 2 (1968). 60-80.

Mayser, Eugen. *Studien zur Dichtung Johanns von Würzburg. Germanische Studien,* Heft 101 (1933). Reprinted Nendeln/Liechtenstein: Kraus Reprint Ltd., 1967.

McConeghy, Patrick. "Aventiure and Anti-Aventiure in Ulrich von Zatzikhoven's Lanzelet and Hartmann von Aue's Iwein." *Germanic Review* 57 (1982). 60-69.

Mentzel-Reuters, Arno. *Vröude: Artusbild, Fortuna- und Gralkonzeption in der "Crône" des Heinrich von dem Türlin als Verteidigung des höfischen Lebensideals.* Frankfurt, Bern, Paris: Lang, 1989.

Mohr, Wolfgang. "Parzival und Gawan." *Wolfram von Eschenbach.* Ed. Heinz Rupp. Darmstadt: Wissenschaftliche Buchgesellschaft, 1966. 287-318.

Muchembled, Robert. *Kultur des Volks - Kultur der Eliten; die Geschichte einer erfolgreichen Verdrängung.* Trans. Ariane Forkel. Stuttgart: Klett-Cotta, 1982.

Naumann, Hans. "Die magische Seite des altgermanischen Königtums." *Wirtschaft und Kultur: Festschrift zum 70. Geburtstag von Alfons Dopsch.* Leipzig: Rudolf Rohrer Verlag, 1938. 1-12.

Neudeck, Otto. "Vergil in deutschsprachiger Literatur um 1300: Ein Zauberer und Magier in heilsgeschichtlicher Funktion." *Germanica Wratislaviensia* 85 (1989). 41-49.

Neudeck, Otto. "Möglichkeiten der Dichter-Stilisierung in mittelhochdeutscher Literatur: Neidhart, Wolfram, Vergil." *Euphorion* 88 (1994). 339-355.

Nock, Arthur Darby. "Paul and the Magus." *Essays on Religion and the Ancient World.* 2 vols. Ed. Zeph. Stewart. Oxford: Clarendon Press, 1972.

Ogilvy, J.D.A. "Unferth: Foil to Beowulf?" *Publications of the Modern Language Association* LXXIX (1964). 370-375.

Perrenec, René "Artusroman und Familie: Daz welsche buoch von Lanzelete." *Acta Germanica* 12 (1979). 1-51.

Peters, Edward. *The Magician, the Witch and the Law.* Philadelphia: University of Pennsylvania Press, 1978.

Peters, Ursula. "Literaturgeschichte als Mentalitätengeschichte? Überlegungen zur Problematik einer neuen Forschungsrichtung." *Germanistik - Forschungsstand und Perspektiven Band II,* Hg. Georg Stötzel. Berlin: de Gruyter, 1985. 179-198.

Price, S.R.F. *Rituals of Power. The Roman Imperial Cult in Asia Minor.* Cambridge: Cambridge University Press, 1984.

Puhvel, Jaan. *Comparative Mythology.* Baltimore: Johns Hopkins University Press, 1987.

Rankin, H.D. *Celts and the Classical World.* Portland: Timber Press, 1987.

Read, Ralph. "Heinrich von dem Türlin's *Diu Krône* and Wolfram's *Parzival*", *Modern Language Quarterly* 35 (1974). 129-139.

Riché Pierre. "La magie à l'époque Carolingienne." *Comptes Rendus de l'Académie des Inscriptions et Belles-Lettres.* Janvier-Mars 1973. 127-138.

Riché, Pierre. *Die Welt der Karolinger.* Trans. Cornelia & Ulf Dirlmeier. Stuttgart: Philip Reclam, 1981.

Röhrich, Lutz. *Erzählungen des späten Mittelalters und ihr Weiterleben in Literatur und Volksdichtung bis zur Gegenwart: Sagen, Märchen, Exempel und Schwänke.* Berne and Munich: Francke Verlag, 1962-67.

Ross, Anne. "The Divine Hag of the Pagan Celts." *The Witch Figure.* Ed. Venetia Newall. London: Routledge & Kegan Paul, 1973. 139-164.

Ruh, Kurt. *Höfische Epik des deutschen Mittelalters.* Vol. II. Berlin: E. Schmidt, 1980.

Rupp, Heinz. "Die Bedeutung der Gawan-Bücher im Parzival Wolframs von Eschenbach". *London German Studies II.* Ed. J.P. Stern. London: Institute of Germanic Studies, University of London, 1983.

Russell, Jeffrey. *Witchcraft in the Middle Ages.* Ithaca (New York): Cornell University Press, 1972.

Scheremeta, Renée. "Historical, Hagiographic Romances? Late Courtly Hybrids." *Genres in Medieval German Literature.* Ed. H. Heinen & I. Henderson. Göppingen: Kümmerle, 1986. 93-102.

Schiprowski, P.E.A. *Merlin in der deutschen Dichtung.* Breslau: Antonius Verlag, 1933.

Schmidt, Klaus. "Frauenritter oder Artusritter? Über Struktur und Gehalt von Ulrich von Zatzikhoven 'Lanzelet'." *Zeitschrift für deutsche Philologie* 98 (1979). 1-18.

Schmitt, Wolfram. *Hans Hartliebs mantische Schriften und seine Beeinflussung durch Nikolaus von Kues.* Diss. Heidelberg 1963.

Schmitt, Wolfram. Magie und Mantik bei Hans Hartlieb. *Salzburger Beiträge zur Paracelsusforschung* 6. Wien, 1966.

Scholz, Bernhard. "The Canonization of Edward the Confessor." *Speculum* 36 (1961). 38-60.

Schröder, Franz Rolf. "Cundrîe." *Festschrift für Ingeborg Schröbler zum 65. Geburtstag.* Ed. Dietrich Schmidtke and Helga Schuppert. Tübingen: Max Niemeyer Verlag, 1973. 187-195.

Schultz, James. "'Lanzelet': A Flawless Hero in a Symmetrical World." *Beiträge zur Geschichte der deutschen Sprache und Literatur* (Tübingen) 102 (1980). 160-188.

Scribner, Robert (Bob). "Cosmic Order and Daily Life: Sacred and Secular in Pre-Industrial German Society." *Religion and Society in Early Modern Europe 1500-1800.* Ed. Kaspar von Greyerz. London: Allen & Unwin, 1984.

Scribner, Robert. "Magie und Aberglaube. Zur volkstümlichen sakramentalischen Denkart in Deutschland am Ausgang des Mittelalters." *Volksreligion im hohen und späten Mittelalter.* Ed. Peter Dinzelbacher & Dieter Bauer. Paderborn: Schöningh, 1990.

Seggewiß, Hermann-Josef. *Godi und Hofdingi: Die literarische Darstellung und Funktion von gode und Häuptling in den Isländingersagas.* Frankfurt: Peter Lang, 1978.

Sherwood, M. "Magic and Mechanics in Medieval Fiction." *Studies in Philology* XLIV (1947). 567-592.

Shils, Edward. *Center and Periphery: Essays in Macrosociology.* Chicago: University of Chicago Press, 1975.

Simek, Rudolf. *Lexikon der germanischen Mythologie.* Stuttgart: Alfred Kröner Verlag, 1984.

Simpson, Jacqueline. "Olaf Tryggvason versus the Powers of Darkness." *The Witch Figure.* Ed. Venetia Newall. London: Routlege and Kegan Paul, 1973. 165-177.

Singer, S. *Allgemeine deutsche Biographie* (XXXIX). Berlin: Duncker & Humboldt, 1971.

Sohm, Rudolf. *Kirchenrecht.* 2 vols. Leipzig: Duncker & Humboldt, 1892-1923.

Southern, R.W. *Medieval Humanism & Other Studies.* Oxford: Basil Blackwell, 1970.

Spargo, John W. *Virgil the Necromancer.* Cambridge: Harvard University Press, 1934.

Sprandel, Rolf. *Gesellschaft und Literatur im Mittelalter.* Paderborn: Schöningh, 1982.

Straub, Veronika. *Entstehung und Entwicklung des frühneuhochdeutschen Prosaromans.* Amsterdam: Rodopi N.V., 1974.

Ström, Åke & Biezais, Harald. *Germanische und Baltische Religion.* Stuttgart: Verlag W. Kohlhammer, 1975.

Ström, Folke. "Kung Domalde i Svitjod och 'kungalyckan'." *Saga och Sed* (1967). 52-66.

Taylor, L. *The Divinity of the Roman Emperor.* Middletown (Connecticut): American Philological Association, 1931.

Thee, Francis. *Julius Africanus and the Early Christian View of Magic.* Tübingen: J.C.B. Mohr, 1984.

Thomas, Keith. *Religion and the Decline of Magic.* New York: Charles Scribner's Sons, 1971.

Thomas, Neil. "Sense and Structure in the Gawan Adventures of Wolfram's 'Parzival'." *Modern Language Review* 76 (1981). 848-856.

Thomas, Neil. "Literary Transformation and Narrative Organization in Wirnt von Gravenberg's Wigalois." *Modern Language Review* 80 (1985). 362-371.

Thoran, Barbara. "Zur Struktur des 'Lanzelet' Ulrichs von Zatzikhoven." *Zeitschrift für deutsche Philologie* 103 (1984). 52-77.

Thorndike, Lynn. "Some Medieval Conceptions of Magic." *The Monist* 25 (1915). 107-139.

Thorndike, Lynn. *History of Magic and Experimental Science.* 8 vols. New York: Macmillan and Columbia University Press, 1923-58.

Thorndike, Lynn. *Michael Scot.* London: Thomas Nelson & Sons Ltd., 1965.

Traister, Barbara Howard. *Heavenly Necromancers: The Magician in English Renaissance Drama.* Columbia: University of Missouri Press, 1984.

Turville-Petre, E.O. "Fertility of Beast and Soil in Old Norse Literature." *Old Norse Literature and Mythology.* Austin, 1964. 244-264.

Van Engen, John. "The Christian Middle Ages as an Historiographical Problem." *American Historical Review* 91 (1986). 519-552.

Vogt, W.H. "Der frühgermanische Kultredner." *Acta Philologica Scandinavica* 2 (1927). 250-263.

Volkmann, Hans. *Germanische Seherinnen in römischen Diensten.* Krefeld: Im Scherpe Verlag, 1964.

Vries, Jan de. "Das Königtum bei den Germanen." *Saeculum* 7 (1956). 289-309.

Vries, Jan de. *Altgermanische Religionsgeschichte.* 2 vols. Berlin: de Gruyter, 1957.

Vries, Jan de. *Kelten und Germanen.* Bern: Francke Verlag, 1960.

Vries, Jan de. *Keltische Religion.* Stuttgart: Kohlhammer Verlag, 1961.

Waddel, H. *The Wandering Scholars.* London: Constable, 1947. Reprinted London, 1968.

Walker, D.P. *Spiritual and Demonic Magic, from Ficino to Campanella.* London: Warburg Institute, 1958.

Wallbank, Rosemary. "The Composition of 'Diu Krone': Heinrich's von dem Türlin Narrative Technique." *Medieval Miscellany: Presented to Eugene Vinaver by Pupils, Colleagues and Friends.* Ed. F. Whitehead. Manchester, 1965. 300-319.

Walshe, M. O'C. "Heinrich von dem Türlin, Chretien and Wolfram." *Mediaeval German Studies Presented to Frederick Norman,* London: University of London Institute of Germanic Studies, 1965. 204-218.

Weber, Max. *Wirtschaft und Gesellschaft.* 5. rev. Auflage. Ed. Johannes Winckelmann. Tübingen: J.C.B. Mohr, 1976. 1. Halbband.

Weiss, Adelaide Marie. *Merlin in German Literature*. Catholic University of America Studies in German, vol. III (1933). Reprinted New York: AMS Press Inc., 1970.

Welz, Dieter. "Lanzelet im Schoenen Walde: Überlegungen zu Struktur und Sinn des Lanzelet Romans." *Acta Germanica* 13 (1980). 47-68.

Weston, Jessie. *The Legend of Sir Gawein: Studies Upon its Original Scope and Significance*. 1897. Reprinted New York: AMS Press, 1972.

Woodman, David. *White Magic and English Renaissance Drama*. Rutherford: Farleigh Dickinson University Press, 1973.

Wolf, Norbert. "Die Gestalt Klingsors in der deutschen Literatur des Mittelalters." *Südostdeutsche Semesterblätter* 19 (1967). 1-19.

Wynn, Marianne. "Parzival and Gâwân - Hero and Counterpart". *Beiträge zur Geschichte der deutschen Sprache und Literatur* (Tübingen) 84 (1962). 142-172.

Wynn, Marianne. *Wolfram's Parzival. On the Genesis of its Poetry*. Frankfurt: Peter Lang, 1984.

Yates, Frances. *Giordano Bruno and the Hermetic Tradition*. London: Routledge, 1964.

MIKROKOSMOS

Beiträge zur Literaturwissenschaft und Bedeutungsforschung

Herausgegeben von Wolfgang Harms

Band 1 Andreas Wang: Der 'Miles Christianus' im 16. und 17. Jahrhundert und seine mittelalterliche Tradition. Ein Beitrag zum Verhältnis von sprachlicher und graphischer Bildlichkeit. 1975.

Band 2 Hans-Henning Rausch: Methoden und Bedeutung naturkundlicher Rezeption und Kompilation im 'Jüngeren Titurel'. 1977.

Band 3 Sara Stebbins: Studien zur Tradition und Rezeption der Bildlichkeit in der 'Eneide' Heinrichs von Veldeke. 1977.

Band 4 Michael Schilling: Imagines Mundi. Metaphorische Darstellungen der Welt in der Emblematik. 1979.

Band 5 Dennis Howard Green und Leslie Peter Johnson: Approaches to Wolfram von Eschenbach. 1978.

Band 6 Fred Wagner: Rudolf Borchardt and the Middle Ages. Translation, Anthology and Nationalism. 1981.

Band 7 Wolfgang Harms/Heimo Reinitzer (Hrsg.): Natura loquax. Naturkunde und allegorische Naturdeutung vom Mittelalter bis zur frühen Neuzeit. 1981.

Band 8 Sara Stebbins: Maxima in minimis. Zum Empirie- und Autoritätsverständnis in der physikotheologischen Literatur der Frühaufklärung. 1980.

Band 9 Marianne Wynn: Wolfram´s 'Parzival': On the Genesis of its Poetry. 1984.

Band 10 Waltraud Timmermann: Studien zur allegorischen Bildlichkeit in den Parabolae Bernhards von Clairvaux mit der Erstedition einer mittelniederdeutschen Übersetzung der Parabolae 'Vom Geistlichen Streit' und 'Vom Streit der vier Töchter Gottes'. 1982.

Band 11 Ruth Kastner: Geistlicher Rauffhandel. Illustrierte Flugblätter zum Reformationsjubiläum 1617 in ihrem historischen und publizistischen Kontext. 1982.

Band 12 Peter Frenz: Studien zu traditionellen Elementen des Geschichtsdenkens und der Bildlichkeit im Werk Johann Gottfried Herders. 1983.

Band 13 Katharina Wallmann: Minnebedingtes Schweigen in Minnesang, Lied und Minnerede des 12. bis 16. Jahrhunderts. 1985.

Band 14 Peter Strohschneider: Ritterromantische Versepik im ausgehenden Mittelalter. Studien zu einer funktionsgeschichtlichen Textinterpretation der 'Mörin' Hermanns von Sachsenheim sowie zu Ulrich Fuetrers 'Persibein' und Maximilians I. 'Teuerdank'. 1986.

Band 15 Norbert Bachleitner: Form und Funktion der Verseinlagen bei Abraham a Sancta Clara. 1985.

Band 16 Dietmar Peil: Der Streit der Glieder mit dem Magen. Studien zur Überlieferungs- und Deutungsgeschichte der Fabel des Menenius Agrippa von der Antike bis ins 20. Jahrhundert. 1985.

Band 17 Sonia Brough: The Goths and the Concept of Gothic in Germany from 1500 to 1750. Culture, Language and Architecture. 1985.

Band 18 Barbara Bauer: Jesuitische 'ars rhetorica' im Zeitalter der Glaubenskämpfe. 1986.

Band 19 Gabriele Hooffacker: Avaritia radix omnium malorum. Barocke Bildlichkeit um Geld und Eigennutz in Flugschriften, Flugblättern und benachbarter Literatur der Kipper- und Wipperzeit (1620-1625). 1988.

Band 20   Eva-Maria Bangerter-Schmid: Erbauliche illustrierte Flugblätter aus den Jahren 1570-1670. 1986.

Band 21   Albrecht Juergens: 'Wilhelm von Österreich'. Johanns von Würzburg 'Historia Poetica' von 1314 und die Aufgabenstellungen einer narrativen Fürstenlehre. 1990.

Band 22   Maria Magdalena Witte: Elias und Henoch als Exempel, typologische Figuren und apokalyptische Zeugen. Zu Verbindungen von Literatur und Theologie im Mittelalter. 1987.

Band 23   Felix Leibrock: Aufklärung und Mittelalter. Bodmer, Gottsched und die mittelalterliche deutsche Literatur. 1988.

Band 24   Herfried Vögel: Naturkundliches im 'Reinfried von Braunschweig'. Zur Funktion naturkundlicher Kenntnisse in deutscher Erzähldichtung des Mittelalters. 1990.

Band 25   Renate Haftlmeier-Seiffert: Bauerndarstellungen auf deutschen illustrierten Flugblättern des 17. Jahrhunderts. 1991.

Band 26   Otto Neudeck: Continuum historiale. Zur Synthese von tradierter Geschichtsauffassung und Gegenwartserfahrung im 'Reinfried von Braunschweig'. 1989.

Band 27   Reinhard Hahn: 'Von frantzosischer zungen in teütsch'. Das literarische Leben am Innsbrucker Hof des späteren 15. Jahrhundert und der Prosaroman 'Pontus und Sidonia (A)'. 1990.

Band 28   Jörg Krämer: Johann Beers Romane. Poetologie, immanente Poetik und Rezeption 'niederer' Texte im späten 17. Jahrhundert. 1991.

Band 29   Silvia Serena Tschopp: Heilsgeschichtliche Deutungsmuster in der Publizistik des Dreißigjährigen Krieges. Pro- und antischwodische Propaganda in Deutschland 1628 bis 1635. 1991.

Band 30   Jörg Platiel: Mythos und Mysterium. Die Rezeption des Mittelalters im Werk Gerhart Hauptmanns. 1993.

Band 31   Alexandra Stein: 'wort unde werc'. Studien zum narrativen Diskurs im 'Parzival' Wolframs von Eschenbach. 1993.

Band 32   Gabriele Dorothea Rödter: Via piae animae. Grundlagenuntersuchung zur emblematischen Verknüpfung von Bild und Wort in den "Pia desideria" (1624) des Herman Hugo S.J. (1588-1629). 1992.

Band 33   Bernd Bastert: Der Münchner Hof und Fuetrers 'Buch der Abenteuer'. Literarische Kontinuität im Spätmittelalter. 1993.

Band 34   Bernhard Jahn: Raumkonzepte in der Frühen Neuzeit. Zur Konstruktion von Wirklichkeit in Pilgerberichten, Amerikareisebeschreibungen und Prosaerzählungen. 1993.

Band 35   Ulrike Dorothea Hänisch: 'Confessio Augustana triumphans'. Funktionen der Publizistik zum Confessio Augustana-Jubiläum 1630. (Zeitung, Flugblatt, Flugschrift). 1993.

Band 36   Ulrike Draesner: Wege durch erzählte Welten. Intertextuelle Verweise als Mittel der Bedeutungskonstitution in Wolframs 'Parzival'. 1993.

Band 37   Eberhard Haufe: Die Behandlung der antiken Mythologie in den Textbüchern der Hamburger Oper 1678-1738. Herausgegeben von Hendrik Birus und Wolfgang Harms. 1994.

Band 38   Sabine Mödersheim: 'Domini Doctrina Coronat': Die geistliche Emblematik Daniel Cramers (1568-1637). 1994.

Band 39   Franz-Heinrich Beyer: Eigenart und Wirkung des reformatorisch-polemischen Flugblatts im Zusammenhang der Publizistik der Reformationszeit. 1994.

Band 40   Regina Pingel: Ritterliche Werte zwischen Tradition und Transformation. Zur veränderten Konzeption von Artusheld und Artushof in Strickers "Daniel von dem Blühenden Tal". 1994.

Band 41   Beate Kellner: Grimms Mythen. Studien zum Mythosbegriff und seiner Anwendung in Jacob Grimms *Deutscher Mythologie*. 1994.

Band 42   Michèle Remakel: Rittertum zwischen Minne und Gral. Untersuchungen zum mittelhochdeutschen "Prosa-Lancelot". 1995.

Band 43   Mara Nottelmann-Feil: Ludwig Tiecks Rezeption der Antike. Literarische Kritik und Reflexion griechischer und römischer Dichtung im theoretischen und poetischen Werk Tiecks. 1996.

Band 44   Stephan Maksymiuk: The Court Magician in Medieval German Romance. 1996.

Melitta Weiss Adamson

Medieval Dietetics
Food and Drink in *Regimen Sanitatis*
Literature from 800 to 1400

Frankfurt/M., Berlin, Bern, New York, Paris, Wien, 1995. 231 pp.
German Studies in Canada. Edited by Manfred Kuxdorf. Vol. 5
ISBN 3-631-48871-8   pb. DM 69.--*

The book explores the connection between cooking and preventive medicine by centering on the food and drink section, *cibus et potus*, in 23 medieval Latin and German *regimina sanitatis*. A brief history of the four-humor theory and the six non-naturals is followed by the analysis of each *regimen*, including information on the text, the role of *cibus et potus* within the non-naturals, its contents (general guidelines on nutrition, dietetic lists of foodstuffs, and culinary recipes), use of the *gradus*-system, as well as sources and dependencies with other *regimina*. In the conclusion the results are arranged in chart-form; an appendix contains the transcription of a 15th-century German translation of Anthimus' "De observatione ciborum."

Peter Lang   Europäischer Verlag der Wissenschaften
Frankfurt a.M. • Berlin • Bern • New York • Paris • Wien
Auslieferung: Verlag Peter Lang AG, Jupiterstr. 15, CH-3000 Bern 15
Telefon (004131) 9402121, Telefax (004131) 9402131
- Preisänderungen vorbehalten - *inklusive Mehrwertsteuer